Experts, Activists, and Democratic Politics: Are Electorates Self-Educating?

This book addresses opinion leadership in democratic politics as a process whereby individuals send and receive information through their informally based networks of political communication. The analyses are based on a series of small group experiments, conducted by the authors, which build on accumulated evidence from more than seventy years of survey data regarding political communication among interdependent actors. The various experimental designs provide an opportunity to assess the nature of the communication process, both in terms of increasing citizen expertise as well as in terms of communicating political biases.

T.K. Ahn is a professor of political science at Seoul National University. His work has been published in a number of journals, including the *American Journal of Political Science*, the *Journal of Politics*, *Political Psychology*, the *Journal of Public Economics*, the *Journal of Public Economic Theory*, and the *Journal of Economy Psychology*. He has received the Paul Lazarsfeld Award from the American Political Science Association for the best paper on political communication. He received his PhD from Indiana University, Bloomington.

Robert Huckfeldt is Distinguished Professor of Political Science at the University of California, Davis. He is the author or coauthor of *Politics in Context*; *Race and the Decline of Class in American Politics*; *Citizens, Politics, and Social Communication* (Cambridge); *Political Disagreement* (Cambridge); and a number of articles. He received the 1979 E.E. Schattschneider Award for the outstanding dissertation in American politics from the American Political Science Association; the 2012 Doris Graber Outstanding Book Award from the Political Communication Section of the American Political Science Association; and outstanding conference-paper awards from the Political Communication Section and the Elections, Public Opinion, and Voting Section of the American Political Science Association. He received his PhD from Washington University in St. Louis.

John Barry Ryan is an assistant professor of political science at Stony Brook University. His work has appeared in journals such as the *American Journal of Political Science*, *Political Behavior*, and *Political Communication*. He has received the Paul Lazarsfeld Award from the American Political Science Association for the best paper on political communication. He received his PhD from the University of California, Davis.

"Against the onslaught of declarations that modern political life is isolated and anomic, this sparkling analysis of networks and experiments shows how networks of ideas and individuals connect our political activities. Ahn, Huckfeldt, and Ryan weave together network surveys and small group experiments to show how political ideas may spread in daily life as well as what structures enhance or restrict that spread. In the end, they present a very compelling vision of modern political life that encompasses politics in the current century, as well as the last half of the twentieth."

– Michael Ward, Duke University

"This book reveals the ways in which pundits, partisans, and political activists are central to forming public opinion and to the resilience of democracy. These biased opinion leaders garner expertise in issues that interest them, and their views are channeled to citizens with little incentive to gather their own information. Anyone seeking to explain public opinion, opinion leaders, partisan bias, political activism, or political communication is going to have to tackle this book. Disputing its findings will be a herculean task. The authors marshal observational data, laboratory experiments, agent-based models, network analysis, and statistical simulations to support their central theoretical claims. The book is an excellent model of social science, using diverse methods to answer well-defined questions."

– Rick K. Wilson, Rice University

Cambridge Studies in Public Opinion and Political Psychology

Series Editors

DENNIS CHONG, University of Southern California and Northwestern University
JAMES H. KUKLINKSI, University of Illinois, Urbana-Champaign

Cambridge Studies in Public Opinion and Political Psychology publishes innovative research from a variety of theoretical and methodological perspectives on the mass public foundations of politics and society. Research in the series focuses on the origins and influence of mass opinion, the dynamics of information and deliberation, and the emotional, normative, and instrumental bases of political choice. In addition to examining psychological processes, the series explores the organization of groups, the association between individual and collective preferences, and the impact of institutions on beliefs and behavior.

Cambridge Studies in Public Opinion and Political Psychology is dedicated to furthering theoretical and empirical research on the relationship between the political system and the attitudes and actions of citizens.

Books in the series are listed on the page following the Index.

Experts, Activists, and Democratic Politics

Are Electorates Self-Educating?

T. K. AHN
Seoul National University

ROBERT HUCKFELDT
University of California, Davis

JOHN BARRY RYAN
Stony Brook University

CAMBRIDGE
UNIVERSITY PRESS

CAMBRIDGE
UNIVERSITY PRESS

32 Avenue of the Americas, New York, NY 10013-2473, USA

Cambridge University Press is part of the University of Cambridge.

It furthers the University's mission by disseminating knowledge in the pursuit of education, learning, and research at the highest international levels of excellence.

www.cambridge.org
Information on this title: www.cambridge.org/9781107068872

© T.K. Ahn, Robert Huckfeldt, and John Barry Ryan 2014

First published 2014

A catalog record for this publication is available from the British Library.

Library of Congress Cataloging in Publication Data
Ahn, T. K., 1966–
Experts, activists, and interdependent citizens : are electorates self-educating? / T.K. Ahn, Robert Huckfeldt, John Barry Ryan.
  pages cm. – (Cambridge studies in public opinion and political psychology)
ISBN 978-1-107-06887-2 (hardback) – ISBN 978-1-107-65772-4 (paperback)
1. Political socialization. 2. Public opinion. 3. Communication in politics. I. Huckfeldt, R. Robert. II. Ryan, John Barry, 1979– III. Title.
JA76.A39 2014
306.2–dc23

2014016705

ISBN 978-1-107-06887-2 Hardback
ISBN 978-1-107-65772-4 Paperback

Dedicated to
John Sprague
and
the memory of
Elinor Ostrom

Contents

Figures

Tables

Origins and acknowledgments

The origin and path of this project reveal the magic of serendipity. Huckfeldt taught a seminar at Indiana University in the mid-1990s on interdependence and communication among citizens – a seminar in which Ahn happened to be enrolled. In spite of Huckfeldt's best efforts at convincing him to undertake a dissertation in the area, Ahn decided instead to work with their friend and colleague, Elinor Ostrom. As a consequence, Ahn also had the opportunity to work with Jimmy Walker and Roy Gardner on the experimental analysis of strategic behavior. Ten years later, Huckfeldt happened to be giving a talk at Florida State, where Ahn was a faculty member. They began a series of discussions on translating the study of network effects on political behavior into an experimental research program. Crucially, this was during the same period that John Ryan happened to arrive as a graduate student at the University of California in Davis, where he subsequently received a doctoral dissertation improvement grant from the National Science Foundation to run a series of experiments on networks and political communication. Finally, during this same period, the project also happened to benefit from a series of related discussions and collaborations with Mayer, Mendez, Osborn, Pietryka, and Reilly – all of whom we gratefully acknowledge as the coauthors of various chapters. Viewed in the rear view mirror, this all seems like a perfectly orderly process, but retrospective judgments obscure the inherently stochastic element within all our journeys – intellectual and otherwise!

The authors are also grateful for the helpful comments, suggestions, and assistance that came from a long list of outstanding colleagues: Chris Achen, John Aldrich, Bill Berry, Cheryl Boudreau, Amber Boydstun, Matt Buttice, Colin Cameron, David Cooper, David Cutts, Erik Engstrom, Stanley Feldman, Ed Fieldhouse, James Fowler, Brad Gomez, Kyu S. Hahn, Matt Hibbing, Ken'ichi Ikeda, Jennifer Jerit, Paul Johnson, Brad Jones, Cindy Kam, Don Kinder, Carol Kohfeld, Howie Lavine, David Lazar, Jan Leighley, Milton Lodge, Scott McClurg, Scott MacKenzie, Zeev Maoz, Jeff Mondak, Diana Owen, Franz Pappi, Won-ho

Park, Charles Plott, Ron Rapoport, Rüdiger Schmitt-Beck, John Scholz, John Scott, Phil Shively, Elizabeth Simas, Paul Sniderman, Walt Stone, Mike Ward, Rick Wilson, Elizabeth Zechmeister, and the late Alan Zuckerman. Finally, we appreciate the support of Lew Bateman, Jim Kuklinski, and Dennis Chong of Cambridge University Press and its Political Psychology Series. In particular, Jim Kuklinski has been the series editor sent from heaven, not only with respect to the current project but also with past projects leading up to it. We are forever and profoundly in debt to his insight and support.

We are also grateful to several publishers, not only for publishing our work in the past, but also for allowing us to build on these earlier efforts in this book. Chapter 1 incorporates arguments originally published by Oxford University Press in Ahn, Huckfeldt, Mayer, and Ryan (2010). Chapter 2 builds on arguments published by Sage Publications in Huckfeldt (2009). Chapter 3 relies on research previously published by John Wiley and Sons in Huckfeldt (2001); Sage Publications in Mendez and Osborn (2010); Springer in Ryan (2011a), and Taylor and Francis in Ryan (2010). Chapter 4 builds on research previously published by Cambridge University Press in Huckfeldt and Mendez (2008) and by John Wiley and Sons in Huckfeldt (2007). Chapter 5 relies on Ahn, Huckfeldt, and Ryan (2010), published by John Wiley. Chapter 6 is based on Ahn, Huckfeldt, Mayer, and Ryan (2013), published by John Wiley. Chapter 8 is based on Ryan (2011b), published by John Wiley. Chapter 9 is an expanded treatment of Huckfeldt, Pietryka, and Reilly (2014), published by Elsevier.

At various points along the way, research funding has been crucial to our effort. Chapter 8 is based on a project funded with a dissertation support grant for John Ryan from the National Science Foundation (SES-0817082). Alex Mayer was supported by a National Science Foundation Graduate Research Fellowship. Field work for the Indianapolis-St. Louis Study was supported by a grant from the National Science Foundation to Robert Huckfeldt and John Sprague (SBR-9515314). T. K. Ahn received support from a National Research Foundation of Korea Grant, funded by the Korean Government (NRF-2012S1A5A2A03). Finally, all three authors received crucial support from their respective institutions during the time of the project – Florida State University, the University of California at Davis, and Seoul National University.

We owe a particularly large debt of gratitude to two individuals who have been with us over the long haul as sources of motivation, inspiration, and intellectual insight. Hence, the book is dedicated to John Sprague and the memory of Elinor Ostrom.

Finally, each of us is grateful to those individuals who play crucial roles in our own lives: T.K. to Mi-young; Bob to Sharon and the other members of their family; and John to Yanna and his parents John and Jeanette Ryan.

I

Experts, activists, and self-educating electorates

T. K. Ahn, Robert Huckfeldt, and John Barry Ryan

> Leadership is a necessary phenomenon in every form of social life. Consequently it is not the task of science to inquire whether this phenomenon is good or evil, or predominantly one or the other. But there is great scientific value in the demonstration that every system of leadership is incompatible with the most essential postulates of democracy.
>
> Robert Michels (1962:364)

Even in the most egalitarian political systems, some citizens are more equal than others. This book addresses the role of opinion leaders as primary movers within the democratic political process – as individuals who are relatively more influential within the networks of communication connecting citizens to one another. These opinion leaders are influential – their opinions matter more – not because they hold elective office, bankroll political campaigns, or serve as advisors to those in power, but rather because their opinions are weighted more heavily in the collective deliberations of democratic electorates. This weighting system is informal rather than formal, and it results from the continuing stream of social interactions that occur among citizens. These opinion leaders have no official standing – their influence emerges instead through the countless social exchanges among citizens that carry political meaning and consequence for individuals as they make up their minds and reach political judgments.

The most effective opinion leaders are both experts and activists. They are politically expert, not necessarily in the sense of an encyclopedic knowledge regarding the technical details of complex policy issues, but rather in their ability to address the contemporaneous political agenda in ways that are helpful and meaningful to others (Ahn et al. 2010). This is not to say that the information they provide is neutral, and indeed one might well question whether political information is ever value-free. Indeed, to adopt an intermediary position between two partisan camps is often acceptable to neither extreme, and is often seen as unsatisfactory by both. Moreover, very few individuals become politically expert

I

out of a politically neutral fascination with politics. More typically, they are motivated to become informed due to their own involvement in the issues of the day.

Indeed, activists become opinion leaders *because* they care about politics and political issues. In many instances they care so deeply that they can hardly avoid becoming engaged with political issues and concerns. Many are like the moths who find the flame of politics and political controversy to be nearly irresistible. Their expertise is motivated by their own political engagement, and it provides them with the ability to arrive at political judgments based on their own subjectively identified interests and political evaluations, as well as the ability to communicate these judgments to others. Their activism is defined not necessarily in terms of any organizational or entrepreneurial engagement in politics, but rather in terms of political interests and commitments that are realized and activated through their communication with others.

These twin characteristics – expertise and activism – make opinion leaders pivotal in the communication process that generates public opinion and in the aggregate reality of democratic politics. Particular opinion leaders may certainly rank higher on one dimension or the other. Some experts are motivated by a fascination with politics that is really quite independent of any judgment regarding the virtue of various political alternatives. Others are complete activists who are quite innocent of well-informed, reasoned judgment guided by expertise. The influence of both extremes is likely to be politically compromised: the neutral expert by a lack of motivation and zeal, and the poorly informed activist by a lack of credibility. Again, the most successful opinion leaders demonstrate a combination of the two – knowledge of contemporary issues coupled with well-articulated preferences and goals. This combination provides both the capacity and the motivation to influence the opinions of others.

The opinion leadership they provide is an irreducible element of democratic politics for the simple reason that interdependence is an irreducible element of social life. If citizens collected and analyzed political information as independent individuals, their decisions would reflect judgments reached through independent means. Political analysts, in turn, could focus solely and wholly on what takes place between the ears of individual citizens, and they could treat the choices of individuals as being independent from one another. Indeed, analysts *do* routinely adopt the implicit or explicit assumption that individual responses to politics *can* be treated independently, but the analyses of this book call these assumptions into question.

Not only are individuals interdependent, but they communicate political information and opinions to one another, and some individuals occupy outsized, disproportionally influential roles within the process. Political communication is not an antiseptic, politically neutral information transfer, and it is not necessarily an exercise in civic enlightenment. Rather, it is an extension of the political process in which some people are more influential than others. At some times and in some circumstances, communication among citizens leads individuals to act in ways that sustain their own beliefs and interests. Echoing Michels' concern, however, the potential also exists for communication that leads individuals to act in ways contrary to their beliefs and interests.

HIGH HOPES AND REALISTIC CONCERNS

Political analysts and philosophers have long been divided on the normative merits of interdependence and social influence among citizens. The quotation from Michels with which we begin this chapter is motivated by his underlying concern that democracy is inevitably compromised by oligarchic tendencies arising under the guise of political leadership, even within the most democratic institutions and processes. His fears reflect Rousseau's (1762 [see Rousseau 1994]) concern that the general will can only be realized if individuals are wholly informed regarding their own interests and act accordingly,without any influence by others. Individuals who are influenced by others, Rousseau fears, might well be led to act against their own interests, thereby obstructing the realization of the general will.

Similar concerns are addressed by students of Condorcet's 1785 jury theorem (see Condorcet 1976). If a group is composed of actors who vote independently from one another, the odds of a majority choosing correctly (given the existence of a correct choice) increases with the size of the group and the competence of the individuals, assuming that individuals are more likely to vote correctly rather than incorrectly. There is disagreement, however, regarding the consequences of relaxing the independence assumption. One view sees interdependence as compromising the democratic optimism of the jury theorem. An alternative view suggests that deference to opinion leaders can, in some instances, improve individual and group competence (Estlund 1994).

Modern concerns regarding the effects of political communication and interdependence among political actors are reflected in the influential political economy literatures regarding "cheap talk" (Johnson 1993). The basic problem posed relates to the potential veracity of the information conveyed by self-interested individuals – that is, if someone is provided with political information and counsel, how do they know whether it speaks to their own interests and concerns or to those of the sender? To the extent that it is the latter, the value of communication in enhancing the capacity of the recipients to realize their own political aspirations is undermined. Correspondingly, to the extent that the recipients *believe* this to be the case, the value of the communication is generally diminished, as well as the recipients' confidence in it. In short, the advice is simply cheap talk that will be disregarded by sophisticated recipients, creating a "babbling equilibrium" without any political value (Lewis 1969).

All of these concerns – the compromising effects of political leadership in democratic processes and institutions, the problematic consequences of interdependence, and the dangers of cheap talk – can be seen in terms of the role played by opinion leaders in democratic politics. Politically activated opinion leaders are not typically motivated by some objective vision of truth, but rather by their *own* vision – that is, opinion leaders are typically motivated to gather information and become politically expert by their own concerns, and the information they obtain often reflects their own preferences. How can it be otherwise? Hence, expertise and activism are often positively correlated – activists tend to be expert.

Moreover, the relationship between expertise and activism is likely to be mutually reinforcing. People who know more are more likely to become opinionated, and the more they know, the more opinionated they are likely to become. They are likely to ignore information that contradicts their own purposes and to embrace information that sustains their own viewpoints. Rather than a search for objectivity, the search for political information is often motivated by existing political beliefs and preferences (Lodge and Taber 2013).

While these concerns regarding the problematic effects of interdependence are legitimate, they sometimes ignore the potentially beneficial aspects of an electorate composed of interdependent individuals. Beginning in the late nineteenth century, many theorists began to adopt a more benign view of social influence and majority opinion. Durkheim's work (1984, 1951) conceives a social aggregate that takes on meaning quite apart from the individuals who compose the group, and one of his primary concerns was the disintegrating effects of modern societies on the social fabric that sustains these groups. Even though Durkheim's concerns were not explicitly political, he establishes a framework for a view which emphasizes the community as being quite separate from individualist conceptions of interests and utilities.

These early concerns persist in contemporary arguments and debates, as well as in the continuing tug of war between individualistic and corporate conceptions of politics and public opinion. As we will see, one body of literature focuses on the potential for social influence to be politically misleading. Echoing Rousseau and Michels, individuals might indeed be led astray from acting in their own interests by an informant or an advisor whose interests are actually divergent from their own (Crawford 1998). At the same time, other efforts reveal the educative potential of social influence and opinion leaders (Berelson et al. 1954; Katz 1957). In an environment where individual citizens are often woefully uninformed, a reliance on relatively well-informed opinion leaders might, under certain circumstances, lead to a better-informed electorate – and in this way, the quality of the interdependent whole might surpass the quality arising from the sum of the independent parts.

Our own argument is that opinion leadership is neither the salvation nor the ruination of democratic politics. Some patterns of interdependence produce political bandwagons and stock market bubbles (Bikhchandani et al. 1992). Others serve to enhance the level of expertise within electorates, as well as to diffuse shared interests within the boundaries of relevant political groups (Lupia and McCubbins 1998). Important contingencies operate on the form and function of communication networks, and qualities of the informant relative to the person being informed constitute a crucial element in the analysis of the information that is conveyed. Are the informant and the recipient in fundamental agreement or disagreement regarding underlying preferences and goals? Is the informant politically expert? Assuming that individuals have multiple informants, do a single informant's views coincide with or diverge from the views communicated by other informants? Is the recipient of incoming information capable of making discriminating judgments regarding the quality of the message?

Downs (1957) argues that citizens are well advised to seek out information from individuals who are both well-informed and share their political preferences. While this prescription provides a useful baseline, it is often violated in practice, primarily because the menu of potential informants is constrained both temporally and spatially. Hence, the costs of locating the ideal political informant are not insignificant, and other priorities may compete. You might prefer an articulate Republican as an associate, but your other preference – for an associate who is keen on hiking in the Sierra – may trump that political preference, even if your hiking buddy turns out to be a liberal environmentalist.

Moreover, when we move from considerations of the individual to considerations of the whole, Downs' ideal may not only be empirically inadequate, but prescriptively inadequate as well. By limiting social communication regarding politics to associates with shared political preferences, individuals limit their opportunities to reconsider and readdress their own fundamental assumptions and preferences. None of these complications negate the fundamental importance of political expertise. In an interdependent world where citizens obtain political information and guidance from others, a range of contingencies operate on the successful translation of individually held interests and preferences into appropriately informed political choices – and one of the most important revolves around the capacities of groups and individuals both to provide and to receive expert political counsel.

POLITICAL EXPERTISE IN THE CORRIDORS OF EVERYDAY LIFE

The concept of political expertise is typically restricted to considerations of political elites and elite decision-making – to the politicians, consultants, bureaucrats, and handlers who populate the corridors of power. While important efforts have certainly been made to introduce the role of expertise into discussions of grass-roots politics among the citizens populating the corridors of everyday life, these efforts have been notable for their failure to penetrate the dominant, enduring vision of democratic politics held among political scientists (Ahn et al. 2010).

This failure is especially striking in view of early efforts in political science and sociology that focused attention on differentiated levels of political capacity among citizens via "opinion leaders" and a "two-step flow" of communication. The earliest two-step model was a simplified rendering in which some people (the opinion leaders) paid attention to politics and the media, while other individuals (virtually everyone else) took their information and guidance from these opinion leaders (Lazarsfeld et al. 1968). This early model was vulnerable to criticisms of political elitism – namely, that it underestimated the capacity of individual citizens consigned to the role of followers. It was also vulnerable to criticisms that it oversimplified the communication processes in which leaders and followers were tied together in complex horizontal as well as vertical networks of relationships where, for example, leaders and followers change roles depending on the particular subject matter. These problems were addressed in later, more sophisticated treatments of opinion leaders and the two-step flow (Berelson et al. 1954; Katz and Lazarsfeld 1955; Katz 1957; Weimann 1982, 1991). Nevertheless, expertise and the role of expert individuals have been slow to penetrate research on voting, public opinion, political communication, and political participation.

This lack of penetration is primarily the consequence of a historical reluctance to consider citizens as interdependent actors in politics. The primary model of a voter in the empirical literature has been a socially disembodied individual whose decisions, judgments, and voting choices are based on individually held preferences, opinions, beliefs, attitudes, and identifications. This atomistic model is probably best seen as an unintentional byproduct of particular observational strategies that have been dominant in political research – most notably randomized sample surveys of large populations that divorce individuals from their social and political environments (Huckfeldt and Sprague 1993, 1995). While relatively few students of politics would advocate an atomistic model on its intellectual merits, traditional methods of data collection have resulted in a *de facto* adherence to a model that separates and isolates one citizen from another in a way that is both theoretically unsatisfying and empirically inadequate.

The welcome news is that rapidly accelerating progress has taken place in alternative modes of data collection and analysis regarding communication among interdependent individuals. These alternatives include contextual studies, network studies, and experimental studies that intentionally locate one citizen relative to other citizens in both time and space, thereby generating new opportunities to revisit opinion leaders and political expertise in the context of horizontal and vertical networks that create multiple-step flows of communication and persuasion (for discussions, see Huckfeldt and Sprague 1993; Huckfeldt 2007a; Ahn et al. 2010). The moment has thus arrived to reconsider and extend the earliest conceptions of opinion leaders, communication, and interdependence within democratic electorates.

THE CIVIC CAPACITY OF VOTERS AND ELECTORATES

The inability of political expertise to gain traction as a useful concept in the study of politics and social communication is even more ironic in view of the historic intellectual investment that has been made in the study of political knowledge, awareness, and belief systems among citizens (Converse 1964; Delli Carpini and Keeter 1993, 1996; Gilens 2001; Kuklinski et al. 2000; Zaller 1992). This body of work, which is typically based on large-scale national surveys and is normally focused on individual determinants and consequences of knowledge and beliefs, has demonstrated levels of political competence that are often disappointing. As Sniderman (1993) suggests, shocked disbelief and opposition to the earliest work ultimately gave way to a new stream of research that takes low levels of civic capacity as a given, turning instead to several important and derivative questions. If voters are so naïve, how are they able to make decisions that often seem well informed (Sniderman, Brody, and Tetlock 1991; Lodge and Steenbergen with Brau 1995)? And, given the incapacities of individual voters, how do aggregate electorates manage to perform in a manner that appears to respond to the political environment in meaningful ways (Page and Shapiro 1992; Erikson, MacKuen, and Stimson 2002; Sniderman 2000)?

This renewed and sharpened focus on the locus of expertise in democratic politics produced a burst of optimism regarding the capacity of citizens and electorates. Even though voters were poorly informed and lacking in encyclopedic knowledge regarding issues and candidates, many hoped they might make sound decisions and choices based on a variety of informational cues and shortcuts. More recent work calls this optimism into question. Kuklinski and Quirk (2000) and Sniderman (2000) draw attention to the failures of cognitive shortcuts in improving the quality of citizen decision-making. Lodge and Taber (2000; see also Taber and Lodge 2006) consider the limitations of human reasoning that arise when individuals must reconcile new and divergent information with their pre-existent beliefs and attitudes. Kuklinski et al. (2000) address the potential for misinformation and its implications for the capacity of electorates.

Within this context, a renewed emphasis on communication networks is potentially relevant to the distribution and diffusion of political expertise among interdependent citizens, as well as to individual and aggregate decision-making. The selection of informants, and hence the construction of networks, not only responds to the preferences of potential discussants, but also to their potential for being informative (Downs 1957). The presence or absence of bias on the part of potential informants does not necessarily reduce their information potential (Calvert 1985a), and empirical studies show that the construction of communication networks responds directly to the expertise of potential discussants. Discussion occurs more frequently with individuals who possess higher levels of interest and knowledge about politics, and it is only modestly depressed by disagreement (see Chapters 3 and 4).

As a consequence, frequently low levels of individually held knowledge are not entirely surprising, and they may be less troublesome. This is particularly the case if the political capacities of individuals are understood in a somewhat larger context. First, citizenship involves more than political knowledge, expertise, and voting. The fabric of a democratic society depends on a range of talents and contributions, supplied both through markets as well as through voluntary communal efforts, and thus productive citizenship is not simply the residue of individuals who are able and willing to read the *New York Times*. If time spent consuming and analyzing information on current affairs comes at the expense of these other commitments – coaching little league baseball, organizing the girl scout troop, or volunteering at the local library – it may very well be a bad bargain for the more complex and variegated fabric of not only democratic politics, but also democratic societies (Berelson et al. 1954: chapter 14).

Moreover, if many individuals do not obtain immediate benefits from consuming information on politics – if they do not place intrinsic value on political information or realize some instrumental advantage – why would we be surprised that the level of political expertise within populations is heterogeneous? At the same time, even when viewed from the vantage point of the most myopic form of individual rationality, the consumption of political information is not irrational for everyone (Fiorina 1990; Downs 1957). Some people enjoy politics more than others, and it is entirely reasonable that these people spend more time on political matters, while others are located in occupations that depend on up-to-date political knowledge. Fortunately, the consumption of political information makes perfectly good sense among *both* those who enjoy politics and public affairs *and* those who value it instrumentally.

What is the solution to the problem of heterogeneous levels of political expertise within populations? Is this heterogeneity a problem? Heterogeneous information levels are potentially mitigated through patterns of interdependence – through complex networks of political communication. The implication is that, by ignoring the relationship between interdependent citizens and varying levels of political expertise, we obscure the capacity of citizens in the aggregate, as well as incorrectly specifying models of political judgment and decision.

None of this means that interdependent citizens necessarily produce beneficial outcomes. Indeed, a politically realistic view of interdependence and social communication acknowledges the potential and reality of individuals who are misinformed by their fellow citizens – in particular, the potential that individuals are persuaded to act against their own interests. Indeed, experts are often activists – they not only invest in information related to their values and preferences, but also hold deeply felt political beliefs which provide the motivation to employ that information in an effort at convincing others. Correspondingly, the very real potential exists for people to be misled by the expert activists in their midst.

Hence, we are not arguing that interdependence among citizens ameliorates all the problems of a poorly informed electorate. Rather, our argument is that an ignorance of individual interdependence within electorates runs the risk of fundamentally misunderstanding not only the nature of citizenship, but also the central abiding strengths and weaknesses of democratic politics. In some instances, social communication allows politically naïve individuals to act as if they were experts without incurring prohibitive information costs. At other moments, social communication encourages individuals to embrace candidates and causes they would be unlikely to support if they were better informed. Hence, social communication among interdependent individuals does not always or necessarily produce an electorate of well-informed individuals capable of acting on the basis of their own objectively and individually defined interests. Rather, it creates an electorate in which the preferences of some individuals – the activists and experts who function as opinion leaders – play outsized roles in the collective discussions of democratic politics. In short, we will argue that political communication among citizens is best understood as an extension of the democratic political process rather than as a value-free exercise in civic education.

EXPERTISE, KNOWLEDGE, AND SELF-EDUCATING ELECTORATES

What is the difference between knowledge and expertise? Knowledge involves an individual's ability to access relevant political information from long-term memory (Lodge and Taber 2000). In contrast, we define expertise in terms of political choices informed by subjectively defined interests, and hence the ability of an individual to act in accord with her own view of the world. Some citizens are politically knowledgeable and hence likely to be expert, and many of these individuals further enhance their levels of expertise based on communication with others. Some citizens possess modest or negligible amounts of political knowledge, but their judgments are informed through various mechanisms, including political discussion (Sniderman et al. 1991; Lodge et al. 1995; Marcus, Neuman and MacKuen 2000; MacKuen and Marcus 2001; Green, Palmquist, and Schickler 2002). Still other citizens base their choices directly on the knowledge and expertise held by others. They act as though they are knowledgeable by imitating the choices of others in their environments, and hence their expertise is socially derived (Fowler and Smirnov 2005; Huckfeldt, Johnson, and Sprague 2004; Boyd and Richerson 1985). While such imitation may not necessarily produce optimal choices, it is a particularly effective strategy for individuals who are unwilling or unable to invest in individually based acquisition of information, but are able to imitate the choices of others who provide appropriate guidance.

These distinctions are important because political communication need not enhance knowledge in order to enhance expertise within the electorate. Indeed, we will argue that individuals do not necessarily become more knowledgeable simply by discussing politics with knowledgeable discussion partners, and there is little evidence to suggest that people automatically weigh the advice of politically knowledgeable informants more heavily when arriving at their own political judgments and choices (Chapter 3). Moreover, an interesting set of studies on "correct" voting (see Lau and Redlawsk's 1997 definition) produces mixed consequences for the effects that arise due to communication with experts (Sokhey and McClurg 2012; Richey 2008; Jackman and Sniderman 2006).

These observations raise a series of questions related to the selection criteria that individuals employ to construct political communication networks, the contextually based supply of experts as a constraint on these selection mechanisms, and the capacity of expert citizens to influence the communication process. Is the expertise of a potential informant relevant to the construction of communication networks? Under what circumstances is expert advice influential, credible, or worthwhile? What are the circumstances and consequences of political communication beyond the boundaries of proximate groups – the conditions giving rise to networks that bridge the divides between groups? What are the implications of these various mechanisms of communication and interdependence for politics in the aggregate?

Our response to these questions is framed around three propositions. First, communication networks are constructed by individual choices and opportunities for interaction that accumulate to form and re-shape patterns of communication, but these choices respond to the availability of potential discussants and their levels of expertise. Second, the messages conveyed through political communication networks are thus neither persistently nor inevitably homogeneous, and the extent of diversity varies systematically as a consequence of both individual and contextual factors. Third, varying levels of diversity, combined with the importance of expertise, carry complex dynamical implications for the diffusion of information, the self-educating properties of electorates, and self-limiting patterns of influence within aggregate populations (Huckfeldt, Johnson, and Sprague 2004).

CONTEXTUAL CONSTRAINTS ON NETWORK CONSTRUCTION

Individuals exercise choice in the construction of communication networks, but choice is constrained by supply, and the supply of discussion partners looms particularly large with respect to network composition. The supply of potential discussants is, in turn, a stochastic function of proximate populations – families, work places, places of worship, sports clubs. Moreover, individuals have multiple preferences in the construction of communication networks, and politics is only one among a long list of preferential criteria – sparkling personalities, trustworthiness, a hatred for the Yankees, and so on. Finally, extended information searches are personally and socially expensive, and hence individuals will typically build networks of association that reflect the contexts within which they reside, regardless of their own political preferences (Greer 1961; Brown 1981).

In short, the distribution of political preferences within networks – either homogeneous or heterogeneous – might arise as a consequence of environmentally imposed supply, quite independently of individual control over associational patterns (Huckfeldt 1983b; Buttice, Huckfeldt and Ryan 2008). None of this means that individuals are powerless to exercise control over the form and content of their communication networks (Finifter 1974; MacKuen 1990). To the contrary, potential methods of control over network construction are crucial to the communication process, and they constitute a primary focus of our effort.

CONSEQUENCES OF NETWORK DIVERSITY

A renewed focus on political diversity within communication networks is inspired by the mismatch between long-standing theory and observation. In their classic study of the 1948 election, Berelson, Lazarsfeld, and McPhee (1954: chapter 7) argue that social interaction produces agreement and homogeneity within small groups. In his analysis of diversity, Abelson (1964, 1979) identifies a seemingly inexorable tendency toward homogeneity within formal models of communication. This same tendency is found in agent-based simulations of communication and diffusion (Axelrod 1997a), where heterogeneity is inevitably extinguished as a consequence of interaction.

More than 25 years of research demonstrate the importance of clustered political preferences within political communication networks. The vast majority of citizens live their lives in settings where most of the people they know hold political preferences and beliefs that reinforce their own inclinations (Mutz 2006). At the same time, the accumulated evidence also points toward persistent levels of residual disagreement, even within the smallest and most closely held social groups (Huckfeldt and Sprague 1995; Huckfeldt, Beck et al. 1998; Huckfeldt, Johnson, and Sprague 2004). Respondents in the 2000 National Election Study were asked to provide the first names of people with whom they were most likely to discuss "government, elections, and politics." Approximately 40 percent of those supporting a major party candidate (Bush or Gore) named at least one discussant who supported the opposite party's candidate, and less than half perceived that all the discussants they had named supported their own preferred candidate (Huckfeldt, Mendez, and Osborn 2004). Similar patterns of preference heterogeneity within networks are demonstrated across time and space within the United States (Huckfeldt and Sprague 1995; Huckfeldt, Beck et al. 1998; Huckfeldt, Johnson, and Sprague 2004), as well as in cross national comparisons (Huckfeldt, Ikeda, and Pappi 2005).

Why is preference heterogeneity important to expertise among citizens? If citizens avoid divergent preferences, the potential for persuasive communication is reduced. This was demonstrated early and convincingly in the work of William McPhee's (1963) vote simulator: disagreement gives rise to continued information search and hence the potential for "influence" in the broadest sense of the term (see also Taber and Lodge 2006). That is, influence occurs not only when individuals are persuaded to change their preferences in response to divergent information, but also when individuals must "counterargue" – either socially or internally. Contrary messages are influential if they force individuals to rethink their own preferences, even if their initial commitments to those preferences are sustained.

LIMITATIONS ON INFLUENCE

Why does disagreement fail to be resolved by persuasion? Why do we not see the *creation* of uniformity within these networks of communication? These are particularly important questions because a range of sophisticated modeling efforts appear to suggest that such a persuasion dynamic is nearly irresistible within large populations (Abelson 1964, 1979; Axelrod 1997a, 1997b; Johnson and Huckfeldt 2005; Huckfeldt, Johnson, and Sprague 2004, 2005). The (perhaps) counterintuitive answer to this question is that complex patterns of communication and influence are, in fact, self-limiting within the context of diverse preferences, and hence interdependence can be seen to sustain heterogeneity!

If disagreement within a dyad leads to a process of counterargument in which the views of other discussants are taken into account, then the influence of communication within any particular dyad is conditioned on communication within all other dyads. In other words, not only is the formation of an individual's preference autoregressive with respect to the distribution of preferences in an individual's communication network (Marsden and Friedkin 1994), but the influence within a particular dyad is autoregressive with respect to the flow of information within the participants' other dyads (Huckfeldt, Johnson, and Sprague 2004). As a consequence, the influence of a contrary message is attenuated by the dominant messages within networks, and heterogeneity is thus sustained.

An example occurs in the work of Mutz and Mondak (2006), who provide a compelling account of the fact that individuals are more likely to encounter political disagreement in the workplace (also see Baybeck and Huckfeldt 2002). Within that context, suppose that Sidney and Lisa are coworkers, and that Sidney is imbedded in a family full of Republicans, while Lisa is imbedded in a family full of Democrats. For a variety of reasons – workplace proximity, shared interests, and so on – Lisa and Sidney regularly communicate about a range of topics, including politics. Neither of them is likely to be convinced by the other to change her political stripes for the simple reason that both still reside within an informational environment dominated by their respective families. Hence, one might argue that agreement as well as disagreement are both socially sustained through complex patterns of social interaction and communication (Huckfeldt, Johnson, and Sprague 2004).

In short, political heterogeneity within networks is a necessary but insufficient condition for political change due to persuasive communication driven by expert opinion. Disagreement provides the occasion for influence, but if expert opinion is not weighted more heavily within the communication process, expert communications would not necessarily translate into the diffusion of expertise. Such weighting might occur if individuals genuflect with respect to citizens with higher levels of expertise – a prospect that we will argue is unlikely – or if the weighting process occurs because the views of expert citizens are disproportionately represented within the process of political communication. Hence, the intentional or unintentional weighting of expert opinion becomes a crucial issue in the analysis of opinion leadership.

INDIVIDUAL, AGGREGATE, AND DYNAMIC IMPLICATIONS

Traditional models suggest that social communication insulates individuals from events in the external political environment. Individual citizens are imbedded within homogeneous groupings of like-minded individuals, and politics is reinterpreted relative to the dominant views in the group. Hence, political information is filtered, conformity encouraged, and group boundaries reinforced (Berelson et al. 1954; Huckfeldt 1983a). The problem is that the persistence of diversity, coupled with the centrality of political experts within communication networks, calls into question this sort of determinate outcome (McPhee 1963).

A number of efforts have pursued the proximate, individual-level implications of homogeneous versus heterogeneous communication networks. While a consensus has not been reached, a diverse set of findings is generating progress in the identification of important underlying issues. Mutz's results (2002a, 2006) suggest that individuals residing in politically heterogeneous networks are less likely to participate and more likely to make decisions closer to the election. Huckfeldt, Mendez, and Osborn (2004) show modestly negative effects of heterogeneity on political interest but no effects on turnout. They also demonstrate higher levels of ambivalence and lower levels of partisanship among those located in heterogeneous networks. Fowler (2005) shows that one individual in a homogeneous network deciding to vote could lead to a turnout cascade, while McClurg (2006) finds that the most important social determinant of turnout is not heterogeneity but rather expertise – people in expert networks are more likely to turn out. Based on his empirical analysis, Kotler-Berkowitz (2005: 167) argues that "networks made up of a diverse set of friends expose people to various non-redundant opportunities and requests for political participation ..." Both Gibson (1992; also 2001) and Mutz (2002b) show that individuals in heterogeneous networks are more likely to be politically tolerant.[1]

While these various results are sometimes difficult to reconcile, they point toward aggregate and dynamic implications of heterogeneous networks for democratic politics that are quite profound. The survival of disagreement within networks of political communication, in combination with the important effects on communication that arise due to the distribution of expertise, lead to a reconsideration of the mechanisms of political interdependence among citizens, the diffusion of expertise within networks, and the aggregate implications of political interdependence among citizens. Indeed, the theory of the consequences of social communication for the dynamics of an election campaign might be fundamentally transformed. Rather than serving as a source of insulation from the external political environment, social communication might even serve to magnify the consequences of the external environment by connecting individuals to extensive and far-reaching networks of political information (Barabasi 2002; Watts 1999).

The intersection of these phenomena – the survival of disagreement, the self-educating capacities of electorates, and the resulting dynamic consequences of interdependent individuals – forces a reassessment of the models and mechanisms of communication among citizens (Mendelberg 2002; Barber 1984;

---

[1] For an interesting effort to reconcile findings, see Gimpel, Lay, and Schuknecht 2003.

Fishkin 1991). It also points toward particular observational strategies for collecting relevant information on these problems. In particular, it is not enough to collect information on individuals, although information on individuals is of course central to progress in understanding political communication patterns. Rather, individuals are understood within the context of communication and interaction – within the groups where they are located. Hence, observational strategies are needed which provide the opportunity to move back and forth seamlessly between individuals and groups, both theoretically and observationally.

EXPERTISE, MOTIVATION, AND COMMUNICATION

One of the enduring innovations of the political economy literature on citizenship is to take information costs seriously in the analysis of political communication and expertise. Within this context, Downs (1957: 229) argues, political discussion minimizes the information costs of political engagement. Those who are astute, he argues, search out **well-informed** associates who possess **compatible** political orientations, and hence citizens become efficiently informed – both individually and collectively.

At the same time, opinion leadership is not simply a consequence of political expertise, but of motivation as well. Not only political knowledge, but also self-reported political interest, correlate highly with discussion frequency and opinion strength in survey analyses of political communication networks. This means that people who are politically expert, opinionated, and engaged are disproportionately represented among the population that dominates the conversational airways of American politics. The fact that people report more frequent conversations with politically expert associates (Chapter 3) may simply reflect the fact that these experts are talking about politics at higher frequencies, and therefore more frequent discussion with experts is virtually unavoidable! Hence we have two different expectations with reinforcing consequences: (1) individuals are likely to seek out experts as political informants, and (2) politically expert, opinionated, and engaged individuals are more likely to broadcast their political opinions and concerns through social communication. It may be either the sender or the recipient of information who initiates political exchanges that accentuate the role of expertise within communication networks.

Political experts are more likely to be emotionally engaged by politics and political issues for several reasons. Affect and emotion vary in systematic and consequential ways across individuals, and they carry important implications for the process of political communication. One reason that disagreement and dialogue occur among citizens is that some individuals cannot resist expressing their opinions, even when it means that a social dispute is the inevitable outcome. That is, when they receive provocative and disagreeable messages through political exchanges, they react on the basis of an automatic and preconscious response, prior to any deliberative calculation regarding the unpleasant disagreement that is likely to follow (Marcus, Neuman, and MacKuen 2000). While these people do not necessarily enjoy communication-induced disagreement, their high levels of engagement in politics and investment in political information serves to make communication inevitable, even when disagreement is the inevitable outcome. This is particularly important because, as McPhee (1963) demonstrates, influence depends on disagreement – you may reinforce your friend's preference if you agree with her, but you will never change her mind unless you disagree.

In short, those who are most engaged by politics and political affairs are most likely to initiate political conversations with the individuals who populate the micro-environments where they are located. This higher frequency of political communication makes them more likely to encounter disagreement – more discussion with more people yields more opportunities for disagreement (Huckfeldt, Ikeda, and Pappi 2005). While one obvious way out of the dilemma is to censor conversations in order to avoid political discussion, the politically engaged citizens who are most emotionally invested will find this to be particularly difficult to accomplish (Chapter 4). Some actors are unaware of events in the external political environment, and hence are immune to the process we are describing. Other actors are so conflict-averse that they steer their way clear of political communication entirely. Still others are engaged and emotionally committed, and these individuals are more likely to seize opportunities to exercise opinion leadership. Indeed, for such individuals, these opportunities may be very nearly irresistible.

SOURCES AND CONSEQUENCES OF MOTIVATION

Fiorina (1990) argues that staying politically informed is at its essence a response to consumer preference – some people value information on its own terms as an end in itself. Why would they value information? One explanation is simply related to an innate interest regarding politics and public affairs – some people simply enjoy politics. Hence, understanding levels of participation and political engagement only in terms of the exogenously imposed information costs can be misleading.

Indeed, as we will see in Chapter 7, the logic of our experimental subjects' behavior cannot be understood wholly as a consequence of information costs. Even among individuals for whom information acquisition is costless, we will see heterogeneous levels of information acquisition. Just as important, we will also see heterogeneity in the communication of information that cannot be understood separately from the idiosyncratic characteristics of the messengers. Some individuals act strategically in their communications while others do not. Some send misleading messages, while others send messages that are straightforward reflections of their own underlying beliefs.

Alternative explanations point toward other factors that lead to political attentiveness and engagement. Some personality types are more likely to be drawn to political discussion and to tolerate – and even welcome – exposure to disagreement (Mondak 2010; Mondak et al. 2010). Analyses using data on the

Big Five personality traits find, for example, that extraverted individuals tend to have large discussion networks and to engage in political discussion with heightened frequency, as well as exhibiting higher levels of exposure to disagreement. More broadly, these same works reveal numerous relationships between personality and various aspects of political engagement.

Moreover, politics elicits strong emotions among some individuals, primarily due to particular patterns of association in memory among objects that are powerfully charged with negative and positive affect. According to Fazio (1990, 1995), attitude strength is defined in terms of the strength of association between an object in long-term memory and the evaluation of that object. In this way, attitude strength can be a provocative factor in the stimulation of political discussion and disagreement, as well as a source of hot cognitions generating an instantaneous emotional response (Kunda 1999; Lodge and Taber 2000).

For example, the mere mention of a "liberal Democrat" or "Rush Limbaugh" or "John Boehner" or "Barack Obama" is likely to stimulate preconscious emotional responses for many people. To the extent that emotional responses to political objects are intense, we would expect political communication to be nearly inevitable. You *may* be able to resist the urge to join a conversation, but you are probably less likely to be able to hide the nature of your emotional response. Hence, just as we would expect some personality types to be active within communication networks, so we would also expect people with strong emotional responses to politics to become more politically active.

These strong emotional responses to political objects often lead individuals to become more actively engaged in a range of political behaviors. In particular, such responses stimulate attentiveness and hence encourage the development of knowledge and expertise (Simon 1983). Expertise is likely to be partisan in nature for the simple reason that emotional responses are unlikely to generate balanced and objective information-gathering and analysis. In short, emotion stimulates engagement, engagement leads to information gathering, and the resulting expertise is likely to be decidedly partisan. As Lodge and Taber (2000) argue, the collection of new information is likely to reinforce previously held attitudes and opinions. This is particularly important because partisan individuals with more extreme attitudes are the people who are most likely to communicate effectively and unambiguously (Huckfeldt, Sprague, and Levine 2000).

As a consequence, the logic of "affective intelligence" (Marcus, Neuman, and MacKuen 2000) extends beyond considerations of individual opinion and behavior to an analysis of the communication processes among citizens, and it suggests that personality and emotion lie very close to political attentiveness, expertise, and influential communication. Those people who feel most deeply and emotionally with regard to political topics are likely to possess more political information, even if they are less likely to be objective and value-free. Indeed, as Lodge and Taber suggest (2000), those who know more are more likely to be more strongly partisan in support of their preferences. Hence, the experts within communication networks possess more information, and they are also more likely to be automatic responders to political stimuli – they are willing to wade into the political thicket of controversy and disagreement.

In other words, affect, emotion, personality, and expertise interact in important ways, producing experts who are more likely to be politically active, as well as activists who are more likely to be politically expert. The personal realization of discomfort and distaste for disagreement is likely to vary quite substantially across various personality types. Even among those who find disagreement distasteful, people who are emotionally engaged are more likely to pay the price, and hence they play central roles within political communication networks. What does this suggest with regard to the profile of the influential citizen expert in democratic politics?

Citizen experts are neither emotionally detached nor politically neutral. This runs at least partially counter to the concept of expertise as it has typically been employed to study the corridors of power, where the professional politicians, bureaucrats, and lobbyists ply their trades. In these contexts, expertise is motivated by instrumental ends, where cool consideration and detached calculation often pay enormous dividends. Indeed, the effectiveness of the professional experts depends on the ability to comprehend the interests of all sides in an effort to realize their instrumental goals more effectively, and the impassioned plea is often just one more tool in the arsenal to achieve these goals (Wilson 1973).

In contrast, emotional engagement is central to the amateur (citizen) expert who operates in the corridors of everyday life. The amateur expert is perhaps no more likely to feel deeply regarding relevant political issues and debates, but feelings and emotions are likely to provide primary motivations for their involvement. Due to the ever-present collective action problems that obstruct citizen involvement, citizens typically lack clear-cut instrumental motivations that survive even the most rudimentary cost-benefit considerations – hence, emotion plays a key role in the survival of a robust democratic politics. Absent the presence of emotion, it is doubtful that cool-headed assessments of the costs and benefits associated with engagement and participation would generate widespread involvement – far fewer individuals would be willing to pay the costs of involvement. Just as altruistic punishment makes it possible for small groups to address collective action problems, so also affective intelligence sustains communication, discussion, and engagement within the electorate by offsetting participation costs (Fehr and Gächter 2002; Ostrom, Walker, and Gardner 1992).

In short, opinion leaders are likely to be *both* experts *and* activists. They do not serve as the reference librarians of democratic politics – individuals who are simply on call to respond to requests for information. Rather, they are frequently the instigators who cannot resist the temptation to become involved when confronted with disagreeable statements or wrong-headed viewpoints. None of this is meant to deny the multiple forms of opinion leaders and opinion leadership. Some tend toward the dispassionately expert, while others tend toward the passionately inept. At the same time, tendencies toward activism and expertise tend to be self-reinforcing, and therein lies an important element of the genius underlying political leadership in the corridors of everyday life.

IMPLICATIONS AND CONCLUSION

While information costs constitute an impediment to participation for many individuals, these costs are highly variable across individuals. As Wolfinger and Rosenstone (1980) suggest, information costs are lower among those individuals for whom the acquisition and processing of information is easier – typically individuals with higher levels of education. And as Fiorina (1990) argues, many individuals may find information about politics to be intrinsically rewarding – they read about the Democrats and the Republicans with the enthusiasm of a basketball fan reading about the Lakers and the Celtics. For these people, the benefits of information far outweigh the costs, and staying informed thus becomes a self-reinforcing behavior.

Moreover, information costs become largely irrelevant for individuals who demonstrate high levels of political motivation. For many individuals, political engagement, interest, and hence discussion constitute preconscious responses to topics about which they care deeply. Political information always comes with costs – one might always prefer sailing a boat on a beautiful day to reading the opinion page of the newspaper. At the same time, and for some individuals, the acquisition of information is less an investment than an emotionally charged response to deeply held attitudes and beliefs.

Hence, we should not be surprised to see the division of labor in the communication of political information suggested by Berelson and his colleagues (1954) so long ago. Individuals with high information costs and/or low levels of emotional involvement will intentionally or unintentionally rely on individuals with minimal information costs and/or high levels of emotional involvement. The resulting patterns of communication may indeed produce an electorate that makes surprisingly expert choices – at least relative to the low mean levels of political awareness among individuals within the electorate (Converse 1964; Zaller 1992; Delli Carpini and Keeter 1996; Page and Shapiro 1992; Erikson, MacKuen, and Stimson 2002). In this way, civic capacity in the aggregate benefits from the diffusion of expert opinion within and throughout networks of political communication.

At the same time, it is important to recall that political communication is not an objective exercise in civic education. It involves people with opinions and interests who are not only learning from one another, but are also persuading one another. The accumulated record, based on surveys and experiments, suggests that the process tends to be driven by knowledge and expertise. That is, the process is skewed in favor of politically engaged participants with more information – the very individuals identified by Lodge and Taber (2000) as being most opinionated and most likely to demonstrate motivated reasoning.

To the extent that the distribution of political expertise within the electorate is correlated with the distributions of particular interests and preferences, the process we have described carries important partisan consequences. Hence, it becomes important to take interdependence seriously in the study of democratic politics. In turn, progress in such an undertaking requires a continuing effort to design and implement novel ways of both locating and observing individuals within the social settings where they obtain political information and make political choices – to study citizens as they occur, as parts of an interdependent social construct.

An adequate understanding of opinion leaders requires a focus on the location of experts and activists within the political communication networks that define the structure and form of interdependence among citizens. Hence, in the chapter that follows we give deliberate attention to the implications of interdependence in politics. We make the attempt to take interdependence seriously as an integral element of political life, and hence as a necessary ingredient in political analysis.

2

The imperatives of interdependence

T. K. Ahn, Robert Huckfeldt, and John Barry Ryan

> ... the norms, preferences, motives, and beliefs of participants in collective beha-
> vior can, in most cases, only provide a necessary but not a sufficient condition for
> the explanation of outcomes; in addition, one needs a model of how these indivi-
> dual preferences interact and aggregate.
>
> Mark Granovetter (1978, p. 1421)

This chapter addresses a series of analytic challenges, opportunities, and
strategies related to the study of interdependence among citizens. Opinion
leadership occurs within a social context, contingent on the particular patterns of interdependence among actors. One individual communicates with
another individual; one or both individuals may or may not be affected by
the exchange; and this leads to a series of questions. Did the recipient of a
message select the informant, or did the informant select the recipient? What
are the criteria that lie behind these choices? Are there competing criteria
in the construction of communication networks? What are the constraints
on the supply of discussants? What are the effects of the communication
within the dyad? Are there higher-order consequences that extend beyond
the dyad – does Joe's message to Tom carry consequences for a message from
Tom to Sam? What are the aggregate consequences and implications for the
diffusion of political information and for the distribution of opinions in the
larger population?

These questions lead directly to a set of challenges that demand our attention –
challenges that serve as the theoretical and methodological imperatives underlying this effort. These imperatives arise as a direct consequence of the patterns
of interdependence among citizen actors who communicate, inform, and persuade one another regarding politics and political issues.

First, interdependence means that we cannot view actors in isolation. Rather,
they must be viewed not only within particular dyadic relationships, but also

more generally within the larger social networks and contexts within which the individual and the dyad are located.[1]

Second, interdependence also implies an underlying process of communication among and between actors. This means, in turn, that interdependence carries important dynamic implications occurring in real time. Hence, this second imperative is related to the observation of interdependence *not only in space but also in time*.

We introduce these issues in the current chapter, and they set the stage for the remainder of our effort. Important progress has been achieved based on studies of networks and contexts that employ network surveys of individuals combined with snowball sample interviews of the people within these individuals' communication networks. These studies provide an important observational platform to employ in observing individual behavior that is contingent on the networks of relationships within which the individual is imbedded. We discuss this progress as it relates to experts, activists, and opinion leadership in Chapters 3 and 4, providing a framework to employ as we move forward.

These network surveys are much less helpful in a direct assessment of the temporal dimension underlying interdependent citizens and opinion leadership. That is, they do not offer an opportunity to observe network formation, communication, and influence in real time – as a process arising among interdependent actors. Hence, in Chapters 5 through 10, we pursue an experimental research strategy based on a series of group-based experiments. These experiments provide an opportunity to undertake a direct frontal assault on problems related to this temporal dimension and its implications for the process of opinion leadership.

In short, the analysis depends both on network surveys and on our experimental analyses. Both provide important insights on opinion leadership, just as both come with inherent limitations. Indeed, we confront the inevitable problems of external and internal validity. The network surveys provide strong external validity based on interviews with individual citizens as well as with those who populate their communication networks, providing valuable information on actual citizens facing real decisions in the context of American presidential election campaigns. While the experiments lack this external validity, they provide a direct observational window on the *process* of communication and influence – something that cannot be replicated in a survey. Our goal is to achieve insight on the role of experts, activists, and opinion leaders in democratic politics, and these two approaches, taken together, provide the platform for our effort.

---

[1] For a discussion of networks versus contexts, as well as their relationships to one another, see Huckfeldt and Sprague 1987.

MOVING BEYOND INDIVIDUAL OBSERVATIONS

The questions motivating our analyses cannot be addressed based wholly on either micro-level observation or on micro-theories of human behavior. Rather, both the survey analyses as well as the experimental analyses focus on the creation and configuration of the networks and contexts within which individuals are imbedded. Networks are defined in terms of the particular connections among and between individuals – not only the dyadic relationships between two associates, but also the higher-order relations among an individual's associates, as well as these associates' relationships with other individuals. Contexts are defined in terms of the composition of the populations and groups within which these networks are constructed, and hence they in turn impose boundaries on the construction of networks.

Our argument is that the consequences of political communication between and among individuals cannot be understood simply on the basis of individuals or even dyads, even though individuals and dyads are crucial to the argument. Rather, both the behavior of individuals and the patterns of influence within dyads are contingent on the locations of individuals and dyads within larger networks of relationships.[2] This means, in turn, that opinion leadership is similarly imbedded within these same networks.

Nearly everyone believes in interdependence, at least in the abstract. Yet the observational imperative of interdependent actors – multiple levels of observation coupled with mappings of relationships among actors – has been the exception rather than the rule in analyses of public opinion, voting, and opinion leadership. Taking interdependence seriously requires an explicit attentiveness to an important set of observational challenges (Huckfeldt, forthcoming). Ultimately, the ability to address interdependence depends on observational strategies that move beyond a strict focus on individuals. This does *not* mean that interdependence negates methodological individualism – our analyses assume that individuals provide the basic unit of analysis (Boudon 1986). Taking interdependence seriously *does* require a focus on the ways in which individuals become politically interdependent with one another, as well as the ways in which that interdependence produces important political consequences for the larger electorate and political system.

The literatures in political economics and political psychology provide important reasons to expect that individuals will be interdependent. From an economic vantage point, enormous efficiencies are realized by relying on information

---

[2] The analysis of dyads generates complex analytic issues not only in the context of communication networks, but also in a variety of other contexts, including systems of international relations (Beck and Katz 2001; Green, Kim, and Yoon 2001; King 2001). Our own perspective coincides with that of Maoz (2010) – not only individuals but also dyads are best seen within the context of larger networks and contexts, in the case of both individual nation states and of individual citizens.

taken from a reliable expert through voluntary social exchange.[3] From the standpoint of social cognition, motivation and emotion loom large in explaining the role of activists who are more likely to engage in political communication with others. And as we have seen, activists and experts are overlapping subsets of the population, with the most influential opinion leaders being both activists and experts. Indeed, many students of interdependence might productively make use of various explanatory devices from both menus in a fairly agnostic fashion (Boudon 1987).

The important point is that interdependence – whether motivated by economic or psychological arguments – is itself a theoretical imperative with important observational consequences (Schelling 1978). An explanation that embraces interdependence among political actors produces distinctive political consequences, and it generates signature implications for political dynamics as well as for aggregate outcomes. Thus, interdependence may be seen as a theoretical statement that stands on its own feet – a fundamental theoretical postulate that drives politics and political affairs rather than simply a derivative conclusion.

OPINION LEADERSHIP, INTERDEPENDENCE, AND DENSITY DEPENDENCE

Identifying patterns of interdependence that give rise to opinion leadership presents enduring challenges in political analysis that are both observational and theoretical. Observation takes place at multiple levels – at the level of individual actors as well as at the level of the various contexts within which actors are located (Huckfeldt 2007a). Density dependence, in turn, provides a conceptual and observational framework which allows a seamless transition between individuals, groups, resulting patterns of interaction, and the complex aggregate whole that is thereby generated.

The concept of interdependence – that individual behavior responds to the behavior and characteristics of others in an actor's environment – is defined here with respect to particular concrete patterns of relationships among actors (Granovetter 1985). This focus is in contrast to less specific forms of interdependence that might arise – for example, among strangers who belong to a societal group that shares a common circumstance, interest, or fate, e.g., members of labor unions. At the same time, these concrete relations take very different forms: intense relationships among close friends, neighbors down the block known only by sight, family members, coworkers, members of the same religious congregation, and so on. Our own effort is based on a conception of interdependence defined in terms of networks of relations among actors, where the particular relations involve informal communication about politics. The participants in

---

[3] Indeed, political economists have been at the forefront in incorporating interdependence within political analysis (Olson 1965; McKelvey and Ordeshook 1985a, 1985b, 1986; Fehr and Gächter 2002).

these networks might indeed be relatives, close friends, or the most casual acquaintances, where the common denominator of association is the communication of political information.

The concept of density dependence is invoked in the spirit of population ecology, where rates of interaction within and among particular species depend on their absolute and relative sizes within local populations, producing systematic patterns of change (May 1973; Maynard Smith 1968, 1974). In similar ways, the rates of interaction and communication between and within political groups often depend on the relative population densities of these groups within shared environments, and the formation of social networks is thus usefully seen as being *density dependent* (Huckfeldt 2009b; Huckfeldt, Ikeda, and Pappi 2005). Hence, if the formation of networks is density dependent, opinions and behaviors that are contingent on communication and interaction are potentially density dependent as well. Individuals who spend their time in environments full of liberals, for example, are typically less likely to interact with conservatives, and hence they may be less likely to be persuaded to adopt conservative views.[4]

Density dependence is thus defined with respect to the compositional and distributional properties of the social contexts within which actors are imbedded, where the social context is conceived relative to either a geographically or non-geographically based population (Eulau 1963, 1986). Most actors are located in more than one social context. They live in neighborhoods. They earn salaries at their places of employment. They attend services at temples or churches or parishes. And each of these contexts may or may not be more or less independent from each of the others (Gamm 1999). Regardless of their potential relationships to one another, each context carries important implications for the networks of association and communication that are central to democratic politics.

What is the virtue of connecting the study of interdependence to the study of density dependence? Particular forms and patterns of interdependence among actors are created at the intersection between individual choice and the constraints and opportunities imposed by the various contexts within which individuals reside. A Republican autoworker in the 1950s realized a radically different set of associational opportunities at the workplace compared to a Democratic coworker (Finifter 1974). And each of them realized a different set of opportunities in comparison to Republican bank tellers at their places of employment. In short, patterns of association are created at the points of intersection between individuals and the environment – between

---

[4] This is not meant to ignore instances in which members of relatively small and isolated groups withdraw from their surroundings to maintain the viability of their groups (Finifter 1974). Indeed, such a response constitutes an alternative form of density dependent behavior (Huckfeldt 1983b).

individual characteristics and associational preferences on the one hand, and the supply of potential associates within the actors' social contexts on the other.

In this way, density dependence provides a point of connection between groups and individuals, thereby making it possible to bridge the micro–macro divide in political analysis (Huckfeldt 2007a). For example, it provides an opportunity to examine the ways in which an opinion leader's influence is contingent on the social and political composition of the environment – that is, one more expert (or one more activist) in a context full of experts and activists may be less influential than the equivalent individual who is surrounded by others who are politically disinterested and naïve.

The assertion that politics is contingent on inherently interdependent processes does not reduce the importance of individuals, individual predispositions, or individual cognition.[5] Moreover, these same individual characteristics and predispositions may become integral elements in explanations of an individual's location within, and relationships to, her political and social surroundings. Indeed, all our analyses are built on an assumption of methodological individualism. Just as individual choice is contingent on patterns of social interaction and communication, so too does social interaction respond to the preferences, choices, and predispositions of individuals.

Density dependence also presents observational challenges. Viewed in the cross-section, how are we to determine whether an individual's liberal communication network is the result of an individual who happens to be located in contexts with abundant opportunities for association with liberals and thus tend to become liberal themselves, or due to liberals who choose both to reside in liberal contexts and to associate with liberals? In addressing this issue, we review a range of evidence taken from earlier efforts: an estimation strategy that employs instrumental variables and a simultaneous equation system, as well as studies based on survey-imbedded experiments.

These problems also lead to particular design features in our laboratory experiments, making it possible to manipulate the population densities that surround individual actors. Hence we are able to consider the implications for both the construction of communication networks as well as for network-based processes of learning and persuasion. In particular, Chapter 6 systematically varies both the density of experts and the distribution of preferences across experimental groups to study the exogenous effects of population densities on network composition and message bias.

---

[5] Genetic predispositions certainly predate an individual's location within most contexts and networks, and we increasingly see powerful evidence regarding the role that genetic inheritance plays in explaining political attitudes (Alford, Funk, and Hibbing 2005; Fowler, Baker, and Dawes 2008). Moreover, patterns of interdependence and activism might also be seen in relationship to genetic predispositions (Mondak 2010).

INTERDEPENDENCE AND STRUCTURES OF INDETERMINACY

Much of politics occurs at the intersection between (1) purposeful action on the part of motivated individuals and (2) environmentally imposed constraints that place boundaries on the choices and options that are available to individuals. This political fact of life is directly related to important forms of density dependence and their consequences for the construction of communication networks, as well as for the impact of these networks on the creation, survival, and communication of political opinions. In general, density dependence at the intersection between individual purpose and environmental constraint creates the potential for structured indeterminacy – well-understood processes that sometimes yield indeterminate outcomes. The crucial observation is that, in Boudon's words (1987: 178), "chance is not nothing." Rather, it frequently involves the outcome of predictable processes that happen to converge in unpredictable ways (Huckfeldt 1990, 2009a).

Indeed, indeterminacy does not mean that a process is inexplicable. *After the event*, an observer (or the participants themselves) can certainly provide a plausible account of the fact that two young people came to know each other and marry. Such explanations often depend on the incorporation of the signal event of a location shared by these individuals at a moment in time. But this shared location in time and space depended on the more or less random event of two individuals pursuing two independent series of choices ending up, perhaps, in the same classroom on the same campus in the same semester. The implications for social interaction and interdependence are two-fold.

First, even when we fully understand all the underlying mechanisms, the particular structures of social interaction may still yield indeterminate outcomes. Again, the choice of campus, class, and semester can be wholly and sensibly explained for each of these two individuals. Rather, it is the more or less random intersection of the two individual sequences that yields the indeterminacy. And hence the identification of indeterminacy within a process does not constitute an explanatory failure – randomness is rather a predictable, integral element occurring within many well-understood processes (Boudon 1986: chapters 6 and 7).

Second, indeterminacy has implications for the actor as well as the observer. You may choose to send your children to safe schools in safe neighborhoods, but the structure of the networks contained within those schools and neighborhoods may (or may not) end up exposing your children to the influences you were trying to avoid. In these and countless other ways, actors often play the odds quite successfully, but that does not change the inherent uncertainty and indeterminacy of processes that are defined in terms of a stochastic component.

In the present context, patterns of communication are products not only of individual preferences regarding appropriate discussion partners, but they are also due to the environmentally stochastic supply of various political preferences among potential discussion partners. Hence, a Democrat may end up talking politics with a Republican colleague for the simple reason that both happen to be

Giants fans, or because they both have schedules that bring them to the lunch room at the same time, or because one or the other provides politically informative insights, or because one or the other talks incessantly about politics. A perhaps unexpected event – a Democrat talking to a Republican about politics – thus occurs not as a meaningless event, nor as an error, nor as the result of a Democrat who likes talking to Republicans, but rather at the point where demand happens to intersect supply in a process of social interaction.

Density dependence also means that the influence of, for example, Democratic and Republican messages within communication networks is contingent not only on the persuasive powers of the message's sender and the sympathies of the message's receiver, but also on the odds that a particular message from a particular informant is reinforced by the distribution of preferences that exist among other informants within the network. In this way, not only is the formation of communication networks subject to density effects within a particular context, but the effects of messages within the communication networks are also subject to density effects within the network (Huckfeldt, Johnson, and Sprague 2004).

Now engage in a mental experiment: suppose that the supply of discussants with particular sets of preferences is unlimited, and that people are infinitely patient in their search for political discussion partners. Under these circumstances, individuals would always get exactly what they want in terms of discussants and communication networks. If the Giants fan who is a Democrat wants to find another Democratic Giants fan, she will do so. So, under these circumstances, homophily will be the ever-persistent state of affairs within communication networks. The problems are that, first, the supply of Democrats who are also Giants fans may be quite limited, at least if you live in Los Angeles, and second, the personal costs of patience are quite high – it may mean social isolation, or at least not having anyone with whom to talk politics (or baseball) at lunch. Moreover, even high levels of patience and selectivity in network construction may be swamped by the stochastic odds attached to the available alternatives (Coleman 1964, chapter 16; Huckfeldt 1983b).[6]

NETWORKS AT THE INTERSECTION BETWEEN DEMAND AND SUPPLY

Hence, networks are endogeneous to *both* individual preference *as well as* the environment, and these various forms of endogeneity are realized in a variety of ways (Erbring and Young 1979). First, the construction of networks depends on the preferences and selection principles of the participants. In the realm of politics, this means that people harbor political preferences that may translate into associational preferences. If the associational preference is for someone with

---

[6] Homophily might also fail to be the result either if people enjoy disagreement or if the value they realize through discussion swamps a minor disincentive due to disagreement (see Chapter 4).

a shared political preference, politically inspired selection principles will translate into higher levels of agreement within networks (McPherson and Smith-
Lovin 1987; Huckfeldt and Sprague 1987). In contrast, if the associational
preference is for someone who is politically informed, the implications for network homogeneity are less clear cut. And if these selection principles work at
cross purposes – for example, the potential informant who is a highly informed
holder of disagreeable views – people face inevitable tradeoffs in their search for
informants.

Second, networks are also endogenous to the environment. For the purposes
of illustration, two factors make it much easier for white voters in Mississippi to
find Republican discussion partners, and for black voters in Mississippi to find
Democratic discussion partners. Patterns of association are structured by race –
whites are more likely to communicate with whites, and blacks are more likely
to communicate with blacks. At the same time, race is also highly correlated
with partisanship and partisan choice in Mississippi, as in the remainder of the
country, and this means that Democrats are much more likely to talk with
other Democrats, and Republicans are much more likely to talk with other
Republicans (Huckfeldt and Kohfeld 1989).[7] Hence, it is less clear whether
Democrats and Republicans *choose* to discuss politics with others who embrace
their political orientations, or whether political homogeneity within political
communication networks is a byproduct of the larger sorting and mixing processes that go on in Mississippi and elsewhere (Achen and Shivley 1995).

Third, the content of messages communicated through networks is subject to
network specialization. People might have one circle of associates with whom
they discuss politics, another with whom they discuss religion, and another with
whom they discuss sports, and so on. This argument was made most convincingly by Katz and Lazarsfeld (1955) in their analysis of personal influence, and
it remains a plausible and often persuasive explanation. The problem is whether,
and to what extent, individuals are able and willing to make the effort to com-
partmentalize everyday life. If you have a question about a particularly important
idiosyncratic topic, say local schools, you may indeed be willing to consult an
expert (Schneider et al. 2002). But would you also be willing to maintain specialized contacts for the wide range of everyday topics that you are likely to discuss
on a more or less continual and casual basis – most notably politics? Moreover,
the extent to which social contacts are compartmentalized also depends on the
relationship among various selection criteria (McPherson and Smith-Lovin
1987) – whether individuals who provide high-quality political information are
also the individuals who make enjoyable associates.

Fourth, people may censor their own conversations. As MacKuen (1990)
demonstrates so compellingly, some people may avoid discussions of politics

---

[7] According to exit polls in the 1984 and 2004 presidential elections, more than 80 percent of
Mississippi whites voted Republican and more than 90 percent of Mississippi blacks voted
Democratic.

(and perhaps religion) in mixed company, particularly with contentious or argumentative individuals. To the extent that people find disagreement to be distasteful, we would expect them to be increasingly conflict averse and hence to avoid political discussion with provocative people whose politics they find objectionable.

At the same time, while disagreement may produce negative feedback that dampens political interest and enthusiasm (Huckfeldt and Mendez 2008), many politically engaged citizens may be unable to resist discussing politics! That is, we will argue that political engagement produces political discussion, and higher frequencies of political discussion yield higher frequencies of political disagreement, even though disagreement attenuates discussion frequency for many individuals (see Chapter 4). Thus, patterns of political communication and disagreement are endogenous to the individual preferences and choices of the participants, but this endogeneity does not necessarily produce a world without disagreement. Among those activists who care about politics and are exposed to heterogeneous preferences, the experience of political disagreement is likely to be a frequent fact of life.

All these issues add to the observational challenges in studying opinion leaders and the construction of political communication networks.[8] We consider a variety of observational strategies to maximize leverage on these problems. Most importantly, we pursue a series of small group experiments conducted in a laboratory setting to address issues regarding the composition of communication networks as well as issues related to a dynamic process of influence arising due to opinion leaders. This experimental effort grows directly out of a set of survey studies relying on evidence from the 1984 South Bend Study, the 1996 Indianapolis-St. Louis Study, and the 2000 National Election Study. Before addressing the methodological details, we turn to a series of theoretical and substantive issues that guide the design of our effort.

INTERDEPENDENCE AND POLITICAL COMPLEXITY

A traditional view suggests that social interdependence creates an electorate that is stable, dependable, and predictable, with individual beliefs and opinions safely anchored in an enduring social fabric. In contrast, an alternative series of arguments identify various forms of interdependence and density dependence capable of producing behavioral patterns that might be complex or unstable or both. Indeed, rather than producing predictability, even *simple* models of interdependence among actors are wholly capable of producing unexpected consequences (Huckfeldt 1990).

Density dependence, its implications for the creation of communication networks, and their combined interdependent consequences for individuals take

---

[8] For quasi-experimental approaches and a field experiment see Lazer (2010); Visser and Mirabile (2004); Levitan and Visser (2009); and Nickerson (2008).

inspiration from ecological studies of interacting species dynamics (Maynard Smith 1968, 1974). May's analyses (1973, 1974, 1975, 1976) were some of the earliest in subsequently burgeoning literatures on chaos and complexity, and they produced a powerful statement regarding the consequences that arise due to even very simple and fundamental statements of interdependence.[9] He demonstrates that changing levels of density dependence account for complex and diverse outcomes, including convergence to locally stable equilibria, oscillating behavior, stable limit cycles, and infinitely complex and seemingly random patterns of behavior that might, indeed, be wholly determinate.

What do these results suggest? There is no *a priori* body of social or political theory to explain these complex patterns that arise due to interdependent actors. To the contrary, results such as these force us to revisit the theoretical implications of interdependence for political theory. To repeat, *interdependence constitutes its own theoretical imperative* – that is, interdependence serves as a fundamental theoretical postulate that underlies politics. This is not to say that every political actor and every political action is best understood in terms of interdependence. Rather, it suggests that interdependent processes will be fundamentally different and more complex than processes marked by independent actors. To the extent that politics is characterized by processes that are frequently imbedded in patterns of interdependence, we benefit by taking interdependence seriously – as a measurement issue certainly, but also as a theoretical issue involving systematic yet remarkably complex dynamic implications (Huckfeldt 1990, 2009a).

More recent work (Axelrod 1997a, 1997b) that has focused on agent-based models is complementary to this work on complex dynamics but from a bottom-up perspective. Rather than specifying a model of aggregate behavior, these efforts incorporate relatively simple forms of interdependence among actors that generate extremely complex consequences in the aggregate (Page 2007). Other efforts in network theory are moving in similar directions as part of the search for a "new science" of networks (Barabasi 2002; Watts 2004).

In this context, agent-based models accommodate themselves quite well to the simulated analyses of social network data, not only in terms of creating networks, but also in terms of network consequences. For example, Huckfeldt, Johnson, and Sprague (2004) show that it is possible for disagreement to survive in lower density communication networks to the extent that the influence of any single informant is conditioned on the opinions in the rest of the network. That is, if nearly all your friends are Democrats, you can resist the pro-Republican messages that come from the friend who is a Republican – and if nearly all her friends are Republicans, she can resist the pro-Democratic message coming from you! Indeed, we might say that disagreement between you and your Republican friend is socially sustained as a direct consequence of the density

---

[9] Also see May and Oster (1976) and May and Leonard (1975).

dependent effects of political communication. The effect of any single message is conditioned on the basis of prior messages – an implication that comports well with the analyses of Lodge and Taber (2000) regarding motivated reasoning in political communication.

In such an interdependent world, not only is diversity sustained, but the complexity of opinion dynamics is enhanced. Moreover, the outcomes of these opinion dynamics tend toward indeterminacy even though the communication mechanisms are simply stated. If we assume that many individuals have not made up their minds at the beginning of a campaign, the conversion of a swing voter from one candidate to another may carry important consequences. These consequences extend far beyond their own conversion, and even beyond the dyadic relationships in which they are imbedded, to include many other dyadic exchanges in which they play no direct role. In short, if the consequence of every dyadic exchange is contingent on all the actors' other dyadic exchanges, the implications are both profound and far-reaching.

This view of political interdependence within the electorate thus serves to redefine the role of opinion leaders in democratic politics, magnifying the importance of the experts and activists in our midst. Indeed, their role in political communication and public opinion is likely to be crucial – for better or for worse – in many of the most important political debates. From one perspective, we are focusing on the stratification of influence within the ranks of the public, thereby acknowledging that democratic publics include their own elites. At the same time, we are focusing on the very real influence that arises within democratic electorates (Druckman and Nelson 2003), thereby providing a response to analyses that often imply a powerless electorate, operating as a passive bystander in the face of the elite manipulators of the public agenda.

OBSERVATIONAL STRATEGIES FOR STUDYING INTERDEPENDENT ACTORS

The consequences of interdependence in politics can seldom be taken into account by simply adding another explanatory variable to the analysis. To the contrary, effective strategies for addressing interdependence yield transformed observational strategies and thus transformed analyses. These observational strategies stand in contrast to past traditions of political analysis that were less well suited to studying the political consequences of contexts, networks, and the relationships among political actors.

Indeed, early behavioral research in political science was dominated by empirical analyses involving only a single level of analysis, giving rise to a "tyranny of the rectangular array" (Huckfeldt 2009b). This typically meant that students of electoral politics and public opinion studied individuals, students of international politics studied nations, students of state politics studied states, and so on. The implications for the study of voters and elections have been particularly profound (see Huckfeldt 2009b).

At the same historical moment when modern individual-level survey data were becoming widely available, Robinson's (1950) discovery of the ecological fallacy alerted social scientists to the danger of inferring the behavior of individuals based on aggregate data. Faced with this methodological challenge, the message was typically translated to mean that the problem could be bypassed by adopting individual-level analyses as opposed to aggregate analyses. Astute analysts recognized, however, that the solution was not that simple.

In his own analysis of the ecological fallacy, Goodman (1953, 1959) showed that the ecological fallacy was only a problem if individual-level behavioral probabilities varied in space. His insight was that if the individual behavioral probabilities do not vary across contexts, the analyst need not worry about an ecological fallacy, and hence one could recover the individual behavioral probabilities from a simple regression of a behavior on a social density. The problem is that, without inferences based on aggregate data, analysts are typically unable to assert that the individual probabilities are constant across contexts, unless they are able to bring individual-level data to bear on the problem. Unfortunately, individual-level data sets are typically insufficient to provide context-specific measures of individual behavior.

The seemingly obvious solution was simply to replace aggregate analyses with individual-level analyses, but this serves to replace the risk of an ecological fallacy with that of an individualistic fallacy. A nationally representative sample will certainly provide a point estimate for the individual probability of a behavior within an individually defined population group. The problem is that if the probability varies as a systematic function of spatially defined patterns of interdependence, the estimate is incorrectly specified unless the relevant contextual variables are included. Hence, to the extent that the behavior of political actors is interdependent, an aggregate analysis runs the risk of committing an ecological fallacy, while an individual analysis runs the risk of committing an individualistic fallacy (Huckfeldt and Sprague 1995). The seemingly obvious fix – always use data at the lowest possible level of analysis – is no solution at all (see Shively 1969; Achen and Shively 1995).

PATH-BREAKING CONTRIBUTIONS

A number of important efforts introduced interdependence within path-breaking analyses during the early period of behavioral research. Key (1949) addressed citizens within states, and states within regional patterns. Berelson and colleagues (1954) conceived individuals as interdependent members of groups. Miller's (1956) paper on one-party politics and the voter, along with Putnam's (1966) analysis of community influence, presented compelling arguments and analyses regarding the implications of interdependence among citizens at the county level. Matthews and Prothro (1966) demonstrated the spatial dependence of racial hostility within the South. The Miller and Stokes (1963) analysis of representation within congressional districts, as well as the Butler and Stokes (1969) analysis of

Labour Party support within constituencies, are similarly astute and multi-layered in their observational frameworks. The Converse analysis (1969) of time and partisan stability produced an intriguing analysis of democratic stability located within contexts defined both in terms of space and time. Jennings and Niemi (1974) created a new research program on the dynamics of political socialization and learning by locating individuals within the political contexts of their nuclear families. A series of efforts in the volume edited by Dogan and Rokkan (1974) produced innovative arguments and startling findings that bear directly on patterns of political interdependence within aggregate populations.

Unfortunately, the observational methodologies of these efforts lay outside the normal confines of political analysis. The substantive recognition of interdependence during this period did not typically translate into common observational practice, and this meant that theoretical and methodological development was stymied. Very few opportunities existed for analysts to connect individuals to their environments, in part because the nationally representative sample often made it inconvenient or impossible to reconnect these environmentally abstracted individuals to the contexts within which they were located. In contrast, the successes cited above, as well as others, are due to the location of individual actors within particular contexts at various levels – families, neighborhoods, American counties, U.S. House Districts, British constituencies, nation states, and so on. And their contributions demonstrate that individual behavior *does* vary systematically across contexts, *independently* from individual characteristics.

This variation of individual behavior across contexts not only points toward the inferential inadequacies of ecological or aggregate population correlations for reaching judgments regarding individual behavior. This same contextual dependence also points toward the inadequacies of individual-level observations – without contextual, density dependent qualifiers – for obtaining estimates of individual behavior that are context specific. Again, when behavior varies across context, a sole reliance on aggregate data runs the risk of an ecological fallacy, and a sole reliance on individual-level data runs the risk of an individualistic fallacy.

The conclusion is straightforward. If individual behavior is interdependent – contingent on others in the individual's context – both observation and analysis gain meaning by taking the underlying sources of interdependence into account. The persistent problem, however, continued to be an inability to demonstrate the mechanisms of interdependence that produced these effects. Without information on individual patterns of social interaction – that is, without social network data – the source of density dependence was difficult to isolate.

NETWORK SURVEYS

Laumann (1973) demonstrated an alternative survey-based observational strategy when he employed an egocentric network battery in the 1966 Detroit Area

Study. In the context of a conventional survey, respondents were asked to provide the first names of three friends, and interviewers asked the respondents a battery of questions about each. The study included a snowball survey for a very small number of the identified discussants, but nearly all the resulting analyses depended on the perceptual data provided by the main respondents. The egocentric network battery, with and without extensive snowball surveys of identified discussants, has provided a useful tool for a series of election studies conducted by political scientists in the United States, Japan, Germany, Britain, and other countries as well (Huckfeldt and Sprague 1995; Huckfeldt, Johnson, and Sprague 2004; Huckfeldt, Ikeda, and Pappi 2005). It also served as the template for a series of studies concerned with social communication defined more generally, particularly due to the occasional incorporation of social network batteries within the national General Social Survey (Marsden 1987; Burt 1986; McPherson, Smith-Lovin, and Brashears 2006).

A primary advantage of egocentric networks combined with snowball surveys is that they provide both validation measures for respondents' perceptions of one another, as well as the opportunity to study biases in these perceptions. Hence, it is possible to address the characteristics of both the senders and the receivers of political signals that give rise to accuracy and inaccuracy in communicated messages. This capability, in turn, makes it possible to address the concerns of political psychology and political communication within the context of a network analysis (Huckfeldt and Sprague 1987).

Even without snowball surveys, network batteries have proven to be useful devices in political analysis for two reasons. In some instances perception is more important than reality. If we want to study the consequences of communication networks that send heterogeneous political signals, we need to possess verified information regarding the signals that are being sent, and this makes the snowball survey indispensable. If we want to understand the sources and consequences of *perceived* disagreement within communication networks for patterns of political activation, the snowball survey is perhaps less central.

Without underestimating the presence of network-generated biases in communication and perception, snowball surveys have demonstrated that individuals are generally quite accurate in their perceptions regarding the political characteristics of other members of their networks. Hence, the snowball surveys serve as validation studies for the use of perceptual measures. For example, respondents are remarkably accurate in the recognition of political expertise on the part of their discussion partners (see Chapter 3). Hence, snowball surveys have been instrumental in documenting the validity of a range of social network measures obtained through egocentric network batteries, making it possible – at least in principle – to conduct analyses that make use of these measures even in the absence of a snowball survey.

Indeed, a great deal of what we know about political communication networks among citizens is based on a series of specially designed election studies carried out in the United States, Japan, Germany, Russia, and South Africa (see Gibson

1992, 2001; Huckfeldt, Beck et al. 1998; Huckfeldt and Sprague 1987, 1995; Huckfeldt, Johnson, and Sprague 2004; Huckfeldt, Ikeda, and Pappi 2005; Mutz 2006). These studies are built around network name generators in which survey respondents are asked to provide the first names and various characteristics of the people in their communication networks. Several of the studies also include snowball surveys – interviews of the discussants thus identified by the respondents to the main survey. Moreover, interviews with the main respondents are typically indexed on a particular spatial locale – a neighborhood, a city, a state, a nation. Hence, it is possible to connect networks and contexts – that is, to connect the creation of communication patterns to the supply of associational alternatives.

These and similar observational strategies offer many opportunities to address a range of important questions from the standpoint of interdependence among citizens. They provide information not only on individuals, but also on relationships among individuals and how these relationships are configured by, and imbedded within, larger environments. Moreover, they accomplish these goals by building on the experience of the National Election Study series, employing concepts as well as observational and measurement procedures that reflect the dominant technology used to study voters in democracies across the world – the sample survey.

At the same time, they share the inherent limitations of any effort employing cross-sectional analyses to make inferences regarding a dynamic process. Hence, the primary analytic strategy of this book is built on a set of laboratory experiments aimed at capturing the dynamic processes involved in communication and persuasion. While these experiments are inspired by the network surveys – and particularly by the network survey analyses of opinion leadership that are addressed in Chapters 3 and 4 – they create new opportunities to take a closer look at these underlying dynamics.

A ROADMAP FOR THE ANALYSIS

First, in Chapters 3 and 4, we review recent research regarding experts, activists, and opinion leadership based on observational strategies using network surveys from the 1996 Indianapolis-St. Louis Study, as well as the 2000 National Election Study, in the context of presidential election campaigns. These survey analyses are particularly useful for understanding opinion leaders as the politically motivated experts and activists who play an outsized role in the social communication process among citizens. A primary strength of these survey analyses is based on their external validity – they generate a highly realistic picture based on interviews with citizens who provide a wealth of information not only on themselves and their own preferences and motivations, but also on the composition of their communication networks. Just as important, snowball surveys provide much of the same information for the individuals with whom these main respondents discuss politics, and hence we are able to delve deeply into the relationships among citizens within the political communication process.

Chapter 3 reviews a set of efforts that consider the ability of citizens to identify political expertise and knowledge among others. If one individual recognizes the presence (or absence) of expertise among other citizens, the potential is created for the enhancement of political capacity within the electorate. The whole might indeed become greater than the sum of its parts, and social communication might provide one element of a solution to the public opinion paradox – individual citizens who appear woefully uninformed compared to an aggregate electorate that behaves in a predictable manner. At the same time, and from a more skeptical standpoint, Chapter 3 also considers whether people who communicate with experts act more effectively on the basis of their own preferences, or whether they act on the basis of the preferences held by the expert informant.

Chapter 4 addresses the collective circumstances and individual-level attributes that create opportunities for opinion leadership, with a primary focus on two sets of factors: (1) the levels of opinion diversity within populations and networks, and (2) the willingness of individuals to confront disagreement over issues that involve diverse opinions. We argue that dyadic discussions between citizens are most enlightening when the distribution of opinion is heterogeneous, and thus opinion leaders have the most opportunities to lead when a political consensus has not been achieved. The most successful opinion leaders do not (or cannot) resist the temptation to engage in political discussion, even when it involves potentially contentious disagreement. This leads to a cyclical dynamic: higher levels of political discussion lead to higher levels of disagreement, but higher disagreement levels simultaneously depress discussion.

While approaches based on network surveys continue to support important research programs, formidable challenges confront any effort aimed at understanding a dynamic process based on self-reported survey data. As we have seen, observational studies of networks, contexts, and political communication confront a series of endogeneity issues (Achen and Shively 1995; Huckfeldt and Mendez 2008), and network batteries and snowball surveys do not resolve all these problems.

The primary limitations of these network surveys are thus two-fold. First, they provide after-the-fact reconstructions of the dynamic relationships that exist between discussion partners – hence, we must base assessments and inferences on the post hoc reports of the respondents, thereby compromising our ability to make dynamic inferences. Perhaps most importantly, we are unable to analyze the *processes* of communication and influence directly as they unfold.

Second, the typical network name generator, with or without a snowball survey, only provides information on first-order relationships, and hence we are typically but not always limited in our ability to reconstruct networks beyond the dyad (Huckfeldt, Johnson, and Sprague 2004, Chapter 5). That is, we know that our main respondent John communicates with Marty, and we have interview data with Marty, but we do not have interview data with Marty's discussion partners. This means that we are only looking at a fragment of a larger network for each of the respondents.

THE SMALL GROUP EXPERIMENTS

A second set of analyses, in Chapters 5 through 10, is based on small group experimental studies with subjects who received modest monetary incentives for their participation. The strengths and limitations of these experiments form a mirror image of those associated with the survey studies. While they do not possess the external validity and realism of the surveys, they provide unparalleled opportunities to make dynamic inferences regarding the processes of network formation, communication, and persuasion. The experimental studies also create the opportunity to identify entire (albeit small) networks of communication, thereby adding a new and important dimension to the analysis. Taken together, the combined analyses create an opportunity to address both the strategic and non-strategic bases of opinion leadership that are anchored in both expertise and motivated activism.

Moreover, both the network surveys and the small group experiments face the same conceptual issues: interdependent actors, communication at the intersection between the supply and demand for information, the central importance of density dependence, stochastic mechanisms underlying network formation, the role of systematic bias in communication, and the complexity as well as indeterminacy of the processes. Perhaps most important, we are able to combine individual incentives, network formation, biased messages, individual persuasion, and aggregate outcomes within the same seamless process.

Our experimental efforts join a movement toward the use of small group studies addressing issues related to network formation, network influence, collective action problems, and other social dilemmas (e.g., Levitan and Visser 2009; Lazer et al. 2010; Fehr and Gächter 2002; Ostrom, Walker, and Gardner 1992). The experiments involve between 7 and 14 participants in the context of a faux election, wherein the participants receive a modest financial incentive if the candidate best reflecting their interests wins the election. The task of the participants is to obtain information regarding which candidate they should support. They have opportunities to acquire information on their own as well as to obtain information from other individuals. All communication among the participants occurs privately, within dyads, over networked computers.

In this context, participants have a monetized incentive not only to obtain information regarding the candidates, but also to influence the views of other participants regarding the candidates, thereby giving rise to the potential for biased communication among participants. The subjects have an opportunity to obtain private information at a cost that that is experimentally manipulated across participants, as well as to obtain information from other subjects that is typically free. This basic experimental platform gives rise to a variety of opportunities for addressing a range of centrally important questions regarding the role of expertise and opinion leadership in political communication. Moreover, because we obtain a complete mapping of all the information flows within the groups, an opportunity is produced to consider higher-order relationships within the networks.

The use of experimental research strategies based in laboratory settings is nothing new to studies of political communication, and a great deal of progress has been accomplished (Boudreau, Coulson, and McCubbins 2008; Druckman and Nelson 2003; Lupia and McCubbins 1998).[10] Our own work pursues an experimental framework based on a Downsian spatial model of political preference and competition. Such a spatial model offers several advantages. First, it allows the explicit modeling of heterogeneous political preferences among citizens, as well as among candidates in an election. Correspondingly, it becomes possible to address the "distance" between any pair of citizens or candidates on a continuum. Second, uncertainty in politics and the level of political expertise can be directly incorporated within analyses (see Shepsle 1972; Calvert 1985b; Baron 1994; Budge 1994, to name a few). Third, the level of political expertise can be represented in various ways, including the amount of information voters have acquired. Finally, and just as important, the level of expertise can be conveniently endogenized by assigning variable information costs among the voters.

An experimental framework built on spatial models provides the opportunity to address a growing literature on communication among agents with heterogeneous preferences (Crawford and Sobel 1982). This literature has inspired a focus on "cheap talk" within political science (Austen-Smith 1990; Austen-Smith and Banks 1996; Feddersen and Pesendorfer 1998; Coughlan, 2000), and it has inspired an effort to link game-theoretic models of communication to enduring issues regarding political deliberation (Johnson 1993; Hafer and Landa 2007). The fundamental issue underlying this cheap talk communication literature is whether individuals with diverging preferences can communicate effectively via non-costly signals, i.e., cheap talk. Thus, by allowing subjects to communicate with each other in an experimental framework built on a spatial model of political competition, we combine several lines of research – psychological and sociological, as well as game-theoretic research on cheap talk.

This framework allows us to pursue a series of important issues which lie beyond the reach of even the most innovative observational studies. Who are the experts, and are the advantages of expertise over-rated? What are the most important (behavioral) criteria for selecting informants – informant expertise or shared preferences between the recipient and the prospective informant? Is the

[10] While laboratory experiments are advantageous because of their increased internal validity, field experiments, survey experiments, and even quasi-experiments have provided important insights regarding the occasions when interpersonal influence is more likely (e.g., Nickerson 2008; Huckfeldt and Mendez 2008; Mondak 1995; Parker, Parker, and McCann 2008).

advice of experts useful when their viewpoints diverge from those of the recipients? Does "cheap talk" hold political consequences for the recipients – do the recipients take it seriously and how do they assess the veracity of messages? What are the effects of group boundaries for the aggregate flow of political information and for patterns of bias in aggregate opinion distributions? Thus, the core of our analysis addresses opinion leadership and expertise based on these laboratory experiments.

AN OUTLINE OF THE EXPERIMENTAL STUDIES

Chapter 5 addresses the challenges of obtaining and evaluating information from other individuals based on information regarding the potential informants' expertise and shared preferences. The costs of obtaining political information vary dramatically across individual subjects, and these costs help explain why some individuals become politically expert while others do not. An attractive alternative, particularly for those with high information costs, is to rely on information and advice taken from others who are politically expert with shared preferences. This chapter focuses on the complications that arise when the network distributions of expertise and preferences are independent. When forced to choose, do experimental subjects embrace shared preferences or expertise in their search for political information? What are the implications for the evaluation of information that conflicts with their own prior judgments?

` Chapter 6 considers the problems that occur when ideal informants, typically characterized by the joint presence of political expertise and shared viewpoints, are unavailable or rare within the immediate groups where individuals are located. In these instances, individuals must often look beyond their own group boundaries to find such informants. The problem is that obtaining information from individuals located beyond their own groups produces additional information costs. Moreover, the availability of ideal informants varies across groups and settings, with the potential to produce (1) context-dependent patterns of informant centrality, which in turn generates (2) varying levels of polarization among groups, and (3) biases in favor of some groups at the expense of others. The aggregate implications of the small group experiments are considered using a simple agent-based model.

Chapter 7 focuses on the complexity of decision and calculation in a setting marked by interdependence among actors. Game-theoretic analyses of communication and interdependence inevitably confront mathematically intractable problems that arise due to the complexity of social interaction and its consequences for politics. While the previous two chapters take inspiration from central insights within this literature, the underlying experimental framework is far too complex to provide definitive solutions to all the strategic challenges faced by the experimental subjects. At a more modest level, this chapter provides an analysis of these strategic choices, thus providing insight into dilemmas faced by both opinion leaders and those who evaluate their efforts at leadership.

Chapter 8 examines the role of parties and partisanship within the context of social communication and opinion leadership. The analysis suggests that partisanship plays a potentially important but frequently underappreciated role. Informed individuals incorporate biased social messages into their candidate evaluations, producing higher levels of incorrect voting in some networks – a consequence that is potentially offset by a reliance on partisan loyalty. In particular, social communication is a useful information shortcut for uninformed independents, but not for uninformed partisans.

Chapter 9 addresses the role of opinion leadership in communication processes characterized by noisy, biased information – processes in which people with variable levels of expertise and strength of preference select informants, as well as being influenced by them. The analysis shows that participants formulate candidate judgments that decay in time, but the decay occurs at a significantly lower rate among the better informed. Moreover, the better informed are less affected by socially communicated messages regarding the candidates. Hence, the influence of experts is due not only to their powers of persuasion, but also to the durability of their own privately formulated opinions. Their role in the communication process is further heightened by the higher value placed by participants on expert opinion, which in turn exposes the recipient to a heterogeneous and hence potentially influential stream of information.

Chapter 10 extends the experimental analysis of Chapter 9 to address the longer term dynamic, interdependent implications of political influence within social networks. Individuals construct their own initial judgments regarding candidates based on public and private information before updating these judgments through a dynamic and sequential process of social communication. We employ a DeGroot model to address the higher-order, dynamic implications of this process for opinion leadership – leadership that reaches beyond the dyad to penetrate the population as a whole. Particular attention focuses on varying levels of information among participants and the implications that arise due to (1) the influence of better-informed individuals; (2) varying levels of reliance on priors and communicated messages; (3) the implications of memory decay for the influence and opinion leadership; and (4) the diffusion of information and patterns of persuasion.

Taken together, Chapters 9 and 10 provide an alternative explanation of opinion leadership that moves beyond a model based on deference to opinion leaders. This alternative is based instead on a structural communication dynamic in which experts form prior judgments that decay slowly in time, the priors of the non-experts decay rapidly, and the experts have a larger number of direct communication links that in turn communicate their views throughout the network.

SUMMARY AND IMPLICATIONS

Network studies of political communication and persuasion address the inherent limitations of citizens in democratic politics. If citizens arrive at decisions independently – as self-contained, fully informed actors – their choices might be explained wholly as a consequence of their own devices. Political decision-making could be understood as the product of individual priorities and the alternatives available to particular individuals. The problem is that relatively few citizens possess either full information, or an unbiased sample of full information, or the well-formed attitudes and belief systems that might guide their choices in a coherent manner (Converse 1964). Moreover, seen from the vantage point of an economic theory of political decision-making (Downs 1957), the high costs of becoming informed, coupled with the minimal likelihood of casting a decisive vote, call into question an expectation that rational citizens would invest heavily in the individual acquisition of information.

Indeed, this problem of citizenship capacity lies at the core of democratic politics, and its analytic implications are quite profound (Gibson 2001). Citizens operate in a complex political environment characterized by inherent uncertainty, and the task of citizenship involves reaching decisions and judgments under uncertainty (Tversky and Kahneman 1973) – uncertainty that is accentuated by the high costs of becoming informed (Downs 1957). The recognition of this challenge has transformed the study of citizens and politics, leading to new directions in scholarship aimed at identifying the means whereby citizens confront the tasks of citizenship (Sniderman 1993; Popkin 1991). Important contributions have been generated by cognitive research regarding attitudes, attitude strength, and the use of heuristics in processing political information and reaching decisions (Krosnick and Petty 1995; Lodge, Steenburgen, and Brau 1995; Sniderman et al. 1991), but this literature also points out the limitations of these informational short cuts (Lodge and Taber 2000; Sniderman 2000; Kuklinski and Quirk 2000).

The study of political communication has been conspicuously absent in the larger discussion of citizenship capacity. This is curious because the study of political communication provides a very direct means to incorporate social capital within the study of public opinion (Coleman 1988; Lake and Huckfeldt 1998; Ikeda and Richey 2005). A primary anticipated benefit that derives from social capital relates to the information that people access through networks of social relationships. These informational benefits are directly related to public opinion because citizens are able to rely on one another for information and guidance in politics. Without social networks, individuals would be forced to bear the acquisition and processing costs of political information on their own (Downs 1957). In this way, social capital that is accessed through networks of communication produces important efficiencies in the creation of informed citizenry.

Ignoring the informational potential of social communication has contributed to a missing link with respect to the study of the knowledge, information, and sophistication that underlie public opinion, in terms of both individual and aggregate opinion. The inescapable fact is that individuals often perform quite poorly in providing adequate responses to survey questions regarding basic

political knowledge, in providing well thought-out rationales for their preferences and opinions, and even in providing thoughtful and stable responses to
questions that solicit their opinions (Converse 1964; Delli Carpini and Keeter
1996; Sniderman 1993). At the same time, and in the aggregate, public opinion
appears to track in predictable, systematic, and seemingly informed ways with
respect to events in the political environment (Page and Shapiro 1992; Erikson,
MacKuen, and Stimson 2002).

Indeed, there are good reasons to suppose that citizens in the aggregate
perform much better than individual citizens in accomplishing their duties as
citizens, and hence to expect that interdependent citizens may enhance the quality
of democratic citizenship. Such an enhancement depends, of course, on the ability
of citizens to know good advice from bad advice, as well as their ability to discern
whether particular advice is in their own subjectively defined self-interests. The
problem is that both of these abilities are problematic.

Moreover, the virtues of an electorate composed of interdependent citizens
depend on the ability for political learning to take place – for individuals to learn
from one another. Here again, questions arise. Lodge and Taber (2000) point
toward the importance of motivated reasoning, particularly among those individuals with the highest levels of citizenship capacity – those citizens most likely
to populate the ranks of the experts and activists in the democratic process.
According to Lodge and Taber (2000), these are the individuals who are *least*
likely to take advantage of new contradictory information to update their judgments regarding politics.

The precise mechanism that leads individuals to depend more heavily on the
political experts in their midst also is unclear. One explanation is that people use
"knowledge proxies" (Lupia 2005, 1992) – they rely on individuals whom they
believe to be trustworthy and knowledgeable. Such an explanation fits in quite
well with Downs' (1957) original argument regarding the role of social communication as a cost-saving device for becoming informed. This explanation raises
other issues, however: in particular, are individuals able to recognize the purveyors of cheap talk (Crawford 1998; Crawford and Sobel 1982)? Are they able
to resist the temptation to take bad advice from a friendly expert who does not
share their own interests?

An alternative explanation for the social diffusion of political expertise is
based on a less intentional formulation. It is not that individuals consciously
look for the political experts in their midst, but rather that these experts tend to
be the politically engaged citizens – they tend to be the activists. In the Lodge and
Taber (2000) formulation, those people who know more are also likely to care
more and to be more committed. Hence, these citizens talk with their expert
associates more frequently because these particular associates talk endlessly
about politics! In this way, experts' opinions become important in the collective
deliberations of democracy because their preferences are self-weighted by their
own motivation and engagement.

Such an explanation offers a combination of good news and bad news. The good news is that expert views are likely to be self-weighted by the tendency of experts (as activists) to be motivated communicators, and hence their views are more likely to be communicated. The bad news is that the less expert recipients of this information may be poorly equipped to recognize its relationship to their own perspectives, orientations, and subjective definitions of self-interest. We address these issues in the chapters that follow.

In conclusion, interdependence may be seen as a theoretical statement that stands on its own feet – as a fundamental theoretical postulate that drives politics and political affairs – rather than simply a derivative conclusion. There are, of course, both economical and psychological versions of theories that explain the existence of particular patterns of interdependence: cognitive dissonance, subjective identification with social groups, information costs, prisoners' dilemmas, and collective action problems. The choices from among these various menus of alternatives are more or less useful depending upon the particular purposes of the investigator and the problem.

The point remains that interdependence – whether motivated by economic or psychological arguments – is itself a theoretical imperative with important observational consequences. An explanation that embraces interdependence among political actors produces distinctive political consequences, and it generates signature implications for political dynamics as well as for aggregate outcomes.

3

Experts, activists, and the social communication of political expertise

T. K. Ahn, Robert Huckfeldt, Jeanette Mendez, Tracy Osborn, and John Barry Ryan

> If, when properly informed, the people were to come to its decisions without any communication between its members, the general will would always emerge . . . and the decisions would always be good.
>
> Jean-Jacques Rousseau (1994: 66)

Rousseau's words sound foreign to the modern ear. He affirms democracy and the will of the people, but places no trust in political communication among citizens. He wants the sovereign to rule in accord with the general will, but believes the people's will to be unknowable unless two conditions are met: (1) the people are properly informed, and (2) they do not speak with one another. Few would dispute the assertion that informed individuals make better decisions, but those of us living in the age of communication and deliberation may find it odd that Rousseau does not trust the people to communicate and reason together. His fear is anchored in political realism. He views political communication as less a civic activity than a political one – an activity leading individuals to vote as their more influential associates want them to vote, rather than deciding according to their own opinions and devices (1994: 67).

In contrast, and nearly two hundred years later, Anthony Downs (1957) argued that communication among citizens is a key to overcoming individual information deficits. An individual can reduce information costs, according to Downs, by transferring these costs to political informants. Downs also is a realist, but he side-steps Rousseau's concerns by establishing strict (but ultimately problematic) criteria for selecting informants – that is, individuals should seek out political experts who share their preferences, or risk receiving faulty information that leads to a mistake at the ballot box.

In this chapter we begin to evaluate these two alternative positions with respect to the democratic virtues of communication among citizens. What are the circumstances under which citizens are informed by social communication? Under what conditions are they likely to be misled? Perhaps most importantly, *should we understand political discussion and communication among citizens as a civic exercise or as an extension of the political process?* The first step in this undertaking is to address the potential influence of experts and activists within the political communication networks connecting individual citizens. The second step is to assess the aggregate implications for the performance of democratic electorates and, in particular, the implications of discussion as a form of delegation.

I. RECOGNIZING EXPERTISE: DO CITIZENS KNOW IT WHEN THEY SEE IT?

The ability of citizens to rely on the political expertise and judgment of others provides a potentially important vehicle for the creation of a self-educating electorate. If people recognize the experts in their midst, the civic capacity of the electorate might be elevated beyond that achieved by individuals reaching political judgments in isolation. Correspondingly, if politically expert citizens are more engaged and thus spend more time talking about politics, the social airways of political discussion will disproportionately represent expert viewpoints. In both instances, individual interdependence has the potential to create added value in democratic politics by enhancing the civic capacity of the aggregate. These beneficial consequences assume that individuals avoid being misled by experts with divergent preferences, and Downs' analysis accomplishes this goal by stipulating that individuals take information from experts with shared preferences. Hence, the political implications of social communication are contingent on the nature of the individual response to information costs and particularly on the individually imposed selection criteria in constructing political communication networks.

The form of the individual-level response is important because political information comes at a cost that varies quite dramatically across individuals (Wolfinger and Rosenstone 1980). One way to minimize these costs is for individuals to obtain information from politically expert associates who share the recipient's political instincts and biases (Downs 1957). And, in order to locate and obtain guidance from these expert informants intentionally, they must accurately recognize the presence of expertise among others.

At the same time, many other individuals – the activists in our midst – are quite ready to offer opinions on a wide range of political issues, regardless of whether their views have been solicited, judged to be expert, or coincide with the recipient's own political viewpoints. Even in these latter circumstances, when the information is unsolicited, citizens operate at a similar advantage if they are able to take information more seriously by recognizing whether it comes from an expert source. In short, regardless of whether individuals are seeking informants, or whether informants are seeking opportunities to express their views, the recognition of expertise among others lies at the heart of politically meaningful social communication.

When recipients recognize the expertise of informants, the whole may indeed become greater than the sum of its parts. That is, to the extent that citizens obtain political information and guidance from other citizens who are relatively more knowledgeable and informed, an asymmetrical process of social communication carries the potential to create a multiplier effect on the distribution of expertise within the electorate. These structured patterns of communication would provide one element to the solution of a continuing public opinion paradox – individual citizens who appear woefully uninformed compared to an aggregate electorate that behaves in a predictable and sensible manner (Converse 1964; Page and Shapiro 1992; Sniderman, Brody, and Tetlock 1991). While those who employ socially communicated expertise may not become more politically expert themselves, they might act on the basis of shared expertise obtained through countless social exchanges (see Katz 1957). In short, social communication creates the potential for modest amounts of political expertise to go a long way in enhancing the performance of democratic politics.

Finally, within the context of political communication among citizens, what *is* expertise? And who *are* the experts? A storehouse of knowledge regarding the institutional and operational details of government certainly plays an important role, but knowledge comes in various forms. One form of expertise is related to paying attention in introductory political science classes, but another is related to ongoing patterns of attentiveness to the world of politics and governance. This latter form of expertise is likely to be most prominent among those who are vitally interested and involved in the political process.

A series of questions thus arises. Are people able to recognize expertise among others, and does this recognition drive political communication? Or are patterns of social communication regarding politics swamped by other considerations, such as the presence of shared political perspectives or the informant's passion for politics? Do individuals seek out expert informants? Or do the politically engaged activists, who are also likely to be politically expert, emerge as a consequence of their own passion for politics? Is the perception of expertise among others biased on the basis of assumptions and beliefs anchored in cultural norms and stereotypes? Finally, what are the aggregate consequences – does social communication create an electorate composed of citizens who are well informed and thus able to act on the basis of their own individually defined preferences?

We address these questions by focusing on (1) the criteria that people employ in making judgments with respect to the political competence of other individuals, (2) the source and potential for biases in these judgments, (3) the consequences of these judgments for the frequency of political discussion with particular individuals, (4) the resulting implications for effective and persuasive communication at both the micro and the macro levels, and (5) the net effect on the capacity of individuals to act on the basis of their self-defined interests and preferences. The discussion builds on previously undertaken efforts, based on analyses of individual citizens who are imbedded within networks of political communication during election campaigns (Huckfeldt 2001; Mendez and Osborn 2010; Ryan 2011a).

Experts, activists, and civic capacity

Political discussion among citizens is a central feature of democratic politics, and a defining ingredient of concerned citizens is their willingness and capacity to enter into a process of collective deliberation with other citizens (Mondak and Gearing 1998; Putnam et al. 1993). Actively engaged citizens seldom go it alone – they seldom engage in the political process as isolated individuals. They communicate, they argue, and they accumulate political information through an ongoing process of social interaction (Lazarsfeld, Berelson, and Gaudet 1968; Berelson, Lazarsfeld, and McPhee 1954). But what are the consequences of this collective process? Are these consequences beneficial to the informed exercise of citizenship and to the functioning of democratic politics? The answers to these questions are central in determining whether the informants and recipients of information act in ways that make political discussion an efficient means of minimizing the information costs of political engagement while simultaneously enhancing the ability of citizens to participate effectively.

The influence of citizens' communication networks might be realized in at least two different ways. According to a purely **demand-driven model**, the consumer of socially communicated information is a strategic actor who seeks to minimize costs by obtaining otherwise costly information at a deep discount from her politically expert associates. According to this model, the self-educating potential of the electorate is jointly contingent on: (1) the ability of citizens to make discriminating judgments regarding the political expertise of other individuals, and (2) the use of political expertise either as a selection criterion in the communication of political information, or as a mechanism for evaluating the quality of the information they are receiving through social communication, or both.

If citizens do not know an expert informant from an ignorant one, they would be poorly equipped to sort out credible analyses and analysts from incredible ones, and hence the effect of political discussion on collective levels of information and expertise would be compromised. Even if citizens *do* recognize political expertise among others, this fact has little consequence unless expertise becomes a factor in the creation of political communication networks. The underlying problem presented by this model is thus two-fold: (1) the extent to which people recognize the presence of knowledge and expertise among others within their networks; and (2) the extent to which they seek out information from those in the networks who are perceived to be the most politically expert.

Alternatively, the civic potential of communication networks might be understood in the context of a **supply-driven model**, as a direct consequence of the **informant's** motivations. Rather than being a passive information source, the activist informant occupies the crucial role in this alternative explanation.

Indeed, the activist informant is a self-appointed opinion leader who cares deeply about politics and becomes a primary actor in the political communication process. While the expert in a demand-driven model provides leadership at the request and as a consequence of actions that arise on the part of the individual being informed, the activist – whether or not she is also an expert – provides leadership as a consequence of her own interest and commitment to politics. Hence, the recipient takes on a secondary role in this model – as someone obtaining information due to the motivation of the activist who regularly shares her views with others.

The model of the activist informant does not negate the importance of either expertise or the identification of expertise. The recipient still benefits from an ability to separate the wheat from the chaff – the capacity to discriminate between the expert activist and the enthusiast who is wholly lacking in expert judgment. Moreover, we would expect expertise and activism to be reinforcing characteristics at the level of individuals. Those who are emotionally engaged and committed to politics are more likely to pay attention (Simon 1983), thereby accumulating higher levels of knowledge and expertise with respect to politics, even though their expertise is likely to reflect the inevitable biases accompanying their own motivation. Moreover, those who are politically expert are more likely to recognize the importance of political issues and political events – they are more likely to be engaged by the political process in a way that makes them active participants in the communication process. Thus, while the stimulus to communication is the passionate commitment of the activist, a primary byproduct may be the social communication of politically expert judgment, even as that judgment carries the inevitable bias of the initiator.

Finally, informants and recipients need not be mirror images of one another, either in terms of activism or expertise. Activists and experts may interact with other experts and activists, but they may also associate with non-activists and non-experts. Indeed, if communication is segregated by activism or expertise – with only activists talking to activists or only experts talking to experts – the synergistic consequences of social communication are undermined.

Identifying and misidentifying political expertise

If people *are* able to recognize a worthy political analyst when they encounter one, the political capacity of the electorate might thus be enhanced by collectively efficient patterns of communication – either by the purposefully constructed networks of political communication that give priority to experts, or by patterns of communication in which experts are taken more seriously, or both. Rather than undertaking extensive and exhaustive research regarding every political issue, individuals may quite reasonably obtain such information "on the cheap" by obtaining it from politically knowledgeable individuals. What are the alternative selection criteria that individuals might invoke, and why might individuals fail to identify experts correctly?

First, the persistent problem is whether individuals know an expert when they see one! Conflict-averse individuals might respond to the discomfort of disagreement by overestimating the political expertise of those with whom they agree, and underestimating the political expertise of those with whom they disagree (Lord, Ross, and Lepper 1979; Kunda 1990, 1999). The implications for democratic politics would not be encouraging. While people may encounter diverse views and perspectives, they might dismiss these views by means of motivated reasoning – people who disagree might be imputed to be politically misguided and ignorant!

Second, and in partial contrast to Downs, Calvert (1985a) argues that information can be useful when it is obtained from someone with whom the recipient *disagrees*. Calvert's insight is that it is often quite helpful to understand people's choices in the context of their own underlying preferences, even when those preferences run counter to your own. For example, if a liberal is uncertain regarding whether the U.S. should withdraw its troops from Afghanistan, it might be helpful to solicit the opinion of a conservative who has spent time thinking about military engagements. If someone who is likely to favor military involvement in general is opposed to it in a particular instance, that information might clarify the particular choice in the context of the particular preference. Thus, *a crucial condition is the accurate recognition of the informant's underlying political orientation*, regardless of whether the informant holds an agreeable or disagreeable viewpoint (Huckfeldt and Sprague 1987). Thus, the relationship between agreement and the expected utility of political information becomes an open question.

Third, some citizens may prefer to discuss politics with people who are politically agreeable, not based on the expected utility of communicated information, but rather based on a preference for agreeable social exchange. Such an explanation fits quite well within a cognitive dissonance interpretation of political communication (Festinger 1957). To the extent that politically inspired disagreement is dissonance-producing, people are likely to sidestep encounters that produce disagreement, and the political implications of such avoidance behavior are quite important. If people avoid disagreement, the vitality of political communication is compromised and the diffusion of political information is truncated. Rather than a full airing of issues and perspectives, political communication might produce political inbreeding and the reinforcement of prior-held beliefs among politically like-minded individuals (Lodge and Taber 2000).

Finally, a great deal of political information is conveyed in ways that are incidental to the primary purpose of the relationship. You may enjoy eating lunch with one of your workplace associates even though she holds political viewpoints that not only are poorly informed, but also run counter to your own. Thus, a great deal of the political information that flows through communication networks may be based on convenience and availability, quite unrelated to any strategic search for information. Hence, the contextually determined supply of potential discussants looms large (Huckfeldt 1983b; Huckfeldt and Sprague 1988), not only in politics but also in the rest of life. Once again, if someone lives and works in Los Angeles, he may have difficulty finding a fellow Giants fan with whom to eat lunch at the workplace.

In summary, if networks of political communication weight the opinions of expert citizens more heavily, the political discussion that occurs among citizens might indeed sustain a discussion of politics on its merits, informed by countless conversations among citizens and the acknowledged capabilities of expert informants (Barber 1984; Fishkin 1991). At the same time, a variety of possible obstacles stand in the way of a self-educating electorate, and this chapter addresses some of the potential roadblocks. In particular, we consider the capacity of individuals to assess the political expertise of the individuals who populate their networks of communication, the factors that compromise this capacity, and the implications for communication in democratic politics.

Observing citizens within networks and contexts

A primary stumbling block to understanding the collective consequences of interdependence among citizens has been a set of dominant observational practices that foreclose the possibilities of observing the social contingencies operating on individual behavior. Public opinion surveys and experimental studies that treat individuals as self-contained decision-making units have unintentionally but inevitably tended to ignore the roles of experts and activists in the communication process among citizens[1] – a communication process that creates complex aggregate outcomes as a consequence of interdependent, interacting individuals.

In order to address these issues fully and empirically, an analysis must take into account information on individual citizens, their discussion networks, their judgments regarding the political expertise of the individual discussants who make up these networks, the frequency with which they discuss politics with particular discussants, and the objectively defined political expertise and activism of these discussants. Several network studies have addressed the problem (Huckfeldt and Sprague 1995; Huckfeldt, Beck, Dalton, and Levine 1995; Huckfeldt, Johnson, and Sprague 2004) by interviewing not only individuals (the main respondents), but also by interviewing the individuals who populate these main respondents' networks – the discussants of the main respondents.

Most of the evidence discussed in this chapter comes from two studies: the 1996 Indianapolis-St. Louis study (ISL) conducted by the Center for Survey Research at Indiana University, and the 2000 National Election Study (NES). The ISL includes two separate samples: a sample of main respondents (N=2,174), who are asked to identify and provide information on their discussion partners, combined with a one-stage snowball sample of these main respondents'

[1] For an example to the contrary, see Carmines and Stimson (1989).

discussants (N=1,475). The main respondent sample is drawn from the voter registration lists of the two study sites, the Indianapolis and St. Louis metropolitan areas, and the discussant sample is located and interviewed on the basis of information provided by the main respondent. A second set of analyses is based on the 2000 NES, which included a similar social network battery, without the snowball interview of the identified discussants.

Interviews in the Indianapolis-St. Louis study were conducted over the course of the campaign, beginning in March 1996 and ending in January 1997. Every respondent to the survey was asked to provide the first names of not more than five discussion partners. A random half of the sample was asked to name people with whom they discuss "important matters"; the other half was asked to name people with whom they discuss "government, elections, and politics" (Burt 1986; Huckfeldt and Sprague 1995; Huckfeldt, Levine et al. 1998b). This procedure provides the opportunity to treat the question wording as an experimental manipulation, allowing a comparison between political communication networks and networks of communication for important – but not necessarily political – topics.

After compiling a list of first names for no more than five discussants, the interviewers asked a battery of questions about each discussant. At the end of the interview, the interviewers asked for identifying information that might be used to contact and interview the discussants. A sample of 1,475 discussants were contacted and agreed to be interviewed based on a survey instrument that was very similar to the instrument used in the main respondent interview.

The 2000 National Election Study employed the traditional pre-election and post-election surveys, and the social network battery was implemented as part of the post-election survey. The same basic network identification questions were used to generate the first names of the discussants, but they were only asked to provide political discussants. Also, the respondents to the NES were *not* asked to provide information regarding the identities of the discussants whom they named.

Both studies include questions designed to measure the political knowledge of the main survey respondents. Drawing on the work of Delli Carpini and Keeter (1993, 1996), the ISL employs a three-question battery that is administered to both the main respondents and the discussants at the end of their respective interviews: Whose responsibility is it to determine if a law is constitutional or not? What are the first ten Amendments in the Constitution called? How much of a majority is required for the U.S. Senate and House to override a presidential veto?

In both studies, interviewers also asked the main respondents to make judgments regarding each discussant's level of political expertise: "Generally speaking, how much do you think (first name of discussant) knows about politics?" The answers to these questions serve as measures of *perceived* political expertise regarding particular discussants. A primary issue for our purposes is to understand the factors that influence these evaluations, and a natural place to begin is with the *objectively defined* levels of political knowledge on the part of individual discussants.

In addition to these questions, the analysis employs a range of information about both the main respondents and the discussants, based on the main respondents' perceptions of the discussants, as well as the self-reports of both the main respondents and the discussants who were interviewed as part of the snowball survey. These data provide, in turn, an opportunity to evaluate the factors affecting one individual's judgment regarding the political expertise of another.

Disagreement and judgments regarding political expertise

What conditions give rise to the communication of political expertise, and to what extent are citizens able to recognize the presence of expertise among others? As suggested earlier, an important argument suggesting that we should *not* trust individual judgments regarding the expertise of others is anchored in cognitive dissonance theory (Festinger 1957) and motivated reasoning (Kunda 1999). Consider the situation in which Tom correctly recognizes that his discussant, Dick, holds an opinion that diverges sharply from his own. One alternative would be for Tom to form a negative assessment of Dick's expertise that would, in turn, justify a disregard of Dick's opinion. Hence Tom forms a negative evaluation of Dick's expertise, based on the demonstrated fact that Dick is not smart enough to adopt Tom's own (presumably) correct views!

This argument is entirely plausible, particularly in light of the fact that disagreement is perceived to occur quite frequently within communication networks. At the end of the campaign, after the election was over, 38 percent of the dyads in the Indianapolis and St. Louis post-election samples involved a main respondent who perceived disagreement with the discussant regarding presidential candidate preference. The likelihood that any given individual would have at least one associate with whom they disagree is correspondingly higher (Huckfeldt, Johnson, and Sprague 2004). Indeed, 52.3 percent had one or more discussants whom they perceived to hold a candidate preference different from their own. In this context, perceived reality is perhaps more important than objectively measured disagreement, but the levels of accuracy are quite high: 78.4 percent of the main respondents *accurately* perceive the presence of agreement, and 72.8 percent of all respondents *accurately* perceive the absence of agreement.

Other factors affecting the recognition of expertise

In addition to the presence of agreement or disagreement, a range of other explanatory factors that might be prime suspects in attenuating or enhancing the social communication and recognition of political expertise need to be considered. The obvious and perhaps naïve hypothesis is that perceptions of political knowledge and expertise are, in fact, driven by political knowledge and expertise! This raises the issue of how expertise should be understood.

Two discussant knowledge measures are included in ISL analyses reported elsewhere (Huckfeldt 2001; Mendez and Osborn 2010; Ryan 2011a): the number of correct answers the discussant scored on the three-item political knowledge battery, and the discussant's level of education. The knowledge battery provides the most obvious measure of an individual's political knowledge, but factual knowledge is only one characteristic of the expert informant, broadly defined. If political expertise is to be perceived in the context of political discussion and political reasoning, well-developed cognitive and communication skills may be equally important, and the discussant's educational level provides an indicator of these skills.

Two explanatory measures of activism are based on the discussants' reported levels of interest in the election campaign, as well as their reported levels of involvement in campaign-related activities (Ryan 2011a). These measures of activism are thus based on evidence of psychological engagement and personal involvement in politics. It is easy to conceive of people who have the knowledge and capacity to participate effectively in politics, but who are simply not interested (Verba, Schlozman, and Brady 1995). Even well-educated citizens with knowledge about the formal institutions and structures of government might demonstrate low levels of campaign involvement and psychological engagement in politics.

Hence, we are able to compare the effects of the informant's political knowledge and educational attainment on main respondent perceptions of political expertise with those arising due to the engagement and involvement of the activist, defined in terms of political interest and campaign activity. Including these measures helps us judge the importance of knowledge and cognitive capacity versus engagement and activism in the recognition of political expertise. If individuals assess expertise in terms of political knowledge and education, controlling for the informant's interest and campaign activity, the recognition of expertise likely depends on the main respondent's independent assessment of an informant's political capacity. In contrast, if individuals identify political expertise in terms of an informant's interest and political activity level, controlling for the informant's knowledge and education, the social communication of political expertise likely depends on the informant's demonstrated motivation and involvement. The latter explanation focuses on the motivation of the informant, while the former focuses on the recipient – the person being informed.

A problem arises because any simple effect due to discussant expertise may, in fact, be a spurious consequence arising due to (1) patterns of association in which experts tend to cluster together and (2) a tendency among experts to infer higher levels of expertise among their associates. Hence, the same measures of knowledge and activism are included as explanatory variables for the main respondents as well: their objectively defined political knowledge as well as their self-reported levels of education, political interest, and involvement in campaign activity.

Finally, accumulated evidence suggests that politics is quite often defined, in cultural terms, as a male activity. In an earlier study, Huckfeldt and Sprague (1995) show that political communication outside the family often is segregated by gender, and both men and women tend to perceive higher levels of political expertise among men than among women. The problem is that these earlier analyses did not include direct measures regarding the knowledge and activism of the discussion partners, and hence the analyses of Mendez and Osborn (2010) provide further insight and leverage on the problem that we rely upon here.

What do the analyses show?

First, a widely prevalent assumption has been that opinion leadership is specialized and contingent on expertise in a particular area (Katz and Lazarsfeld 1955). While this may certainly be true for many socially communicated topics (e.g., Schneider et al. 2000), it does not appear to be as obvious for general political discussion. The network discussants in the ISL study are no more likely to be judged as expert than the discussants who are identified as part of an "important matters" network. Hence, after measures of discussant expertise are taken into account, there is little evidence to suggest that political communication networks are differentiated from more generalized communication networks on the basis of *perceived* levels of expertise that are independent of objectively defined levels of expertise. (This is an important issue, to which we will return later in this chapter and Chapter 4.)

In contrast, the objective measures of informant knowledge, as well as the measures for the informant's interest and campaign involvement, produce important and substantial effects. Higher levels of involvement, interest, knowledge, and education on the part of the informants produce higher perceived levels of expertise on the part of the main respondents. At the same time, *none of these expertise and activism measures produce discernible effects for the main respondents.* In other words, these perceptions of others are anchored in the political characteristics of the individuals being perceived, not in terms of the individual who is doing the perceiving. This is a particularly important result because it points to perceptions of expertise among others that are anchored in reality, not in misperception.

This is not to say that the perceptions are free of bias, however. Most importantly, both men and women are more likely to perceive men as being more politically expert – *even after knowledge and activism are taken into account* (Mendez and Osborn 2010).[2] Indeed, the gender bias in evaluating informant

---

[2] Somewhat more than a third of the dyads are mixed gender, and only one-third of these mixed gender dyads are male main respondents naming female discussants. Hence the evidence is limited. It appears, however, that the gender bias arises due to generally high expertise ratings given by

expertise is nearly as important as the effect due to objectively defined expertise on the part of the discussant. Both male and female main respondents rate the expertise of women to be less than the expertise of men – and indeed female main respondents rate female informants more negatively than do male main respondents! The importance of this result is difficult to overstate, inasmuch as it is over and above the effects arising due to objectively defined activism and knowledge on the part of the discussant (Mendez and Osborn 2010).

How important are the effects that arise due to activism and objectively defined expertise on the part of the discussants? The somewhat larger effect arises as a consequence of discussant activism, measured as the combined effect of the discussants' levels of political interest and campaign activity, but the effect arising due to the discussant's education and political knowledge is only slightly less important. Informant interest and activism increase the probability of perceiving that the informant knows a "great deal" by .56, and the change due to informant knowledge and education is .42. In comparison, the increase in perceived expertise due to agreement on presidential vote choice between the main respondent and the discussant is only .09 (Ryan 2010).

Do these results suggest that perceptions of expertise are biased by the informant's level of political engagement and by shared preferences among the individuals within the dyad? This may be the case, but we might also consider alternative, more generous interpretations. First, expertise on the part of the disengaged may simply not communicate well – that is, how are we to know that associates are expert if they are too uninvolved to demonstrate their expertise? Alternatively, activism may serve as an indirect measure of expertise. Those who are engaged and involved are more likely to develop a familiarity with the issues of the day – and hence they are more likely to become expert! This form of expertise, which is a byproduct of activism, may be particularly relevant and useful in the context of political communication among citizens.

Similarly, the fact that the main respondents are less likely to believe that informants with divergent political preferences are expert also is amenable to alternative interpretations. On the one hand, people may justify disagreement by pointing toward an individual's supposed lack of political expertise. On the other hand, if people believe their own views are correct, is it surprising that they consider those with other views to be less expert? In either event, the effect of disagreement is anemic in comparison to the effects of activism and knowledge on the part of the informant.

Taken together, these results suggest that informants are not passive actors. Rather, it appears that an important element in the *social communication* of political expertise is the *existence* of political involvement and expertise on the

women to men combined with the particularly low ratings that men give to their wives. Female main respondents rate male main respondents as knowing a "great deal" about 50 percent of the time regardless of their relationship with the man. Men place their wives in the highest category only 22 percent of the time, compared with 34 percent of the time for their other female discussants.

part of the informant. Political expertise diffuses not only due to the demand-driven motivation of those who are in search of political information and guidance, but also as a result of the supply-driven activists who are intrinsically motivated to share their beliefs. At the same time, gender provides an important overlay of cultural bias on these reality-based perceptions. Indeed, we see convincing evidence of a systematic bias based on gender – a bias that persists even when objectively defined levels of expertise are taken into account.

In summary, a modified version of the naïve hypothesis receives dramatic support. The best predictors of *perceived* expertise are the measures of objectively defined activism and knowledge on the part of the informant. Opinion leaders are not figments of imagination constructed in the eye of the beholder. To the contrary, discussants with higher levels of interest, involvement, knowledge, and education are perceived to be more expert by their associates, and the cumulative effects of these four factors swamp the combined effect of perceived agreement. At the same time, we also see dramatic and persistent patterns of perceptual bias based on gender, and, as a consequence, the political capacity of women is regularly undervalued.

Expertise and discussion

Are citizens more likely to discuss politics with people whom they believe to be politically expert? If not, a potential mechanism for producing a social multiplier effect on the effects of individual expertise becomes immaterial – that is, the demand-driven model of socially communicated expertise becomes irrelevant, and only a supply-driven model is left to account for the communication of politically expert judgment. In this context, we consider the relationship between perceived expertise and the frequency of political discussion.

After asking respondents how many days each week they talked with the particular discussant, the interviewers went on to ask: "When you talk with (discussant first name), do you discuss political matters: often, sometimes, rarely, or never?" The simple relationship between the perceived expertise of the discussant and the reported frequency of political discussion is quite pronounced: 38.6 percent of respondents who believe that their discussants know a great deal report the highest frequency of political discussion, but only 6.4 percent of those who believe their discussants know "not much at all" report the highest frequency. While individuals are more likely to report frequent discussion with discussants whom they believe to be politically expert, the question arises, does this relationship persist when other explanations are taken into account? Indeed, a variety of other factors might be related to both perceived frequency and perceived expertise, and hence the relationship may be a spurious consequence of other circumstances and conditions.

First, both the politically interested and the politically partisan are likely to be engaged by the debates and dramas of politics, and hence they are more likely to engage in political discussion. Those who are interested and involved are *also* more likely to be perceived as being politically knowledgeable, and thus activism may help to explain the relationship between perceived expertise and reported frequency of discussion.

A second alternative explanation is that the effect of perceived knowledge is the (familiar) residue of political agreement and shared political orientations. That is, perhaps we talk more with people who share our viewpoints, and perceived expertise is simply the rationalization for this behavior. From the standpoint of reducing cognitive dissonance, it is easier for one person to avoid or dismiss another's disagreeable viewpoints if she believes that the other person does not know much anyway.

The results show that, while education generates no direct effect on discussion frequency for either the main respondent or the informant, knowledge, interest, and campaign activity are important on the part of *both* the informant *and* the main respondent. Not only are respondents more likely to discuss politics more frequently with knowledgeable activists, but they are also more likely to discuss if they are knowledgeable activists themselves. While gender does not produce any direct effects on discussion frequency within dyads, we see an important effect in which spouses are more likely to discuss politics. Finally, main respondents report more frequent political discussion with individuals identified as being part of explicitly political discussion networks, as opposed to "important matters networks."

These results are not particularly surprising. While perceptions of expertise are driven primarily by characteristics of the informant in question, the frequency of discussion depends on both halves of the dyad. In other words, the likelihood of political discussion responds to the characteristics of both participants in the dyad.

When the main respondent's perception of informant expertise is introduced into the analysis as an explanatory variable, the consequences are quite profound. Not only does the perception of expertise produce a substantial effect, it also erases the effects for objectively defined knowledge, education, interest, and campaign activity on the part of the informant. Quite simply, the impact of informant characteristics on discussion frequency is filtered through the main respondent's perception regarding political expertise on the part of the informant. At the same time, psychological engagement and campaign involvement on the part of the main respondent continue to demonstrate strong effects on the frequency of participation.

The magnitudes of these effects are quite striking. The effect of perceived expertise on the part of the informant is comparable to the effect that arises due to the main respondent's level of engagement, based on reported interest and engagement. In comparison, the effect of disagreement on the probability of frequent discussion is extremely small, while the increase among marriage partners is quite dramatic.

In summary, when it comes to the reported frequency of political discussion within dyads, we see that characteristics of *both* the main respondent *and* the informant are important. Main respondents report higher rates of discussion with knowledgeable, interested, involved informants, but they are also more likely to report higher rates of discussion if they are knowledgeable, interested, and involved themselves. The consequences of informant characteristics are, in turn, filtered through the main respondents' perceptions of the informants' expertise levels. In short, political communication is anchored in both the reality and the perception of expertise and engagement. We see a communication process instigated by individuals who gravitate toward political discussion with people whom they perceive as experts, and a process in which some experts – those who are politically activated – instigate political discussion as well.

Expertise and communication effectiveness

What are the consequences of expertise for the effectiveness and influence of the political communication process among citizens? One measure of effectiveness is the accuracy with which political messages are communicated. If Tom and Dick talk about politics at work, and Tom believes that Dick supports the Democratic candidate when he actually favors the Republican, then political deliberation has quite clearly misfired. The question thus becomes, are the preferences of politically expert discussants more likely to be perceived accurately, thereby enhancing communication effectiveness? A second measure of effectiveness is influence – we might expect that expert messengers would be more influential in affecting the preferences and behavior of the message's recipient, and the question thus becomes, are experts more influential?

Three effects on effectiveness measured as correct perception have been demonstrated: spousal relationships, location in an explicitly defined political communication network, and discussant campaign activity. The first effect is straightforward – as we have seen, spouses talk about politics with high frequency, and hence they know one another's political preferences. Second, discussants who are part of explicitly defined political communication networks are more likely to be perceived accurately as well.

The third effect, due to discussant campaign activity, builds on earlier results showing that strong partisans tend to communicate more clearly. Individuals with extreme candidate preferences, extreme partisan identifications, and accessible partisan attitudes are less likely to send ambiguous political signals, and hence they are more likely to be perceived accurately (Huckfeldt, Sprague, and Levine 2000; Huckfeldt 2001). Campaign activists tend to be involved on the basis of strong partisan orientations, and their preferences tend to be clearly perceived.

Several other factors are important as well – actual agreement within the dyad based on the self-reported voting preferences of main respondents and discussants, and the level of perceived support within the remainder of the network for the vote preference reported by the discussant. The results show that discussants are more likely to be perceived accurately if they share the perceiver's political preference. Moreover, they are also more likely to be perceived accurately if their preferences are perceived to be more widely shared among other members of the main respondent's network.

How can we explain the effects that arise due to agreement in the dyad and in the network? Many socially communicated political messages are shrouded in ambiguity. In ambiguous circumstances, people are more likely to perceive others within the context of their own social frame of reference. If you vote Democratic, you are more likely to assume that your friends and associates – with whom you share many characteristics in common – are likely to vote Democratic as well. If you believe that most of your friends and associates vote Democratic, you are less likely to notice that one of them may actually be a Republican. In short, lacking clear and unambiguous signals from an associate, you are likely to assess messages from that individual within the surrounding social context. This is another empirical footprint of an autoregressive theory of social influence (Huckfeldt, Johnson, and Sprague 2004), and a major theme in subsequent analyses.

The importance of the political activist makes itself felt at these points of ambiguity. The activists in our midst are, quite simply, less likely to melt into the background. They are more likely to be recognized for what they are – committed supporters of candidates, causes, and parties. Informants can have little direct influence if their preferences are misperceived (Huckfeldt and Sprague 1995). Thus, by engaging in political communication with those experts and activists who make their preferences clearly understood, citizens increase the likelihood that their own opinions and viewpoints will be influenced. And, in this way, the preferences of politically expert discussants are weighted more heavily in the collective deliberations of democratic politics.

Influence within the dyad

In contrast to accurate perception, persuasion within the dyad requires an assessment of the effect due to the informant's political preferences on those of the main respondents – that is, do the informant's preferences and choices directly affect those of the main respondent? As we would expect (Campbell et al. 1960), the main respondents' reported votes closely parallel their reported party identifications. At the same time, even after taking account of the main respondents' own partisan loyalties, an important effect also arises due to the discussant's reported vote.

Other analyses demonstrate, however, that the influence of the informant is not contingent on the informant's level of expertise – that is, ***politically expert discussants are no more likely to be influential than the politically inexpert.***[3] At the same time, the effect of the discussant's vote on the main respondent's vote

---

[3] Analyses of the 1984 South Bend study (Huckfeldt and Sprague 1995) as well as unpublished analyses of the ISL show that discussant expertise has no effect on dyadic vote agreement.

is contingent on the vote preferences held by the remainder of the network. Based on the 2000 NES, for example, the probability that a respondent shares an associate's preference for Bush or Gore in 2000 depends on the percentage of the remaining network that supports the same candidate. Indeed, this probability increases among political independents by approximately 40 points, from a probability of .4 when no one else in the network supports the candidate, to a probability of approximately .8 when everyone else in the network supports the candidate (Huckfeldt, Johnson, and Sprague 2004: 54–60).

In short, these results suggest that the direct persuasive power of an informant is fundamentally contingent on the distribution of preferences in the remainder of the network. Voters do not genuflect on the basis of expert judgment, accepting the credibility of an expert informant's message. Recall the earlier discussion of attribution effects – even the wrong-headed views of experts are subject to a variety of explanations that might account for their errant views. For example: "Joe knows a lot about politics – too bad he is a liberal!" To the contrary, the views of discussants would appear to be validated by an autoregressive process in which they are supported by other individuals within the main respondent's political communication network (Huckfeldt, Johnson, and Sprague 2004). In short, *even expert judgment is subject to external (social) validity checks.*

This does not mean that discussant political characteristics are without influence. We have already seen that the main respondents acknowledge expertise among their associates based on an objective judgment regarding the knowledge and activism of the informant. They talk more frequently with informants whom they acknowledge to be experts, and they are more likely to recognize the opinions of experts and activists more accurately. Hence, these results do not suggest that knowledge and activism are inconsequential or lacking in influence. To the contrary, the analysis simply suggests the presence of boundaries on the influence of expert opinion, and these boundaries are socially imposed. The political process is democratic not only because votes are counted to determine the winning and losing candidates, but also because the opinions of individuals are subject to a social ratification process in which any message from any single source is judged relative to every other source.

The important results are thus five-fold. First, citizens communicate more frequently with those whom they perceive to be politically expert. Second, their perceptions are based in reality, driven primarily by actual levels of activism and knowledge among others. Third, this asymmetrical quality of communication, in which people rely more heavily on locally defined experts, increases the effectiveness of expert communication as well as the ultimate, if not direct, influence of politically expert citizens. Fourth, a continuing source of bias in the political communication process arises due to the dramatic effects of gender, which underestimate the political expertise of women and discount their viewpoints at a most basic level. Finally, we see only minor effects on discussion frequency arising due to disagreement, and hence the process carries the potential to expose individuals to influential viewpoints that are at variance with their own sentiments and interests.

Implications for political communication among citizens

Political communication within networks of social relations carries the potential to enhance the individual and collective capacities of citizens to play meaningful roles in democratic politics. First, citizens are more likely to talk with others whom they believe to be politically expert, quite independently from either the reality or the perception of political disagreement. Indeed, the effect of perceived discussant expertise on the frequency of political communication is much more substantial than the effect of perceived agreement.

Second, apart from the dramatic gender bias, citizens judge their discussants to be politically expert based on objectively defined and relevant characteristics of potential informant – their levels of political knowledge, interest, and involvement. In contrast, the perception of political disagreement produces a relatively minor and inconsequential effect on the perception of expertise. Apart from the gender bias, political discussion is contingent on the reality-based judgments of participants regarding the informational value of alternative informants, and hence the political relationships among citizens are frequently asymmetric with respect to political expertise.[4]

What are the substantive implications of the analysis for democratic politics? First, at the level of collective electorates, the whole really *is* more than the sum of its parts. Alternatively, to anchor this argument in its Durkheimian roots (1951: 320), "the group formed by associated individuals has a reality of a different sort from each individual considered singly." Hence, one of the reasons that "democracy works" is that its citizens do indeed rely on "horizontal networks of relations" for meaningful political engagement (Putnam 1993). In a political society where individuals are isolated and cut off from one another, democratic politics will either operate suboptimally, or it will cease to function at all (Mondak and Gearing 1998). The intellectual corollary for political science runs along similar lines: a scholarly treatment of citizenship that focuses solely on isolated individuals ignores the collective potential of democratic politics, and it underestimates the capacity of citizens who are located in complex networks of political interdependence (Axelrod 1997).

Second, the capacities of individuals to render meaningful judgments regarding the expertise of alternative information sources are quite striking. People are not generally lost in a cloud of misperception when they engage in social

---

[4] Other analyses demonstrate a perhaps surprising level of non-reciprocity within dyads. In the South Bend study, Huckfeldt and Sprague (1995: 167–168) estimate that only 15 percent of non-relative dyads and 21 percent of non-spouse relative dyads were estimated to name the main respondent as *their* discussant. In the ISL, 29 percent of non-spouse relative dyads and 31 percent of non-relative dyads were estimated to be reciprocal (Huckfeldt, Johnson, and Sprague 2004: 119).

communication about politics, and neither is the information they obtain simply a mirror of their own preferences. Rather, they recognize a valuable source of political information when they encounter one, quite independently of whether they share the source's political bias, and they proceed to utilize these informants more fully.

The glaring exception arises due to the systematic gender bias that pervades political communication among citizens. The political expertise of women is consistently undervalued, with two important implications: first, women as individuals are less likely to be recognized as serious contributors to the larger political discussion in American politics, and second, the quality of the political conversation is thus compromised because an important voice is systematically underrepresented.

What are the implications of this analysis for the nature and consequence of political disagreement among and between citizens? The comparative informational value of political communication within and between groups holding different preferences is a complex and perhaps not fully resolved question (Downs 1957; Calvert 1985a), and hence any empirical expectation is correspondingly clouded. Some people in some settings may seek out political discussants who hold compatible political biases. Other people in other settings – and perhaps the *same* people in other settings – may very well seek out discussants with divergent political biases, particularly if these individuals are judged to be politically expert. In short, the empirical effect demonstrated here – a modestly positive relationship between perceived agreement and reported frequency of discussion – may indeed be a net effect that summarizes heterogeneous responses and strategies of information acquisition.

Moreover, the modest and positive effect of agreement on perceived expertise does not necessarily reflect a response anchored in dissonance reduction. Rather, it may reflect an individual's quite reasonable (or at least comprehensible) assessment regarding a discussant who is judged to make faulty political judgments. In short, one need not assume that *any* effect arising due to disagreement is necessarily a response to the psychic discomfort of political disagreement, and there is little evidence of such psychic discomfort anywhere in this analysis. The perception of disagreement is relatively widespread; the presence of disagreement does not extinguish political communication; and judgments regarding expertise are primarily driven on the merits of the particular case, with only a minor effect due to disagreement.

Thus, political disagreement among and between citizens may not be particularly important in the production of cognitive dissonance. As Ross and his colleagues (1976) suggest, motivated conformity is most powerful when disagreement is most difficult to explain. In the Asch experiments (1963), the subjects who were unaware of the experimental manipulation had no plausible explanation for the seemingly faulty judgments of those individuals who reported that the long line was shorter than the short line. In contrast, a multitude of possible explanations are available to account for a discussant's wrong-headed political viewpoints, thereby rendering the existence of political disagreement entirely comprehensible and not troubling. Joe likes the Democratic candidate because he *always* likes Democrats. Sally likes Republicans because she is a conservative, or because she is from Georgia, or because she is a Tea Party activist. In short, disagreement is more easily accommodated when it can be explained, and in the day-to-day world of democratic politics, disagreements based on subjective judgments of issues and candidates may frequently approach the point of infinite explicability.

The evidence presented here sustains the role of social interdependence for the vitality of democratic politics. Not only do people exchange their own viewpoints through a process of social interaction, but they also acquire information and access to expert judgment. At the same time, this chapter also provides evidence of systematic bias and inefficiency in social communication. A pattern of social interaction and communication emerges that repeatedly devalues the political contributions of women. This devaluation creates biases in the political process because it systematically excludes a distinctive voice in the process. It creates inefficiency because important sources of expertise are unrecognized and hence underutilized. While the individual and collective capacity of citizens is enhanced through horizontal patterns of social communication, the democratic potential of this interdependence is compromised by imbedded biases linked to gender.

Finally, the network surveys suggest that respondents are either unwilling or unable to implement Downs' advice fully. While they frequently communicate with experts and activists regarding politics, they are much less likely to discriminate with respect to shared political viewpoints. Hence, they are much more likely to report frequent communication with experts who hold divergent preferences than they are to report frequent communication with non-experts who hold coincidental preferences. Thus, not only are voters exposed to divergent political messages, but these divergent messages are likely to be conveyed by experts and activists. We turn now to these political implications.

II. DISCUSSION AS DELEGATION: AGGREGATE IMPLICATIONS

Many individuals lack the time, motivation, ability, or opportunity to become politically informed (Luskin, 1990), and many others find that the uncertain value of informed participation is outstripped by the high costs of becoming informed. As an alternative to these costs, Downs (1957) suggests that low-cost information is readily available through political communication with others. In pursuing this alternative, individuals are to some extent delegating their political choices to others, either by using political discussion to guide their decisions, or by simply mimicking the behavior of others. According to this perspective, it is important that individuals select politically expert agents who share their own viewpoints (Boudreau 2009; Lupia and McCubbins 1998). A problem arises, however, when individuals find themselves in settings where experts with shared preferences are difficult to locate (Huckfeldt 1983b; Mutz and Mondak 2006). As a result, many individuals experience difficulty in constructing a communication network composed of politically like-minded informants, and hence the efficacy of delegation is called into question.

Sokhey and McClurg (2012) analyzed the 2000 National Election Study using a method employed by Lau and Redlawsk (1997) to evaluate how an individual's discussion network affects the probability she will vote "correctly" – how individuals would vote if they knew exactly where the candidates stood on the issues relative to their own positions. In support of Downs' theory, individuals are less likely to make a correct decision if they experience disagreement within their networks – indeed, if citizens fully implemented Downs' advice, their communication networks would be free of disagreement! Perhaps more importantly, they find no effect for the expertise of the discussion network.

How do individuals use information from discussion networks with diverse preferences and varying information levels? Richey's (2008) argument, and our own, is that a discussion partner is more likely to be influential to the extent that the messages from the particular informant conform to the other messages an individual receives. This is certainly not a perverse decision rule. If an individual's associates are more often right than wrong, one would expect that the majority opinion would be correct (Young, 1988).

Yet such a process would differ from Downs' (1957) expectations in two important ways. First, expert discussion partners might not necessarily exercise greater influence. Rather, the influence of an expert, or any other informant, would depend on the correspondence between the expert's message and all other messages received by the respondent (Lodge and Taber 2000). Second, the political preferences within discussion networks may very well be heterogeneous, and hence the overall partisanship of an individual's discussion network should be a strong indicator of how the individual actually voted, independent of the individual's own predispositions. Hence their perceptions of the political world might be strongly influenced by the partisan lens through which their associates view the world – the outcome Rousseau feared.

Individuals, aggregates, and expertise

The analysis on which we rely (Ryan 2010) employs the 2000 National Election Study (NES). The key explanatory variables are the respondent's partisanship and objective knowledge, as well as measures of the perceived partisanship and perceived expertise of their discussion networks. Respondent partisanship serves as a measure of personal bias. Objective knowledge takes account of the information a respondent obtains from sources other than his or her network – primarily information from the media (see Price and Zaller 1993).

The 2000 NES included a series of questions, similar to those in the ISL study, regarding political discussion networks. Respondents identified up to four discussion partners in response to the question regarding the first names of the people with whom they discuss "government, elections and politics." Interviewers also asked respondents how much these each discussant knew about politics. The ISL analysis shows that these perceptions accord very closely with reality, only modestly affected by agreement between discussion partners. Respondents also told interviewers which presidential candidate they believed each discussion partner was supporting.

Two key questions arise. First, do poorly informed individuals with expert discussion partners vote the same way that informed individuals vote – do they vote as though they were informed? Second, what role does the partisan heterogeneity of a discussion network play in affecting the vote? The partisan composition of a network should affect what political messages an individual receives, and, more importantly, which messages the individual accepts and which she rejects. Hence, diverging from Downs' prescription, we allow for the possibility that networks might be politically heterogeneous.

Network expertise and vote choice

Downs' (1957) argument is that individuals may still vote as if they are political experts without putting in the effort to gather political information or evaluate the candidates. By relying on the efforts of expert discussion partners who share their preferences, individuals might vote as these better-informed advisors vote. The question thus arises, how important are shared preferences? Do individuals with expert discussion partners vote the same way that informed individuals vote, even if they are located within politically heterogeneous networks?

Using a strategy developed by Bartels (1996) and later utilized by Althaus (1998, 2004), Ryan (2010) compares the actual (reported) vote to three different simulated votes: (1) a simulated electorate's vote in which all individuals are fully informed but located within their idiosyncratic (and often politically heterogeneous) networks; (2) a simulated electorate in which individuals possess their idiosyncratic levels of information but are located within homogenously expert networks with idiosyncratic (and often heterogeneous) political preferences; and (3) a hypothetical electorate in which respondents and their idiosyncratic (and potentially heterogeneous) networks are both fully informed. We are particularly concerned with a comparison between the first and second simulations.

Indeed, the difference between fully informed individuals and individuals in fully informed networks is larger than any of the other possible comparisons. Hence, at the individual level, there is a pronounced difference between how respondents would vote if they became fully informed themselves and how they would vote if they relied on expert discussion partners. The lesson is not that either set of hypothetical respondents is making "better" decisions. Rather, a network comprised of knowledgeable informants is not a facsimile for becoming informed on one's own. That is, there is no escaping the socially contingent effects that arise due to social communication, and thus it appears that political influence, and hence bias, emerges within the process. In short, we are addressing a political process rooted in persuasion rather than a civic exercise rooted in civic enlightenment.

Implications and conclusions

The major ingredient in Downs' prescriptive argument relates to informant selection based on *both* expertise *and* shared political preferences. As we have seen, political communication among citizens *is* disproportionately influenced by the experts and activists who are motivated to discuss politics. In contrast, while many individuals may very well prefer to speak with experts *who share their preferences*, the constraints of context and supply often mean that they end up discussing politics with people who hold politically divergent positions (Huckfeldt and Sprague 1988). Moreover, it is an oversimplification to expect that individuals will vote as if they are themselves informed by relying on the advice and counsel of their expert discussion partners as a shortcut, for the simple reason that many of these experts will not share their underlying political goals and preferences. While it is certainly possible and reasonable for individuals to rely on the political counsel of their associates, the frequent result is that they vote as their associates would vote.

This means that an individual's particular location within a communication network is a fact of political significance. Indeed, voters are often profoundly influenced by the political messages communicated through these networks (Huckfeldt, Johnson, and Sprague 2004). If an individual's associates are like-minded in their support for a party or candidate, the individual will likely support that same party or candidate. To the contrary, a substantial number of partisans will defect if their discussion partners are on the other side. Lacking a partisan screen on incoming information, the independents are particularly susceptible to these networks. In short, social communication does not necessarily lead voters to choose the candidate whom they would prefer if they were fully informed. Rather, their votes are contingent on the complex interactions of their own views regarding politics and the particular messages communicated through these networks.

At the same time, vote decisions are based on subjective judgments that take into account a myriad of complex interdependent factors, making it ultimately quite difficult to argue that a voting decision is a mistake based on abstract conceptions of preferences and interests. How many Democrats, for example, would be willing to assert that Warren Buffett and the other billionaires who tend to vote Democratic are fundamentally misguided? If an individual obtains information, considers it, and is persuaded to vote in a particular way, it is difficult to argue that democracy has failed – even if one believes that Warren Buffett is delusional.

Along with Boudon (1986), we view the rationality of social and political behavior to be anchored in the comprehensibility of the actor's own frame of reference with respect to her own behavior. In this context, social communication regarding politics is an integral part of a fundamentally *political* process involving argumentation and persuasion rather than an essentially *civic* process involving individually based enlightenment. This does not mean that enlightenment never occurs, but rather that it is not an inevitable or integral outcome in an inherently political process.

Downs (1957) suggests transferring the costs of becoming informed to informants, thereby allowing individuals to act as if they were informed without going through the effort of becoming so. This vision of voters as single-minded seekers of low-cost information creates some problems. If it is accurate, we would expect to see communication networks made up of experts with homogeneous preferences. This is most certainly *not* what we see, and it is much less than clear that we would be better off in a world where uninformed voters regularly delegate their vote decisions to a politically homogeneous panel of experts. To the contrary, the supply of like-minded experts is frequently limited, people have multiple associational preferences that have nothing to do with politics, and people with limited knowledge may have difficulty figuring out which political discussants are in fact like-minded. In short, imposing strict political criteria on the selection of associates imposes prohibitive costs on the task of constructing a communication network and is thus self-defeating if the goal is to minimize information costs.

Finally, while we do not share Downs' optimism regarding the potential for social communication to turn any citizen into the equivalent of an independent expert, neither do we share Rousseau's fear that the democratic process will be subverted by interdependent citizens. Choosing a candidate is an inherently subjective decision. While the *most* expert individuals may be well-versed on the current state of affairs, they are often wildly mistaken regarding challenges that may lie in the future (Tetlock 2005). In this context, the mixed record of experts and the limitations on their ability to influence others may not be such bad news. While the process may often lead to suboptimal decisions, an excessive reliance on politically homogeneous panels of like-minded activists and experts does not necessarily constitute a cure.

Indeed, as we will argue in Chapter 4, political controversy and disagreement lie near the core of the process, and the opportunity for opinion leadership depends on heterogeneous distributions of opinions and beliefs in the political environments where communication occurs, as well as the willingness of potential opinion leaders to engage political issues that generate discord and disagreement close to home. In short, political heterogeneity within communication networks is a central feature of a democratic process anchored in politics and persuasion.

4

Unanimity, discord, and opportunities for opinion leadership

T. K. Ahn, Robert Huckfeldt, Jeanette Mendez, and John Barry Ryan

> Politics takes place in space and time and also probably is not at equilibrium.
>
> John Sprague (1980: 23)

While the communication and diffusion of public opinion ultimately depends on the capacity of opinion holders to convey clear and unambiguous messages (Huckfeldt, Sprague, and Levine 2000), the recipients' assessments of these messages also depend on opinion distributions in the larger population (Mutz 1998). Public opinion on some issues – both in the aggregate and among individuals – can seemingly be taken for granted. In many settings, large majorities with relatively few dissenters support the general principle of equal rights for women, and absent the presence of a clear message to the contrary, it is a good statistical bet that any particular individual will report an opinion supporting women's rights. Indeed, within contexts or networks dominated by a clear majority view, those individuals holding minority opinions and preferences are more likely to be misperceived (Huckfeldt and Sprague 1995; Huckfeldt, Johnson, and Sprague 2004). Hence, one of the continuing disadvantages of the political minorities is that their own minority status is exaggerated within the collective deliberations of democratic politics (Miller 1956; Noelle-Neumann 1984).

In contrast, when opinions are locally diverse, people lack reliable contextual information to use in reaching a judgment regarding the opinions of other individuals. For example, people in many settings disagree with respect to the right of a woman to have an abortion, and a clear majority sentiment does not exist. In situations such as these, judgments regarding the opinions of others necessarily become more reliant on information conveyed within dyads through discussion and communication. Opinion leadership, in turn, depends on the capacity and willingness of an individual to express opinions regarding issues in these politically diverse settings.

The problem is that diverse opinions arise over controversial issues, and a long and continuing line of research in political psychology asserts that people tend to avoid discussion of controversial topics (Mutz 2002a; MacKuen 1990). Hence, in circumstances where discussion would be most valuable in illuminating the opinions of others, many individuals might become less willing to run the risk of contentious disagreement.

In short, opportunities for opinion leadership are more likely to arise when there is no clearly dominant majority opinion – in settings where the surrounding distribution of opinion is diverse and controversy is not uncommon. As a consequence, the potential for opinion leadership depends on the willingness of potential opinion leaders to engage issues imbedded in conflict and controversy. Hence, this chapter considers the manner in which individuals discern the opinions of their associates, in both politically heterogeneous and homogeneous settings, as well as addressing the circumstances that give rise to opinion leadership.

I. THE ROLE OF OPINION VARIANCE WITHIN COMMUNICATION NETWORKS

Our initial concern lies with the consequences of disagreement and opinion variance for the communication and diffusion of public opinion. This purpose requires that a preliminary question be addressed: Why should meaningful patterns of political disagreement persist among citizens in democratic politics? The answer to this question is important because several arguments imply that disagreement may be a rare event within communication networks.

First, as we have seen, cost-conscious consumers of political information can minimize their information costs by obtaining information through conversations with fellow citizens, and Downs (1957) suggests that a rational individual will obtain information from politically expert individuals who hold politically compatible viewpoints. Thus, to the extent that individuals rely on people with compatible views, one would expect very little disagreement to occur (but see Calvert 1985a).

Second, from the alternative vantage points of conformity theory (Asch 1963) and cognitive dissonance theory (Festinger 1957), disagreement has been seen as a psychologically punishing experience that people seek to escape. They might avoid disagreeable encounters, misperceive disagreeable messages, and modify their own viewpoints in an agreeable direction. Indeed, the utility of cross-cutting cleavages as an explanation for opinion change is anchored in arguments such as these (Mutz 2002a, 2002b; Berelson, Lazarsfeld, and McPhee 1954). That is, cross-cutting cleaves expose individuals to disagreement, making individuals aware of alternative views, opinions, and points of orientation. The influence (and discomfort) of disagreement, in turn, has the net effect of moderating individual passions, muting stridency, and diminishing the potential for rancorous conflict.

Finally, substantial research traditions based on dynamic models of opinion change (Abelson 1979; Axelrod 1997) point toward the experience of opinion heterogeneity as a transient, unstable state within a system defined in terms of interacting individuals. These models generate stable equilibria among interacting individuals only when disagreement is eliminated, opinion variance disappears, and uniformity is the stable end result.

Not only are the implications of these analyses troubling to those who value the free give-and-take of political information (Mendelberg 2002), but they are also difficult to reconcile with the empirical record. Walsh (2004) demonstrates a lively, informal, and sustained process of discussion, disagreement, and deliberation among individuals involved in ongoing patterns of social interaction. An accumulated series of network studies shows that, while individuals are likely to agree with most of the people in their communication networks, the experience of disagreement tends to be widespread and persistent (Huckfeldt and Sprague 1995; Huckfeldt, Johnson, and Sprague 2004; Huckfeldt, Ikeda, and Pappi 2005). Indeed, the 2000 National Election Study showed that, among those respondents who provided information on their political communication networks, more than one-third of the Bush and Gore voters named at least one discussant who supported the opposite candidate, and less than half reported unanimous support for their favored candidate (Huckfeldt, Johnson, and Sprague 2004).

A number of factors sustain politically diverse preferences within communication networks. First, disagreement is not a prohibitively painful or costly experience for everyone. A lively engagement in politics might be expected to outweigh related disagreement costs for many individuals. Second, even if people would rather discuss politics with those who are like-minded, this preference often competes with a range of other preferences and purposes. You may enjoy eating lunch with a friendly and politically knowledgeable coworker because you share a range of non-political interests, and hence you tolerate her wrong-headed political views. Third, and just as important, the selection of associates is a stochastic process, and the distribution of opinions among potential discussion partners severely limits individual control. If you are employed at a workplace full of Republicans, it may be difficult (but not impossible) to find a Democratic workplace associate with whom to eat lunch (Finifter 1974; Mutz and Mondak 2006; Huckfeldt and Sprague 1995).

Finally, communication networks are often characterized by low network densities, where many individuals are not directly connected (Granovetter 1973; Burt 1992) – that is, two coworkers may regularly discuss politics at work without sharing any other associates in common, and they may regularly and persistently disagree if their opinions are anchored by the dominant viewpoint existing within their separate circles of associates. This is important because the political message conveyed by any particular associate is more likely to be both correctly understood and persuasive to the extent that it is reinforced by the messages conveyed from other associates (Huckfeldt, Johnson, and Sprague 2004). In short, influence within a dyad is *not* automatic, and disagreement might be sustained as part of a stable dynamic equilibrium.

As a consequence, people cannot necessarily assume political unanimity within their networks of political communication, and hence it becomes important to consider the consequences of opinion heterogeneity for the flow of information within and beyond the boundaries of political communication networks. These consequences, in turn, depend on the inherent ambiguity of the political communication that occurs among and between citizens.

Contingent ambiguity in political communication

Political communication among and between citizens is a potentially efficient method whereby individuals might become politically informed (Downs 1957); it plays an influential role in the formation and diffusion of political preferences (Berelson, Lazarsfeld, and McPhee 1954; Druckman and Nelson 2003; Levine 2004); and it is central to patterns of political engagement and mobilization (Rosenstone and Hansen 1993; Huckfeldt and Sprague 1995). Notwithstanding these important functions, political communication often occurs in a context marked by high levels of ambiguity. The source of this ambiguity is an important issue in the analysis of political communication because it speaks directly to the potential of collective decision-making in democratic politics, as well as to patterns of unanimity and discord.

First, social communication regarding political topics is often informal and offhand, with politics seldom serving as the centerpiece for relationships and social encounters. This is not to say that politics is unimportant or insignificant, but only that it competes with other subjects and purposes for air-time in the conversational lives of most citizens (Huckfeldt, Johnson, and Sprague 2004). Political salience matters, and the importance of these other factors is likely to be more pronounced in the context of public opinion regarding complex policy issues than it is, for example, in the context of the vote for president. While many individuals are able to make accurate judgments regarding the presidential votes of their associates, it may be more difficult to reach judgments regarding opinions on a wide array of issues that are rarely discussed.

Second, both experts and activists are likely to be quite different on this dimension. Politics is likely to be a central preoccupation for most of these individuals, and, particularly for the activists, it is likely to become a recurrent topic of consideration in social encounters. Hence, we see some people who send mixed or ambiguous signals, while others communicate clearly and unambiguously. In other words, the signal strength and clarity of socially communicated political messages are likely to be contingent on an individual's personal level of investment in politics and political information as well as their motivation and interest regarding particular issues and topics.

Finally, the ambiguity of political communication may be individually motivated, either by conscious strategy, or by social discomfort, or by both

(MacKuen 1990; Mutz 2002). When people encounter associates with divergent political viewpoints, they may change the subject, unwittingly misperceive the message, or consciously censor their own response to avoid an uncomfortable social exchange. Indeed, a rich and enduring tradition in the analysis of political communication calls into question the capacity and willingness of individuals to perceive political messages accurately when these messages run contrary to their own preferences (Festinger 1957; Klapper 1960; Huckfeldt and Sprague 1995).

Context, inference, and environmental priors

Given the ambiguity of social communication and the uncertainty that it produces, the context of the communication becomes particularly important for understanding the judgments that individuals reach regarding the opinions of individual associates. Individuals are located within communities, counties, and other macro-environments that are characterized by particular distributions of public opinion with respect to important political issues. They do not encounter these opinion distributions directly, but rather through networks of communication drawn from these larger populations (Huckfeldt and Sprague 1995).

Hence, political communication occurs within social contexts that are specific to a series of nested environments: political messages are conveyed within the context of particular dyads, located within larger networks, imbedded within larger environments of opinion. Each of these environments, in turn, has the potential to influence the inferential judgments that citizens make about the opinions of other individuals. Without actually hearing a friend's opinion on organized prayer in public schools, one might infer – correctly or incorrectly – that she holds the same opinion as is held by others. One might assume, for example, that since most of your friends are pro-life, it must be a larger community sentiment, and hence any particular associate is likely to be pro-life as well, even though you have never actually discussed the matter with her. In short, ambiguous political messages and the uncertainty they produce create a setting in which prior information, taken from larger surrounding environments, becomes particularly influential in forming judgments regarding the preferences held by other individuals.

The use of prior information may not come naturally or easily for many individuals in many settings, and a rich tradition of experimental research indicates that people often fail to employ prior information successfully (Tversky and Kahneman 1974). This raises a question: How important is prior information taken from the environment to political communication among citizens? Tversky and Kahneman (1982) argue that the effect of a base rate (or prior information) depends on the particular inferential context. Prior information is more likely to be employed when individuals interpret the information as revealing something quite important regarding the likelihood of an event due to "external-situational factors" independently of the immediate circumstances ("internal-dispositional factors") affecting the inference (1982: 159). This chapter's argument, as well as arguments offered later (see Chapters 9 and 10), is that prior judgments often become important relative to an autoregressive process of political communication among citizens (Huckfeldt, Johnson, and Sprague 2004), and this view generates several implications.

First, environmental information is most informative when the opinion distribution is most consensual. To the extent that your own opinion, the opinions of your associates, and the opinions of the public at large tend to be in agreement, there is less need to collect information from individual associates regarding their opinions. You might assume, more or less reliably, that since everyone holds the same opinion, communication with any particular individual proves to be less necessary to the formation of a judgment regarding that individual's opinion. Indeed, to the extent that one expects everyone to hold a particular opinion or belief, it might be difficult to believe that anyone would hold an opinion to the contrary!

Second, and conversely, the environment is least informative when opinion is most divided. To the extent that a higher level of variance exists among and between your own opinion, the opinions of your own associates, and opinions in the larger community, prior information taken from the environment will be less helpful in forming judgments regarding the opinions of particular individuals. In these circumstances, a deeply divided distribution of opinion is likely to provide little guidance, and hence the process of communicating with a given associate becomes particularly important in forming a judgment about that individual's opinion.[1]

This creates a problem, of course, if controversial opinions are believed to be inappropriate subject matter for political communication. In other words, *if people fail to communicate their opinions regarding controversial subjects, then communication fails just when it would be most important.*

The Indianapolis-St. Louis study

As in the previous chapter, our discussion draws on previous analyses of the 1996 Indianapolis-St. Louis (ISL) Study (Huckfeldt 2007b). To review, early in the main respondent survey, interviewers asked each survey respondent to provide the first names of their discussion partners. A random half-sample was asked to name people with whom they discuss "important matters"; the other random half was asked to name people with whom they discuss "government, elections, and politics" (Burt 1986; Huckfeldt, Levine et al. 1998). The interviewers took up to five names before asking a battery of questions about each discussant in the sequential order in which the discussant was named. After completing this initial battery of questions on each discussant, the interviewer went on to ask the main respondents a series of questions regarding their own political opinions, views, and political activity.

---

[1] More precisely, the utility of the environmental prior is weighted by its variance, where high levels of opinion variance undermine confidence in the prior (Bullock 2009).

Near the end of the survey, after the respondent had answered extensive batteries of questions regarding other issues unrelated to the network battery, the interviewer asked a final battery of questions regarding the previously identified discussants. The purpose of this battery was to obtain the respondent's perception regarding each of her discussants' opinions on a particular political issue. For each respondent, this issue was randomly chosen from a list of four possibilities: a woman's right to an abortion, government aid for blacks and other minorities, equal rights for women, and organized prayer in public schools. The text of the question was:

We are about finished, and now I would like to ask you a few more questions about the (people/person) you named earlier. On a scale of 1 to 5, where 1 is strongly oppose and 5 is strongly favor, what do you think (discussant name's) opinion is regarding (the randomly assigned opinion)?

Finally, the interviewer asked the respondent a follow-up question regarding each discussant:

When you talk with (name of discussant), do you discuss these sorts of issues often, sometimes, rarely, or never?

Each of the respondents was asked to provide information regarding their discussants' views on only one randomly chosen policy issue out of four possibilities: prayer in schools, minority programs, equal rights for women, and the right of every woman to have an abortion. The distributions of responses to these policy issues – which constitute a random sample of the opinions in the two metropolitan areas – vary dramatically in the level of controversy. In both cities, the most controversial is a woman's right to an abortion and the most consensual is equal rights for women, with the other two issues lying within a more moderate range.

These procedures yield the following measures for each of the 1,475 dyads in the data matrix: (1) the respondent's perception regarding the opinion of the interviewed discussant on one of the four issues, selected at random; (2) the self-reported opinion of the discussant and the respondent on the same randomly selected issue; (3) the respondent's judgment regarding the frequency with which "these sorts of issues" are discussed with each discussant; and (4) the respondent's perceptions of their other discussants' positions on the same issue, regardless of whether the other discussants were interviewed.

Discussion and diversity within the networks

The relationship between opinion diversity within communication networks and opinion diversity within the larger population is a particularly important issue. To the extent that individuals exercise control over the political composition of their communication networks, one might expect to see little relationship between network diversity and levels of diversity in the larger population. If individuals successfully seek out politically sympathetic discussants, or if they avoid political controversy and disagreement, communication networks should be politically homogeneous and agreeable, regardless of opinion distributions in the surrounding population. Alternatively, to the extent that such control is incomplete, or to the extent that people are less motivated to exercise such control, the dispersion of opinion within networks should reflect the dispersion of opinion within the larger population.

Several analyses, both of the ISL study as well as the Cross-National Election Studies of the early 1990s, show that larger networks tend to be more politically diverse – that is, people with more extensive networks of communication are more likely to encounter divergent political viewpoints (Huckfeldt 2008; Huckfeldt, Ikeda, and Pappi 2005). Moreover, the composition of larger networks more closely reflects the underlying composition of the larger community (Huckfeldt et al. 1995). Even when the particular features of the networks and the respondents are taken into account, the analysis of the ISL study shows a strong and direct tie between the diversity of aggregate opinion distributions in the larger community and the diversity of opinion distributions within communication networks (Huckfeldt 2008).

The distribution of abortion opinions in the ISL study is the most diverse of the four issues, both within networks and within the larger population, and equal rights for women is the least diverse, with the minority aid issue and prayer in schools issue lying between. Little evidence exists to suggest that individuals escape controversy by sequestering themselves in politically agreeable settings. Controversial issues in the larger political environment penetrate even closely held networks of political communication, especially among those who are located in larger networks.

A related issue revolves around the consequences of opinion diversity regarding a particular issue for the frequency with which that issue is discussed. Even if individuals are unable or disinclined to exercise lock-grip control over the political composition of their communication networks, they may still censor their conversations, thereby reducing the frequency with which they discuss controversial issues. Hence, in response to divergent opinion regarding a particular issue, individuals might simply move on to consensual topics that are better suited for polite conversation. Analyses of the ISL study suggests that people *are* less likely to discuss controversial issues (Huckfeldt 2008) – opinion diversity in the larger environment is associated with lower frequencies of communication (see Mutz 2002a; MacKuen 1990).

Hence, while individuals report higher levels of network disagreement regarding controversial issues, they also report discussing these issues less frequently. Individuals appear to avoid controversy, *but the existence of opinion diversity still manages to penetrate their own reports regarding opinion distributions within closely held networks of political communication.* Regardless of decreased rates of discussion regarding controversial issues, the respondents are likely to be aware that the controversy exists, and hence the political communication occurring within these networks serves as an extension of the political process occurring in the larger political environment. Rather than sequestering individuals from disagreement, opinion distributions within these networks expose individuals to the political controversies of the day (Anderson and Paskeviciute 2005, 2006; Visser and Mirabile 2004). In summary, even though diversity within networks is truncated with respect to diversity in the larger environment, the diversity of opinion in the larger community translates into higher levels of diversity within communication networks.

The factors that drive perception

Individuals reach judgments regarding the opinions of their associates based on several primary sources – their own opinions, the opinions of the other individuals within their communication networks, and the actual opinion of the associate in question (Huckfeldt, Johnson, and Sprague 2004). From one perspective, the first two factors – an individual's own opinion and the opinions of other associates – provide shortcuts for one individual to use in assessing another individual's opinion. As long as the distribution of an opinion is characterized by unanimity, such shortcuts are likely to be highly reliable. In contrast, when the distribution of opinions on a particular issue is widely dispersed, these shortcuts become less reliable.

The question thus arises, do individual inferences regarding a discussant's opinion rely more heavily on the actual opinion of the particular discussant when an issue is marked by discord rather than unanimity? Analyses of the ISL study show that the effect of an individual discussant's opinion on the main respondent's perception is enhanced as the standard deviation of the opinion increases for the sample as a whole (Huckfeldt 2007b). That is, the discussant's self-reported opinion is most important with respect to abortion – the opinion with the highest standard deviation. In contrast, it is least important with respect to equal rights for women – the opinion with the lowest standard deviation.

In summary, *the actual opinions of discussants become more important to the main respondent's perception of the discussant when the distribution of opinion in the larger population is more heterogeneous.* Respondents are less able to rely on a surrounding consensus in reaching judgments regarding the opinions of others, and hence the actual opinions held by individuals become relatively more important to these judgments.

In a similar way, respondents are more likely to recognize divergent preferences accurately if they are located in heterogeneous micro-environments – this is another way of saying that the communication of individual opinion is most efficacious when disagreement is more common. If people seldom encounter opinions that are different from their own, they are unlikely to recognize divergent preferences when they *do* encounter them. Thus, individuals are more likely to misperceive disagreement as agreement in relationship to environments and issues characterized by unanimity rather than discord. In this sense, conditions approaching unanimity can be seen as an obstacle to the accurate communication of any divergent opinions, a catalyst for misperception, and thus a hurdle for opinion leadership.

Opinion diversity and the potential for change

In summary, the political communication networks and micro-environments where individuals transmit, receive, and process information about politics do not necessarily provide safe havens from the controversies that buffet the larger political environment. Issues that provoke controversies in the larger environment also provoke disagreement closer to home. While people are less likely to report frequent discussions regarding issues that are more controversial, they are also more likely to report higher levels of disagreement regarding these controversial issues within their communication networks. In short, politics is driven by conflict and disagreement, not only at the level of elites and formal institutions, but also at the level of citizens and the informal institutions of political communication that lie at the heart of democratic politics.

Thus, opportunities for opinion leadership are more likely to occur in settings marked by discord and disagreement. The views of opinion leaders are most likely to be recognized accurately at the same time that the opinions of others are less likely to be anchored securely in a unified climate of opinion. These are, in short, the moments most likely to produce influential opinion leaders in the formation and change of aggregate sentiment. In the remainder of this chapter our focus turns to the characteristics of the successful opinion leader – to the qualities most likely to produce influence in the context of diverse opinions.

II. OPINION LEADERS AND CONTROVERSY – MOTHS AND FLAMES

Some people are located, either by intent or by accident, within closed social cells of politically like-minded associates. Others find themselves in politically diverse settings where participants deftly avoid political discussion in an effort at keeping the peace. Still others, in similarly diverse settings, resemble the moth and the flame – incapable of resisting the temptation to address politics, even when contentious disagreement is the inevitable result. Hence, the underlying model is that political discussion stimulates argumentation, while argumentation impedes discussion, and the combined dynamic helps explain the influence of opinion leaders as well as the patterns of persistent disagreement in democratic politics.

Within this dynamic, opinion leaders play an outsized role due to their own high levels of interest in politics. Indeed, due to their willingness to pay the costs of political engagement, we might say that opinion leaders are frequently self-appointed. That is, many opinion leaders may be those individuals who thrive on the give-and-take of political discussion, thereby providing, in the reported words of Reggie Jackson, "the straw that stirs the drink."[2] This manifestation of self-selection, which points to self-selected opinion leaders and their implications for political communication, runs counter to the other commonly offered arguments regarding endogeneity in studies of communication that point toward conflict avoidance and the creation of political homogeneity within social groupings. Hence, we return to the problem of endogeneity by focusing on the construction of communication networks.

Self-selection and clustered preferences

A persistent problem in the analysis of opinion leaders and socially communicated political information revolves around several interrelated endogeneity issues. The core of the problem is anchored within a two-fold dilemma. On the one hand, citizens are *not* hapless bystanders, either in the acquisition of political information, or in the selection of information sources. To the contrary, they are intentional and frequently judicious in the acquisition and analysis of political information, and they do not automatically absorb any information that happens to be available. On the other hand, the extent of individual control over the flow of information is incomplete, and the potential thus arises that a heterogeneous stream of information might sneak in through the back door, producing important consequences for the informational biases encountered by particular citizens (Achen 1986; Achen and Shively 1995; Huckfeldt and Sprague 1995).

At its most basic level, this problem arises whenever we observe a tendency toward clustering in the distribution of preferences among associated individuals. At least since the influential work of the Columbia sociologists (Lazarsfeld, Berelson, and Gaudet 1968; Berelson, Lazarsfeld, and McPhee 1954), analysts have recognized that individuals who are located adjacently within small-scale social organization, such as friendship groups and communication networks, are likely to share political preferences. The problem with an observation such as this is that it inevitably leads to a chicken-and-egg problem. Did agreement predate discussion, leading to purposeful patterns of communication that were created to avoid the unpleasant and disquieting experience of political disagreement? Or was communication structurally induced, leading to agreement through a process of persuasion and adjustment (Huckfeldt 1983b)?[3]

These issues are not simply methodological curiosities – they are fundamentally important both to opinion leadership and to the nature of citizenship in democratic politics. To the extent that patterns of communication are tightly constrained by pre-existent patterns of political agreement, the potential for political learning and persuasion is radically curtailed. If citizens talk only to those with whom they agree, the opportunity to consider alternative viewpoints

---

[2] Whether or not Jackson actually uttered this self-characterization is somewhat controversial.

[3] McPherson and Smith-Lovin (1987) refer to this as the difference between choice homophily and structural homophily.

is eliminated, and the potential for political innovation and electoral change is extinguished. Indeed, if agreement is a precondition for communication, there *is* no opportunity for persuasion (McPhee 1963).

Two questions are fundamental: Do individuals locate themselves within political communication networks where they are shielded from the experience of political disagreement? If and when individuals come into contact with others holding disagreeable political views, do they monitor their interactions to avoid political communication? Both of these questions address important endogeneity problems, and several different strategies have been employed in analyses based on the 1996 ISL study.

Selecting in, selecting out, and contextual effects

In two classic contextual analyses, Tingsten (1963) and Langton and Rapoport (1975) showed that workers in Stockholm and Santiago were more likely to vote for parties of the left if they lived in working-class neighborhoods. The abiding issue raised by studies such as these relates to the particular mechanisms that produce these individual-level political variations across space, and endogeneity problems thus prove to be the fly-in-the-ointment for many analyses of political information and influence.

Two models have dominated the interpretation of evidence that demonstrates political clustering among citizens. According to the first model, various mechanisms of political communication and influence produce politically interdependent preferences, which in turn lead to patterns of political clustering across space. Thus, returning to the work of Tingsten (1963) and Langton and Rapoport (1975), one argument is that workers living among other workers are more likely to come into contact with workers, and this increased frequency of contact produces shared political loyalties, preferences, and choices.

According to a second model, evidence of political clustering is a byproduct of unmeasured individual-level characteristics and predispositions – frequently the result of individuals who choose to locate themselves, either directly or indirectly, within environments characterized by particular distributions of social and political preferences (Hauser 1974; Achen and Shively 1995). Such a self-selection process occurs when partisans intentionally locate themselves among people with shared leanings, but it might also occur in far more subtle ways (MacKuen 1990; Gamm 1999).

In summary, workers living in the working class areas of Santiago and Stockholm may have been more likely to interact with other workers who persuaded them to vote on the basis of class-based preferences. Alternatively, the workers living among other workers may have been there as a consequence of simple or complex sorting and mixing processes that are correlated with the political behavior in question. The problem is that each of these explanations is attractive, plausible, and less than wholly convincing – that is, it would seem unlikely *either* that individuals are wholly able to control the information they receive through social communication *or* that they simply accept whatever the environment happens to provide.

One might hope that more precise measures regarding individual locations within social networks would help resolve these problems, but this is certainly not the case. A variety of analyses have shown that political clustering occurs within communication networks: partisans tend to discuss politics with fellow partisans (Baker, Ames, and Renno 2006; Mutz and Martin 2001). Is this because individuals are influenced to adopt preferences that correspond to the political bias of the information they obtain, or is it because individuals construct communication networks to reinforce their own partisan predispositions (Downs 1957), or both?

Individual control over patterns of political communication within networks of association and communication might occur in at least two ways: (1) in the construction of communication networks, and (2) in patterns of conflict avoidance within communication networks. In the first, individuals construct their communication networks to exclude others who hold disagreeable political opinions and preferences. In the second, even if individuals associate with others who hold divergent preferences, they practice conflict avoidance – they bob and weave to avoid uncomfortable conversations. Both mechanisms produce the same result – disagreement *does not* occur, and hence persuasion *cannot* occur.

What are the micro-motives that might be marshaled in support of social influence and self-selection interpretations for contextual effects? Most explanations revolve around arguments rooted in cognitive dissonance (Festinger 1957), social conformity (Asch 1963), or the political economy of choice (Downs 1957). The cognitive dissonance interpretation is that individuals cannot tolerate disagreement and seek to avoid or resolve it, and the social conformity argument is that individuals typically bend their own preferences to fit their surroundings (but see Ross et al. 1976). The classic political economy argument (Downs 1957) is that people can be expected to choose politically expert discussants who hold political preferences similar to their own.

Hence, the end result has typically been a strong expectation that individuals will be located within politically homogeneous surroundings. Either because they dislike disagreement, or because they engage in a strategic search for information, people tend to seek out other individuals who hold politically agreeable views. If political disagreement does manage to sneak in through the back door, conformity arguments suggest that such disagreement should be resolved in relatively short order (Huckfeldt, Johnson, and Sprague 2004).

Perhaps the most immediate problem with these various expectations is that political heterogeneity is *not* a rare event within discussion networks – less than half of the two-party voters in the 2000 National Election Study identify all their political discussants as holding the same vote preference, and more than one-third name a discussant who supports the opposite party's candidate (Huckfeldt, Mendez, and Osborn 2004). Hence we address research based on the ISL

(Huckfeldt and Mendez 2008) that focuses on two self-selection mechanisms as means for managing heterogeneity: individual control over the construction of discussion networks, and individual control over the frequency of political communication with the individuals located within these networks.

After being asked how many days they talked with each discussant during a normal week, the main respondents provided answers to the following sequence of questions:

When you talk with (discussant name), do you discuss political matters:
  often, sometimes, rarely, or never?
When you discuss politics with (discussant name), do you disagree:
  often, sometimes, rarely, or never?

The first question provides the main respondents' perceptions regarding the relative frequency of political discussion within the dyad – relative, that is, to the frequency with which more general interaction occurs. The second provides the main respondents' perceptions regarding the frequency of disagreement, relative to the frequency of political communication.

Endogeneity and network construction

The substantive content of the name generator was randomly assigned to respondents, and hence it can be treated as an experimentally supplied treatment. That is, a randomly assigned half-sample was asked to provide the names of the people with whom they discuss "important matters," and the other half-sample was asked to provide the names of the people with whom they discuss "government, elections, and politics." The questionnaire was organized to minimize the political content that occurred before the name generator, and hence the main respondents were not being encouraged to think about politics and elections before they were asked the question. We are not assuming that an individual's list of "important matters" discussants will necessarily be different or separate from their "government, elections, and politics" discussants. To the contrary, we are employing the randomly applied network name generator to address the issue empirically.

The question thus becomes, are networks of political communication distinct from more generalized networks of communication? If they *are* distinct, do people construct networks of political communication to be politically homogeneous? Other analyses of the experimental name generator show important differences in patterns of response (Huckfeldt, Levine et al. 1998). This analysis extends those earlier efforts to consider the implications for patterns of diversity and disagreement within discussion networks. Do people construct political communication networks to eliminate disagreement and the communication of political information that diverges from their own points of political orientation?

In Table 4.1, several compositional measures for the respondents' networks are regressed on a dummy variable that measures the form of the name generator that is used to solicit network information from the main respondent.

TABLE 4.1. *Effects of randomly applied network name generator on political composition of network. All compositional measures are based on main respondent reports. (Coefficient t-values are in parentheses.)*

	Percent same presidential vote	Mean political discussion frequency	Mean political disagreement frequency	Mean political knowledge
Constant	.63	2.72	2.51	2.21
	(46.40)	(133.75)	(120.82)	(158.35)
Politics name	.02	.19	.06	.04
generator	(.94)	(6.60)	(1.95)	(1.86)
R^2	.00	.02	.00	.00
SE of estimate	.40	.61	.61	.42
N	1361	1739	1697	1732

Percent same presidential vote: the percentage of identified discussants who are perceived to support the same presidential candidate as that supported by the main respondent, for main respondents who support a major party candidate

Mean political discussion frequency: "When you talk with [discussant name], do you discuss political matters: often (scored 4), sometimes (3), rarely (2), or never(1)?"

Mean political disagreement frequency: "When you discuss politics with [discussant name], do you disagree: often (scored 4), sometimes (3), rarely (2), or never(1)?"

Mean political knowledge: "Generally speaking, how much do you think [discussant name] knows about politics? Would you say: a great deal (scored 3), an average amount (2), or not much at all (1)?"

Note: The unit of analysis in this table is the individual respondent. Respondents are eliminated from the analyses if they do not report any discussants in response to the network name generator. The first column only includes respondents who supported a major party presidential candidate.

Respondents who replied to the politics name generator are coded 1, and respondents who replied to the "important matters" name generator are coded 0. Hence, the slope is directly interpretable as a difference in means between the groups of respondents responding to each, where the intercept is the mean for the important matters name generator, and the sum of the intercept and the slope is the mean for the politics name generator. What does this analysis show? In general, the differences are quite modest. With the exception of political discussion frequency within the network, the coefficients for the dummy variable produce marginal t-values that vary between 1.86 and 2.17. The magnitude of the differences are minimal, with little evidence of any dramatic differences between the two half-samples.

Focusing on the model in the first column of Table 4.1, each main respondent was asked to provide judgments regarding which presidential candidate each of their discussants supported. On this basis, and on the basis of the respondents' *own* reported candidate preferences, the first column of Table 4.1 considers percentage levels of shared candidate preferences within the networks for main respondents who supported a major party candidate. Respondents report perceived levels of shared candidate preferences that indicate 63 percent agreement in important matters networks and 65 percent agreement in political networks, but the difference is not statistically discernible, with a t-value of .94.

The second column of Table 4.1 provides the largest difference in network composition between the name generators. Reported frequencies of political discussion produce mean levels that are higher in the politics networks (2.91) than in the important matters networks (2.72), with a large t-value. But even here, the effect of the name generator falls short of being dramatic.

The third column of Table 4.1 supplies an analysis of the reported frequency of disagreement while discussing politics within the networks. In this instance respondents report levels of disagreement frequency that are slightly higher in political networks (the mean is 2.57) than in important matters networks (the mean is 2.51).

The fourth column of Table 4.1 provides limited evidence of a difference in the mean levels of political expertise within the discussion networks. Each respondent was asked to provide their judgment regarding how much each of the discussants knows about politics. The results show that, on average, the important matters discussants are perceived to know slightly less than the political discussants – the means are 2.21 and 2.25 respectively.

What conclusions might we draw on the basis of these results? The most obvious is that "important matters" discussants are not dramatically different from "politics" discussants in terms of shared candidate preferences, political discussion frequency, disagreement frequency, and levels of perceived political knowledge.

None of this means that there are no differences in the construction of the networks – indeed, other analyses of the ISL data suggest otherwise (Baybeck and Huckfeldt 2002; Huckfeldt, Levine et al. 1998). Neither do we intend to suggest that people fail to turn to different people for different purposes (see Klofstad et al. 2009 for arguments to the contrary). Katz and Lazarsfeld (1955), as well as other analyses of the ISL study (Huckfeldt 2001; Chapter 3 of this volume), point toward patterns of discussion that are tied up with interest and expertise regarding subject matter, as well as with individual purpose in the use of socially communicated information. The segregation of politics and political life from other matters of everyday concern should not be overstated, however. Most importantly, Table 4.1 offers little evidence to suggest that people are particularly careful to construct networks of *political* communication that consistently reflect their own political preferences.

This becomes a moot point if *all* networks of communication, regardless of substantive content, are constructed to minimize disagreement and maximize shared political viewpoints. This does not, however, appear to be the case. In terms of Table 4.1, supporters of the major party candidates perceive that 63 percent of the discussants in the important matters networks hold their own candidate preferences, and 65 percent in the politics networks hold their own candidate preferences. Hence, while these networks reflect political clustering, they do not present particularly high levels of internal homogeneity and partisan isolation. Other analyses show that 42 percent of all Clinton voters report at least one discussant who voted for someone other than Clinton, and 37 percent report at least one discussant who voted for Dole. In comparison, 36 percent of all Dole voters report at least one discussant who voted for someone other than Dole, and 31 percent report at least one discussant who voted for Clinton.

The presence or absence of disagreement within political communication networks has become an issue of some controversy, as well as an ongoing topic of interesting analysis. To be clear, we are not arguing that sorting and mixing processes are not influential in creating preferences that are clustered by social units that range from dyads to friendship groups to neighborhoods and beyond. To the contrary, our argument is that patterns of interdependence among citizens constitute a fundamental element of political life, and they are reflected in substantively significant and theoretically important tendencies toward clusters of like-minded citizens within communication networks. Most people are typically located in social settings where their preferences are within the majority. Within this context, however, the patterns of interdependence that sustain disagreement are just as important as the factors that lead to shared preferences, and opinion leaders play a crucial role in giving voice to political diversity.

How extensive is disagreement within political communication networks? Direct evidence with respect to this issue has accumulated over nearly 30 years. For example, among those respondents to the 2000 National Election Study who were interviewed after the election and identified at least one discussant, only 41 percent of the Gore voters were located in networks where they perceived that everyone supported Gore, and only 47 percent of the Bush supporters were located in networks where they perceived that everyone supports Bush. Moreover, 35.5 percent of all Bush voters named at least one discussant who supports Gore, and 36.7 percent of all Gore voters named at least one discussant who supports Bush (Huckfeldt, Mendez, and Osborn 2004).[4]

These levels of agreement and disagreement are similar to those shown in the 1996 ISL study. And, as Huckfeldt, Ikeda, and Pappi (2005) demonstrate, these patterns are quite comparable to those found among major party supporters in other nations and at other times – in the United States in 1992, in Japan in 1993, and in Germany in 1990. Moreover, in each of these national settings, respondents within larger networks were increasingly less likely to report homogeneous agreement. Thus, citizens with more extensive networks of communication are more likely to encounter diverse preferences.

Finally, a simple regression of discussant partisanship on main respondent partisanship for the dyads in this study yields a slope of .43 (t=17), with R^2 of .20, and a standard error for the estimate of 2.08. Hence, we see very strong

---

[4] Mutz (2005) objects to a measure of agreement defined in terms of the proportion of identified discussants who agree with the respondent, thereby including discussants with undetermined preferences as part of the base. Hence, we include an alternative measure here. A more complete consideration of these issues can be found in Huckfeldt, Ikeda, and Pappi (2005).

evidence of clustering in these data. Democrats are more likely to talk politics with Democrats, and Republicans with Republicans. We would expect nothing less!

Within this context, however, 22 percent of the discussants named by strongly partisan respondents self-identify as independent partisans, weak partisans, or strong partisans of the opposite party. The slope of the regression line falls far short of 1, and the typical distance from the regression line is more than 2 steps on the seven-point partisanship scale. In summary, it would misrepresent the evidence to suggest that individual citizens are overwhelmingly imbedded within politically homogeneous networks, or that political communication networks are dramatically more homogeneous than generalized discussion networks.

Endogeneity and censored patterns of communication

On the basis of the evidence presented thus far, the construction of political communication networks appears to be only weakly endogenous with respect to political preference. This is not to suggest, however, that agreement and political preference do not play substantial roles in the communication that occurs among citizens. In the remainder of this chapter, we consider another form of endogeneity – the censoring of political conversations in anticipation of political disagreement. Most readers recognize this phenomenon from personal experience – the avoidance of political discussions that we know will produce arguments and contentious exchanges. The problem is presented in a particularly compelling form by MacKuen (1990) in his analysis of political conversations. In the analyses that follow we consider the possibility that, even within networks of political communication, the frequency of political communication and the potential for political disagreement may be related in complex ways.

We turn from an analysis of individuals and their aggregated communication networks to an analysis of the individual dyads that are included within these networks. Hence, the unit of analysis is a dyadic communication link, based on interview data obtained from both the main respondent who reported the link and the discussant who was thus identified. We begin by reporting that the simple correlation between the frequency of political communication and the frequency of disagreement within 1,422 dyads is .06, where both discussion frequency and disagreement frequency are based on the previously discussed main respondent reports. The curious fact about this correlation is that it is greater than zero. One would expect, based on the arguments of Downs (1957) and Festinger (1957), that disagreement should inhibit communication and hence produce a negative correlation.

At the same time, the dyadic relationship between discussion frequency and disagreement frequency is likely to be complex. Higher frequencies of expressed disagreement within a dyad might be expected to inhibit political discussion between two individuals. Conversely, the more frequently people talk about

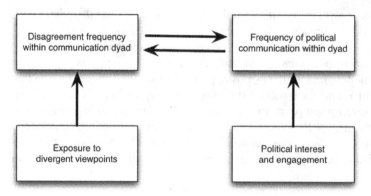

FIGURE 4.1. The simultaneity of discussion and disagreement.

politics, the more likely it becomes that disagreement will occur, almost by definition. In short, more political talk yields more opportunities for political disagreement, but more disagreement yields censored patterns of communication and a reduced frequency of political discussion.

We report here on an analysis undertaken to address these issues, drawing on the ISL study (Huckfeldt and Mendez 2008). Based on the likelihood of simultaneity between the frequency of political discussion and the expression of disagreement, both endogenous variables – discussion frequency and disagreement frequency – are located within a larger system that also includes important exogenous variables.[5] As Figure 4.1 suggests, the reported frequency of political discussion within a dyad is explained not only by the level of political disagreement within the dyad, but also by other characteristics of both discussion partners: their self-reported levels of political interest, their levels of political knowledge, their educational levels, and the frequency with which they report discussing politics with *other* individuals. Moreover, Table 4.1 showed that the frequency of political discussion is somewhat higher in political discussion networks than in important matters networks, and hence the form of the name generator question answered by the main respondent is included as well.

In contrast, the expression of political disagreement within a dyad is not only affected by the reported frequency of discussion within the dyad, but also by the reality of divergent preferences. This reality is conceived as the level of correspondence (or divergence) between the self-reported partisan orientations of the main respondent and the discussant, and it is measured with three variables – the main respondent's party identification, the discussant's party identification, and the multiplicative interaction between the two. In addition, to allow for the possibility that some people may be more inclined to engage in political argumentation, we include a measure for the mean level of disagreement reported by

[5] See Huckfeldt and Mendez (2008) for details.

the main respondent with her other discussants. Finally, the form of the name generator question is once again included.

Hence, the statistical model is based on the following exclusion restrictions. First, the model assumes that political interest and engagement produce an indirect effect on disagreement frequency within dyads by affecting the frequency of political discussion within the dyad, but no direct effect. Second, the model assumes that the existence of divergent orientations within the dyad, measured as a difference in reported partisanship, produces an indirect effect on the frequency of political communication by affecting the frequency of expressed disagreement, but no direct effect.

Are these restrictions justified? In the first restriction, we are arguing that political interest and engagement do not motivate individuals to seek out disagreement in an intentional manner. Rather, people who are interested and engaged *do* participate in higher frequencies of political discussion, and this in turn exposes them to higher levels of political disagreement. In terms of the second restriction, we are simply arguing that a tree falling in the forest has no effect on what the hiker hears unless she is there to hear it. Unless divergent preferences are expressed as disagreement in political conversations, we should not expect them to have an effect on political discussion frequency.[6] The results of the model's estimation produce a pattern of pronounced and reciprocal effects between disagreement and discussion frequency – more talk yields more disagreement, but more disagreement yields less talk. Moreover, this same pattern of effects is obtained based on a variety of specifications, estimation methods, and alternative simultaneous equation models.

What does this suggest regarding the positive coefficient obtained from a simple correlation of discussion frequency with disagreement frequency? A simple regression of one variable on the other presents a weak and incorrectly specified measure of association that is actually the residue of pronounced and separate effects with opposite signs. And this alternative pattern of effects is sustained based on a variety of specifications, methods, and models.

The dynamical implications of moths and flames

The important dynamic footprint in the simultaneous relationship between discussion and disagreement is that higher frequencies of political discussion enhance the likelihood of disagreement, while higher frequencies of political disagreement diminish the likelihood of discussion. In the language of dynamic systems, political disagreement produces negative feedback on political discussion, but political discussion produces positive feedback on political

---

[6] A discussion of these exclusion restrictions within the context of the reduced form equations for the model, as well as other measurement and statistical issues, are included in the appendix for Huckfeldt and Mendez 2008.

disagreement. Hence, discussion and disagreement are dynamically interdependent and joint in their distributions over time (see Huckfeldt, Kohfeld, and Likens 1982; Smith 1974).

We can safely assume that the frequencies of disagreement and discussion are inherently self-limiting, producing a locally stable equilibrium, where both are sustained at intermediate levels (see Huckfeldt and Mendez 2008). This equilibrium is likely to be frequently disturbed, however. Assuming that one of the individuals within the dyad pays heed to the events of politics, the day-to-day events and dramas periodically increase the level of political discussion. But as discussion increases, so does the likelihood of disagreement, thereby dislodging the dyad from its equilibrium. A typical pattern appears in which, after such a disturbance, the time paths for discussion and disagreement overshoot their respective equilibria but then recover and converge back to them in a pattern of longer-term oscillation. As long as the parameters defining the relationships remain unchanged, the dyad ultimately returns to its original equilibrium value.

What are the substantive implications of these dynamical patterns? The relatively straightforward dynamic logic underlying discussion and disagreement produces relatively complex recoveries to equilibrium. The time paths become even more complex as the frequency of political events increases, thereby adding more perturbations along the way. These complex time paths are due to random disturbances from equilibrium within the context of the simple dynamic structure underlying discussion and disagreement: more talk yields more disagreement, but more disagreement yields less talk.

Most important, *this dynamic tension serves to eliminate neither discussion nor disagreement*. Political discussion is not a stark choice between communication without disagreement or disagreement without communication. Rather, *the dynamic logic of discussion and disagreement is capable of sustaining both in a stable equilibrium relationship*, and this fact helps to explain the persistence of political disagreement within the patterns of communication that exist among citizens in democratic politics (Huckfeldt, Johnson, and Sprague 2004).

Implications and conclusions

What keeps disagreeable dyads from turning to other, less controversial subjects of conversation? What keeps political communication from being extinguished in disagreeing dyads? People who are interested in politics are more likely to discuss politics, regardless of the circumstances in which they are imbedded. All else being equal, disagreement serves as negative feedback on the frequency of disagreement, but all else is not equal, particularly with respect to levels of political engagement and civic capacity across individuals. Hence, we see a dynamic tension in which frequent discussion makes disagreement more likely, but frequent disagreement makes discussion less likely.

The dynamic tension between disagreement frequency and discussion frequency is particularly important because, as we have seen, many individuals are located within politically heterogeneous communication networks. The construction of political discussion networks is only modestly endogenous with respect to political disagreement. Political discussion networks do not demonstrate substantially lower levels of political disagreement than communication networks that are not defined politically. Moreover, while partisans are more likely to talk about politics with other like-minded partisans, the levels of political disagreement within both types of networks are quite substantial.

The analysis reviewed in this chapter shows that censoring does indeed occur, both in terms of network construction and in terms of the negative feedback on discussion frequency that is produced by disagreement. At the same time, opinion leaders engaged by politics and political discussion are more likely to talk politics, in spite of disagreement. Indeed, their commitment and fascination motivates them to discuss more frequently, and the frequency of discussion stimulates more frequent disagreement. Much like the moth and the flame, those engaged by political discussion are destined to encounter substantial doses of disagreement and argumentation along the way. And these encounters play a central role in sustaining the vitality of political conversation and opinion leadership among citizens.

Finally, this chapter makes two fundamental points. First, contexts and networks characterized by higher levels of political diversity create more opportunities for opinion leadership. Second, the individuals who are most likely to take advantage of these opportunities are those experts and activists who are engaged by the political process, even in the face of political disagreement and discord.

In summary, while network surveys provide a useful and crucial platform for the analysis of interdependence and opinion leadership within democratic electorates, many questions remain. In particular, as after-the-fact reconstructions based on the inevitably biased and faulty recall of survey respondents, the surveys are inherently limited in their capacity to provide evidence for dynamic inferences regarding the nature and source of political influence. Second, social interaction, social communication, and political influence occur within a process, and hence it becomes important to observe the process in real time as it unfolds. Finally, while the surveys explicitly address interdependence among actors, opportunities for addressing interdependence beyond dyadic relationships within larger networks of relationships are limited. For all these reasons, in Chapter 5 we turn to an experimental strategy for studying opinion leadership.

5

Informational asymmetries among voters

T. K. Ahn, Robert Huckfeldt, and John Barry Ryan

> To be sure, many voters act in odd ways indeed; yet in the large the electorate behaves about as rationally and responsibly as we should expect, given the clarity of the alternatives presented to it and the character of the information available to it.
>
> V.O. Key, Jr. (1966: 7)

The costs of becoming politically informed are highly variable across individuals, and information costs are lower among those individuals for whom the acquisition and processing of information is easier – typically individuals with higher levels of education (Wolfinger and Rosenstone 1980). Not only are information costs highly variable across individuals, but for many the costs are even negative (Fiorina 1990). Indeed, some individuals find the acquisition of information to be quite rewarding, often enjoyable, and sometimes irresistible. Hence, in the spirit of Downs (1957) and Berelson et al. (1954), we would expect to see a division of labor in the communication of political information. Individuals with high information costs might rely on communication with individuals who have minimal or even negative information costs.

While informational asymmetries thus arise systematically within networks of political communication, they also give rise to uncertainty, bias, and strategic behavior. This chapter addresses the implications of these asymmetries for political communication and influence. Are individuals more likely to trust their own judgments if they are well informed? Does the quality of their judgments reflect their own investments in political information? Is the construction of networks driven by levels of expertise, or by the compatibility of views that exist among potential informants? Are those who rely on socially mediated information more likely to be misled? How do the recipients of socially communicated information assess its reliability and utility?

The analysis in this chapter is the first in a series of analyses based on small group experiments in which subjects participate as voters in a series of faux elections. In each experiment, they decide to vote for one of two candidates, and they are rewarded with a modest financial incentive if the winning candidate holds a position closer to their own. The positions of the voters and the candidates are located on an arbitrary seven-point scale without any substantive or ideologically based endpoints, and participants are able to engage in limited communication with one another via networked computers – that is, they are only able to provide one another with estimates of candidate positions. In contrast, the candidates are non-reasoning computer objects that do not engage in any strategic behavior. None of the experiments involve any deception, and participants are fully informed regarding all experimental procedures. In short, these elections are abstract renderings of an actual election, but their design is informed by previous field research such as that discussed in Chapters 3 and 4.

In each of the experiments, the two candidates hold fixed positions on a one-dimensional preference space, but these positions are unknown to the experimental subjects. Hence the first task of the voters is to inform themselves regarding candidate positions. The information comes to the participants in three different forms: (1) publicly available information that is free and unbiased but with high variance; (2) privately acquired information that may cost more but is unbiased with a lower level of variance; and (3) socially communicated information that is free with indeterminate variance and bias.

SOCIAL COMMUNICATION AND INFORMATION COSTS

The collective benefit of a more highly informed citizenry cannot be withheld from individuals who do not themselves become informed. These benefits occur at two different levels. At the level of the overall electorate, democracy is more likely to thrive when citizens are better informed, and an ignorant electorate will compromise democratic control (Delli Carpini and Keeter 1996). At the level of politically meaningful groups with divergent political interests, it is in the collective interests of a particular group if its members are informed regarding the shared interests of group members. In both instances, the problem of political information costs thus constitutes a collective action problem (Olson 1965; Johnson 1996).

A central ingredient of this particular collective action problem revolves around the cost structures surrounding political information, as well as the implications that derive from both publicly available information and shared information among interdependent individuals (Berelson et al. 1954; Downs 1957). First, the individual acquisition costs of political information vary widely across different individuals. Some individuals acquire the information as a byproduct of pursuing other instrumental activities, while other individuals obtain recreational value from political information – they are the political enthusiasts who enjoy following politics and hence realize inherent benefits from the information independent of its utility in reaching political decisions (Fiorina 1990).

Second, these variations in costs take on additional meaning because people who find the collection of political information to be costly often can rely on information and guidance provided by others (Katz 1957). Unlike the classic free-rider situation, many individuals in this setting are ready and willing to pay information costs and share information. At one extreme, they are political junkies for whom information is its own reward (Huckfeldt and Sprague 1995).

Problems arise because group interests do not always translate directly and unambiguously into a particular political choice among individual group members. Consider three coworkers who share economic and professional interests but little else: a pro-life Democrat, a Republican who is a secular humanist, and an independent who belongs to the ACLU. Regardless of their shared occupational circumstances, they may have a difficult time identifying the points at which their individually held preferences and interests intersect and diverge. Two questions thus arise: Can any one of them trust either of the others for political advice and guidance? Are informationally impoverished individuals able to form judgments regarding the quality and reliability of the advice they receive?

These are important issues, particularly when people obtain information from informants with divergent preferences. While Downs' (1957) solution is to select an expert with shared preferences, such informants might not be readily available in many social contexts. As we have seen in previous chapters, one might need to choose between a political expert with divergent preferences and a political novice with convergent preferences. The results in Chapter 3 suggest that individuals are more likely to obtain political information from expert individuals even when their political preferences are divergent. Other arguments suggest that, under particular circumstances, information with a distinct bias may be quite useful, even if the bias of the informant does not necessarily coincide with the bias of the recipient (Calvert 1985a).

In situations such as these, it is in the interests of the recipient to employ processing strategies that offer protection from being misled. Indeed, neither the interests of individual citizens nor the collective interests of democratic electorates are well-served by a process potentially rife with misinformation. The crux of the difficulty is that individuals who are bereft of information may have a difficult time assessing the quality of information and advice they receive from other citizens. And thus we end up with yet another version of *Catch-22* – individuals without information need information in order to evaluate the information they receive from others (Heller 1961).

SOURCES AND CONSEQUENCES OF UNCERTAINTY

The analysis is thus based on cost-conscious individuals who make political choices based on their own understandings of their interests. Even though their interests are defined unequivocally, the subjects confront a three-fold dilemma in the effort to realize these interests. First, their willingness and ability to invest in information acquisition and analysis are limited, and hence they confront substantial levels of uncertainty regarding appropriate choices. Second, Downs' (1957) ideal of well-informed, like-minded informants is often difficult to attain. Stochastic distributions of expertise and preferences are not necessarily correlated among potential informants, and hence the like-minded expert may be unavailable. Third, and as a consequence, the subjects' incomplete information regarding the appropriate candidate choice is complemented by a heterogeneous stream of socially communicated information that may carry significant and unknown levels of bias, or honest error, or both. The issue is not that actors are irrational, but rather that the rational course of action is unclear, and hence the implementation of rationality is inevitably based on perception and judgment (Simon 1957, 1985).

In the communication process we have described, individuals make a series of implicit yet complex judgments. These include (1) introspective judgments regarding their own levels of expertise; (2) imputed judgments regarding the levels of expertise among informants and potential informants; and (3) strategic judgments regarding the level of bias that accompanies the information obtained from the various informants. In uncertain situations such as these, we might expect individuals to employ heuristic devices as shortcuts to make judgments and reach decisions (Kahneman and Tversky 1973; Tversky and Kahneman 1973; Sniderman 1993).

The use of heuristic devices sometimes helps to explain why citizens lacking detailed knowledge are often able to hold meaningful opinions and reach sensible judgments (Sniderman, Brody, and Tetlock 1991), but these heuristics also demonstrate inherent limitations as aids to low-information decision-makers (Sniderman 2000). Moreover, heuristic devices produce distinctive biases within the decision-making process (Kuklinski and Quirk 2000; Huckfeldt, Johnson, and Sprague 2004), and hence they often generate important political consequences. Our goal in this chapter is to identify the ways in which citizens might employ heuristic devices within processes of political communication among citizens, as well as the implications of these heuristic devices for patterns of interdependence and influence (Mondak 1995).

EXPERIMENTAL DESIGN

Each of our small group experiments involves seven subjects who interact with one another via networked computers. All the experiments include two computer-generated candidates running for election, each with a fixed integer position on an undefined one-dimensional preference space numbered from 1 to 7. Subjects receive a cash incentive if the candidate closest to them wins the election and a cash penalty if the other candidate wins. Hence, their immediate goal is to cast a vote for the candidate who most closely matches their own randomly assigned position on the same seven-point scale.[1]

---

[1] The appendix to this chapter includes the instructions provided to experimental participants.

Information comes to the subjects in three different forms: publicly available information that is free but of low quality; privately acquired information that may cost more but is of higher quality; and socially communicated information taken from other individuals that is free with uncertain quality.

We conducted ten sessions of these computerized small group experiments, with seven subjects participating in each session. The experimental design builds on a spatial voting model in which voters and candidates have positions on a single-dimensional preference space, voters cast their votes in an election, and the voters' payoffs depend on which of the two candidates win the election. The exact positions of the candidates were not known to the participants, creating a need among the subjects to obtain information.

Subjects were paid a show-up fee of $5.00 and given an additional opportunity to earn more money based on the decisions they and other subjects make during the experiment. In all sessions, the baseline experiment was repeated for 15 rounds.[2] The experimental program was written using z-Tree software (Fischbacher 2007). Subjects were paid volunteers recruited from undergraduate political science classes at the University of California, Davis. The range of total payoffs was between $7.75 and $25.50, and a session lasted about 60 minutes.

THE UNDERLYING SPATIAL VOTING MODEL

Candidates and voters have preferences which are represented as integer numbers from 1 to 7 on a one-dimensional preference space. At the beginning of a session each subject was assigned a preference such that there is one voter with ideal point 1, one voter with ideal point 2, one voter with ideal point 3, and so on. Thus, the seven subjects are evenly distributed on the scale. Once assigned, a subject's preference remained unchanged for the duration of the experiment. We will refer to the subjects as voter 1, voter 2, etc., where voter j means the subject's preference (or ideal point) is j.

The two candidates, Candidate A and Candidate B, were not real human subjects, but computer-generated positions. Candidate A's position was randomly drawn *in each round* from a set $\{1, 2,\ldots, 6\}$. Candidate B's position was also randomly drawn *in each round*, independently of Candidate A's position, from a set $\{2, 3,\ldots, 7\}$. The candidates' positions took only integer values; subjects were told that the candidates were computer-generated positions, redrawn in each period from the respective intervals, but the voters did not know the exact positions of the candidates with certainty.

Each subject cast a vote for either Candidate A or Candidate B in every round. Voting was costless, and abstention was not allowed. Also, the subjects had a

---

[2] The experimental sessions included 70 subjects who participated in sessions that involved 15 rounds for a total of 1,050 subject-rounds. Analyses are pooled with a clustering correction for multiple observations on the same subjects (Rogers 1993).

well-understood incentive to vote for the candidates whose positions were closer to their own positions.

At the beginning of each round of voting, subjects were endowed with 100 ECUs (Experimental Currency Units). Subjects were allowed to use up to 50 ECUs out of the endowed 100 ECUs to purchase information on the candidates' positions. (Information purchase and exchange will be explained in detail later.) After voting, if the winning candidate's position was closer to a voter than the losing candidate's, the voter earned 50 extra ECUs. If the winning candidate's position was farther away from the voter's position than the losing candidate, 50 ECUs were subtracted from the voter's account. If the two candidates were equally distant from the voter, then the voter neither gained nor lost ECUs due to the outcome of the election.[3]

A voter could conceivably earn 150 ECUs maximum in a round: the initial 100 ECU endowment plus 50 more ECUs if his favorite candidate wins, assuming that the subject does not spend any ECUs to purchase information on the candidates' true positions. The minimum possible payoff for a subject in a period is 0 ECUs; this happens when a voter spends 50 ECUs on purchasing information, and her favorite candidate loses the election. At the end of the experiment, the subjects were paid (in cash) the show-up fee plus their total earnings during the experiment.[4]

OBTAINING INFORMATION ON CANDIDATES' POSITIONS

While the true positions of the two candidates are unknown, the voters have three potential sources of information on which to base their votes: (1) public information about the possible candidate positions; (2) private information that they have an option to purchase; (3) information shared by their fellow subjects.

First, the fact that the two candidates' positions were drawn from different intervals could potentially help a voter absent other forms of information. We provide all subjects with this information for several reasons. This information mimics the manner in which publicly available information provides even the most modestly attentive citizens with at least some diagnostic information – even the least-informed individuals often recognize that one candidate is more likely to lie on the left and another on the right. Moreover, it provides subjects who do not purchase information with the ability to form a prior judgment that is at least modestly informed. This public information should be more helpful to voters with more extreme positions (i.e., voter 1 and voter 7) than to those in the middle

---

[3] Subjects were paid based on their actual distance from the candidates, not how they voted. So, for example, if Candidate A was closer to subject *j*, but the subject voted for B, subject *j* was paid based on whether or not Candidate A won.

[4] The conversion rate between ECUs and dollars was 100 ECUs equals U.S.$1.00.

(voter 4). For example, voter 7, in the absence of any other information, should always vote for Candidate B.[5]

Second, voters were allowed to spend up to 50 ECUs to obtain additional information on the candidates' true positions. Subjects were randomly assigned three different information costs. In each session, two voters paid zero costs to obtain information (these are referred to as low information cost voters), two paid 5 ECUs for each piece of information (medium information cost voters), and three paid 25 ECUs for each piece of information (high information cost voters). Once assigned, a subject's information cost remained unchanged for the entire experiment. The maximum allowed information purchase was four pieces of information, but no subject was allowed to spend more than the 50 ECU limit on information purchases per round. Thus, subjects with high information costs were able to purchase no more than two pieces of information.

When a voter purchases a piece of information, it arrives in the form (a, b) where a is an estimate of A's true position and b is an estimate of B's true position. Let α and β denote the true positions of candidates A and B in a round. Then the signals a and b are randomly and independently drawn from a uniform interval $[\alpha - 3, \alpha + 3]$ and $[\beta - 3, \beta + 3]$, respectively. The signals took only integer values. Subjects were told how the signals were drawn as well as the fact that the signals on average reflect the true positions of the candidates.

Third, and finally, each subject has an opportunity to request information from one other subject. Before they make this request, all subjects are shown the preferences of each subject, as well as the number of pieces of information purchased by each subject. After all subjects have made their requests, the subjects are told if anyone requested information from them, and the preferences of the requestors are revealed. The subjects are not required to comply with the request, and they are not required to provide truthful information.[6] When there are multiple requestors, a subject is not required to provide the same information to all requestors.

Hence, subjects may provide no information, truthful information, or misleading information. When one subject agrees to the information request from another subject, the information provider sends a message in the form of (a, b),

---

[5] There are 36 possible combinations of the two candidates' positions and the joint distribution is uniform; in 21 out of these 36 possibilities, Candidate B would be closer to voter 7 than Candidate A.

[6] By "truthful" we mean that the information provider's best guess is conditional on the information he has and his cognitive ability. Thus, truthful information may not be objectively "correct," in the sense of reflecting the candidates' real positions. We allow informants to provide misleading information because the introduction of bias within communication is central to our objectives. Does such an experimental procedure reflect real world conditions? When conservatives try to convince liberals to support their preferred (conservative) candidates, they often try to convince these liberals that their preferred candidates are not so conservative as liberals might think (see Brady and Sniderman 1985). Such a dynamic parallels the situation faced by our subjects. While such a situation is not necessarily seen as being dishonest in the actual world, it is certainly central to efforts at political persuasion.

where *a* is the provider's estimate regarding the true position of Candidate A and *b* is the provider's estimate regarding the true position of Candidate B.

SUMMARY OF PROCEDURE

In short, the following steps occur during the experiment. At the beginning of the experiment, subjects were assigned their respective, mutually exclusive, integer preferences on a one-dimensional preference space from 1 to 7. Information costs are randomly assigned to subjects such that two subjects have low costs, two have medium costs, and three have high costs. Once assigned, these positions and information costs remain unchanged for each subject for the duration of the experiment. The candidate positions are set between 1 and 7, and subjects are accurately informed that Candidate A's position lies between 1 and 6 inclusively, while Candidate B's position is set between 2 and 7 inclusively.[7] Then, in each of the 15 rounds per session, the following steps occur:

1. The two candidates' positions are drawn from the respective intervals.
2. Subjects are given an opportunity to purchase information at the assigned cost.
3. After the subjects have received the information, they are asked to provide their judgment of where they believe each candidate's position to be. This information is not communicated to other subjects.
4. After being shown all the subjects' positions on the scale, as well as the amount of information each has purchased, they are allowed to request information from one other subject. The subject need not comply with the request, and they need not provide accurate information.
5. After receiving information from one another, the subjects are provided a summary of the information they have received, and they vote for one of the candidates.
6. The outcome of the election is revealed to the voters. If the winning candidate's position is closer to a voter than the losing candidate's, the voter receives additional 50 ECUs as a reward. If the losing candidate's position is closer to a voter, 50 ECUs are taken from the voter's account. If the voter's position is equally distant from the candidates' positions, they neither lose nor gain ECUs as a result of the outcome. Finally, subjects are informed of their net earnings, both in the round and cumulatively.
7. The candidate positions are reset, and subjects proceed to the next round.

The value of information can be measured in terms of its variance around an unbiased central tendency. Each bit of individually purchased information is drawn from uniform distributions with midpoints centered at the candidates'

---

[7] Hence, the notification that the two candidates' positions lie in different intervals is public information, available to all, that Candidate A is somewhat more likely to lie to the left, and Candidate B is more likely to lie on the right.

true position and boundaries that are symmetrical to the midpoints. This means that individuals must make judgments regarding candidates based on multiple pieces of unbiased but noisy information. In contrast, when individuals rely on the judgments of other subjects, they not only depend on the mix of noisy information that serves as the basis for these subjects' judgments, but also on the ability and willingness of the source to compile this information in an unbiased manner. This basic structure provides an opportunity to address a series of issues related to asymmetries in information among subjects, as well as the implications of these asymmetries for political communication.

This experimental framework is an admittedly incomplete representation of the context in which real-world political decisions are made by citizens. At the same time, it captures several features of the process that are central to our purposes. First, it produces variation in information costs across individuals. Second, it provides public information that is free and potentially useful in a low information environment. Third, socially mediated information is free, but it carries the potential both to be inaccurate due to the informant's own limited information, and to be strategically biased – particularly when the informant and the recipient hold divergent positions.

THE COST AND VALUE OF INDIVIDUALLY OBTAINED INFORMATION

The first issue that arises relates to the value of the privately acquired information. We address this question by considering the subjects' prior judgments regarding candidate positions. These judgments are "prior" in the sense that they are made by the subjects based wholly on privately obtained information, prior to communication with other subjects.

The randomly assigned information costs make a substantial difference in the amount of information purchased by individual subjects. More than 78 percent of those without information costs obtain the maximum amount of information, but only 21.3 percent of those who pay 5 ECUs purchase the maximum. Those who pay 25 ECUs are only eligible to purchase two pieces of information, but 26.9 percent do not purchase any at all. As a consequence, the mean acquisition is 3.5 pieces among subjects for whom information is free, 2.2 for subjects who pay 5 ECUs, and 1.1 for subjects who pay 25 ECUs. In short, subjects economize in purchasing information, and the amount of information they purchase is a direct function of cost.[8]

Is this information helpful to the subjects in forming judgments regarding the locations of the candidates? We address this question on the basis of subjects' initial judgments regarding the candidates' positions. Recall that they provide

---

[8] Why do the subjects without information costs fail to take all the information that is available? There are, of course, other costs not captured in the experimental manipulation – in particular the basic cognitive costs of processing and integrating additional information.

TABLE 5.1. *Absolute value of difference between prior and candidate position. Standard errors for coefficients are corrected for clustering* A. *By the amount of information purchased.*

	Candidate A		Candidate B	
	Coefficient	T-Ratio	Coefficient	T-Ratio
Information Purchased (dummies)				
One piece	−0.336	−2.15	−0.481	−2.49
Two pieces	−0.638	−4.32	−0.939	−4.98
Three pieces	−0.652	−3.93	−1.026	−3.77
Four pieces	−0.889	−5.8	−1.249	−6.56
Constant	1.712	12.14	1.966	10.84
N (clusters)	1050 (70)		1050 (70)	
R^2	0.07		0.14	

B. *By initial and additional information purchased.*

	Candidate A		Candidate B	
	Coefficient	T-Ratio	Coefficient	T-Ratio
First piece (dummy)	−0.390	−2.59	−0.576	−3.12
Additional pieces	−0.172	−6.71	−0.237	−6.98
Constant	1.712	12.15	1.966	10.85
N (clusters)	1050 (70)		1050 (70)	
R^2	0.07		0.14	

these judgments *after* obtaining the individually purchased information but *prior* to obtaining the information communicated by another subject. A measure of judgmental error is formed by taking the absolute value of the difference between this prior judgment and the true candidate position, which is unknown to the subjects.

The effect of information on judgmental errors is initially considered in Part A of Table 5.1, where an error is defined as the absolute value of the difference between the candidate's true position and the subject's judgment. The amount of information purchased by a subject is represented with a set of dummy variables, where the excluded category consists of subjects who did not purchase any information. This analysis shows that subjects who purchase more information are likely to make smaller errors regarding the candidate positions. The results show continued improvement in the level of error reduction as the amount of information purchased by a subject increases, but the net improvement from zero to one piece of information exceeds the improvement realized due to any other single piece of information subsequently purchased.

The consequences of information for error reduction are thus re-specified in Part B, where a dummy variable is defined for those who purchase one or more pieces of information, and a second variable is defined as the number of *additional* information purchases. If a subject did not purchase any information, they would score zero on both, but a person who purchased three pieces of information would score 1 on the dummy variable and 2 on the count variable. This specification shows, once again, a large effect for the first piece of information. In terms of judgments regarding Candidate A, purchasing one piece of information reduces the error by .39, and each additional information purchase reduces the error by .17.

In summary, information costs inhibit information purchases. Those who purchase more information are less likely to make errors in judgment regarding candidates, but the returns from information are diminishing (see McKelvey and Ordeshook 1985a). This is *not* because individuals fail to learn from additional pieces of information. Other analyses of these experimental data (not shown here) indicate that participants weigh each piece of information equally – the content provided by each piece of information received is as important as the content provided by any other piece.[9] Rather, in the stochastic world that we have created, a single piece of unbiased information is likely to be quite valuable, but the value of additional information is greatly diminished. Hence, depending on the underlying cost structure for the particular subject, the additional investment in information may not generate substantial efficiency gains, and we should not expect dramatic improvements in judgment as a participant purchases one or two additional pieces of information.[10]

CRITERIA FOR SELECTING INFORMANTS

The diminishing benefits of additional information raise an important question – who qualifies as a reliable expert? We expect that democratic politics and the capacity of electorates are more likely to be enhanced by communication among and between citizens if individuals disproportionately communicate with politically expert associates.[11] Informant selection criteria are particularly complex in the context of political communication due to its inherently partisan nature. Differences of opinion lie at the essence of democratic politics, and the management of disagreement plays an important role in the structure of communication

---

[9] We address the dynamic process of information acquisition in Chapter 10.

[10] One might expect participants to develop insights that would lead to the evolution of strategies over the course of the experiment. As the appendix shows, however, there is only limited evidence to suggest that learning occurs.

[11] This is not intended to minimize the educative functions of communication per se. Even when individuals communicate with people who know very little about politics, they are forced to consider, evaluate, and make relative assessments regarding relevant issues and topics. These cognitive processes, in and of themselves, are likely to produce more complex and thoughtful assessments regarding politics and political affairs.

TABLE 5.2. *Requests for information within dyads. Standard errors for coefficients are corrected for clustering (logit models.)*
A. *Whether ego asks alter for information during a round, by the amount of information alter purchased during the round, and the absolute distance between the preferences of alter and ego (logit model, with standard errors corrected for clustering on egos).*

	Coefficient	t-ratio
Amount of information purchased by alter	0.591	7.08
Distance between ego and alter	−0.312	−4.30
Constant	−2.300	−9.49
N	6300	
χ^2	54.46	
p	0.000	
Number of subjects (egos)	70	

B. *Predicted probability of asking for information (based on estimates in Part A of this table.)*

Distance between alter and ego	Information purchased by alter	
	0 pieces	4 pieces
1	0.07	0.44
6	0.02	0.14

networks and the conveyance of political information through these networks (see Chapter 4).

In *An Economic Theory of Democracy* (1957), Downs suggests that rational individuals seek out information from knowledgeable informants who share their political biases. Within the context of this experiment, and from the vantage point of cheap talk, one might thus expect that individuals would dismiss information taken from informants with divergent perspectives (Johnson 1993). After all, the subjects have incentives to make sure that the candidates closest to them win the election, and thus it would be reasonable to expect that the reliability of informants would be contingent on the positions of informants relative to the recipients of information.

We evaluate this argument with a logit model in Part A of Table 5.2, based on dyad data taken from the study. In this analysis, each dyad in every round is treated as an observation, thereby yielding an n-size of 6,300. A clustering correction takes account of multiple observations on the subjects requesting information, yielding 70 clusters (subjects defined as "egos"). The model in this table assesses whether or not one subject asks for information from another subject (the "alter"), based on the amount of information purchased by the potential informant, as well as by the distance between the preferences of the two subjects in the dyad.

While both factors produce statistically discernible effects, the predicted probabilities in Part B of Table 5.2 show that the amount of information purchased by a potential informant is actually the more important explanatory factor. One subject is more likely to request information from another to the extent that the potential informant has purchased more information. The model predicts that if two individuals hold adjacent positions, the probability of requesting information from an individual who has not purchased any information is .07, but this probability increases to .44 if an individual has purchased four pieces of information. In contrast, if a prospective informant has purchased four pieces of information, but the two subjects' preferences are separated by the maximum of 6 points, the probability drops to .14. In short, mirroring the previous results discussed in Chapter 3, expertise tends to be more important than agreement – subjects are two times more likely to communicate with expert individuals holding divergent preferences (.14) than with inexpert individuals holding like-minded preferences (.07).

The participants thus behave as Downs (1957) would expect when expert informants are available who share their own preferences. But when push comes to shove – when they must choose between (1) expert informants with divergent preferences and (2) a lack of expertise among informants with convergent preferences – they regularly throw caution to the wind and opt in favor of the disagreeable experts. These results seem to suggest that the self-educative potential of democratic electorates might be anchored in the tendency for expertise to trump agreement in the construction of communication networks. The issue that naturally arises is the extent to which these experts provide trustworthy information and guidance.

THE RELIABILITY OF EXPERT ADVICE

Do informants act as candid conduits of information, or do they provide information that reflects the level of correspondence between their own preferences and the preferences of the subjects requesting the information? That is, to what extent do informants communicate biased information? For the purposes of this analysis, our focus is on the divergence between the prior judgment of the informant and the message they send to the subject who is requesting guidance. If the informant is being entirely straightforward, the messages they communicate should be the same as their own prior estimates of the candidates' positions, and hence there should be no difference between the prior and the message – that is, the subjects form a prior estimate based on public and privately purchased information. Immediately after forming that prior estimate, people ask them for information, and they are then given the opportunity to obtain information from others. If communication is driven by their candid assessments, message content should be predicted by the prior estimate and nothing else.

TABLE 5.3. *Biases in communicated messages: the absolute difference between informant prior and the communicated message regressed on the absolute difference in the positions of the informant and recipient. Standard errors for coefficients are corrected for clustering*

	Candidate A		Candidate B	
	Coefficient	t-ratio	Coefficient	t-ratio
Difference between positions of informant and recipient	0.164	2.61	0.157	3.29
Constant	0.654	6.22	0.514	4.59
N		903		903
R^2		0.03		0.03
Number of clusters (subjects)		68		68
Standard error of estimate		1.332		1.273

Note. The mean absolute difference between the informant's message and the informant's prior is 1.00 for Candidate A (standard deviation = 1.35) and .85 for Candidate B (standard deviation = 1.29).

The dependent variable in the Table 5.3 regressions is the absolute difference between the informants' prior judgments and the candidate messages that they send to the recipients. The explanatory variable is the absolute difference between the ideal positions of the informants and the recipients. The positive coefficients with substantial t-values suggest that divergence between the priors and the communicated messages reflect divergent preferences between the informant and the recipient. While this provides clear evidence of biased communication, the extent of the bias is relatively constrained. The maximum distance between two subjects is an interval of 6 units, and hence the maximum predicted bias in the information due to divergent positions between informant and the recipient would be approximately .96 for each candidate. While the bias in the messages is constrained, the distance between the two candidates is often relatively small – the mean absolute distance is 1.75. Hence, even minimal levels of bias can be consequential when candidates converge.

These results suggest that the quality of the communicated message is attenuated by the existence of divergent positions between the informant and the recipient. While relying on expert information creates the potential for a self-educating electorate, this potential might be compromised by messages that misinform the recipient. Hence, an important issue is the capacity of recipients to make sophisticated judgments regarding the value of these messages.

COPING WITH ADVICE FROM SUSPECT SOURCES

In their effort to obtain expert guidance, subjects run the risk of exposing themselves to cheap talk and misinformation (Johnson 1993; Farrell and Rabin 1996). Why would individuals take such a chance? Our argument is that subjects might employ several different heuristics as coping mechanisms in order to evaluate the reliability of the information they receive from others, based primarily on their own privately held information and expertise. That is, privately held information is likely to occupy a central role in the assessment of socially communicated information, and this privately held information becomes important in two different ways.

First, a "credible prior" heuristic suggests that subjects place more confidence in their prior judgments when they invest more heavily in the private information on which the priors are based. In contrast, individuals who fail to purchase information might place little confidence in these priors, depending more heavily on the information they obtain from other individuals.

A second "credible message" heuristic is based on an evaluation of messages relative to priors. The recipient might be less likely to infer credibility to socially communicated information when the messages are at variance with their own views – that is, we expect that individuals will be less likely to trust a message that diverges sharply from their own judgments regarding the state of the world. Correspondingly, well-informed subjects might be the most likely to resist incoming messages that conflict with their own priors.

A third "credible messenger" heuristic is that individuals might be suspicious of messages that come from informants with divergent preferences. This is, in effect, a less exacting version of the previous heuristic. It suggests that, even though subjects take information from informants with divergent preferences, they continue to evaluate the messengers as well as their messages. Hence, they are more likely to infer credibility to messages coming from informants with preferences that are proximate to their own, regardless of content.

First, we evaluate the "credible prior" heuristic, based on the amount of information purchased by the recipient. A logit model is employed in the first column of Table 5.4 to regress the subject's vote on the subject's prior and the message received from the informant, with interaction effects for information purchases. The model shows a discernible interaction effect for the prior but not for the message, suggesting that subjects place more confidence in their prior when they make a greater investment in information. The magnitudes of the prior's effect on the probabilities of voting for Candidate A are shown in Figure 5.1A across different levels of information purchases. Well-informed subjects clearly place more confidence in their own priors, and hence we treat low- and high-information subjects separately in the analyses that follow.[12]

The models in the second and third columns of Table 5.4 evaluate the credible message and credible messenger heuristics, where the subject's vote is regressed on a series of explanatory variables, separately for high-information and low-information subjects. The second column model includes subjects with 3 or 4 information purchases, and the third column model includes subjects with 0, 1,

---

[12] We consider factors affecting the strength and durability of priors in Chapter 10.

TABLE 5.4. *Subject vote by priors and socially communicated information, with interactions for heuristic devices. Standard errors for coefficients are corrected for clustering (logit models).*

	All Subjects		High Information		Low Information	
	Coef.	T-Ratio	Coef.	T-Ratio	Coef.	T-Ratio
Subject priors regarding candidates	0.157	1.70	0.677	3.25	0.331	4.82
Messages regarding candidates	0.565	4.47	1.419	3.35	0.637	3.40
Amount of information purchased	−0.009	−0.13				
Amount of information X prior (credible prior heuristic)	0.169	2.73				
Amount of information X messages	−0.079	−1.69				
Distance between subjects			0.006	0.05	0.233	2.39
Deviation between prior and message			−0.067	−0.35	−0.032	−0.32
Message X distance between subjects (credible messenger heuristic)			−0.202	−2.79	−0.037	−0.81
Message X deviation between message and prior (credible message heuristic)			−0.340	−2.37	−0.021	−0.45
Constant	−0.059	−0.30	0.109	0.26	−0.494	−1.63
N (Clusters)	903 (70)		326 (33)		577 (57)	
χ^2, d.f., p	71.5, 5, 0.00		19.3, 6, 0.00		94.28, 6, 0.00	

S= subject's preference (position on 7 point scale)
   I= informant's preference (position on 7 point scale)
   P_a= subject prior regarding position of Candidate A
   P_b= subject prior regarding position of Candidate B
   M_a= Informant message regarding position of Candidate A
   M_b= Informant message regarding position of Candidate B
   The subject's combined prior regarding candidates= $abs(P_b-S)-abs(P_a-S)$
   The combined messages regarding the candidates= $abs(M_b-S)-abs(M_a-S)$
   Distance between subjects= $abs(S-I)$
   Deviation between priors and messages= $[(P_a-M_a)^2 + (P_b-M_b)^2]/2$
   Dependent variable is coded 1 if the subject voted for Candidate A.

or 2 information purchases. The explanatory variables in the second and third columns include the subject priors regarding the candidates; the messages regarding the candidates; the distance between the preferences of the subject and the informant; the divergence between the message and the recipient's prior; the multiplicative interaction between the message and the preference distance (the credible messenger contingency); and the multiplicative interaction between the

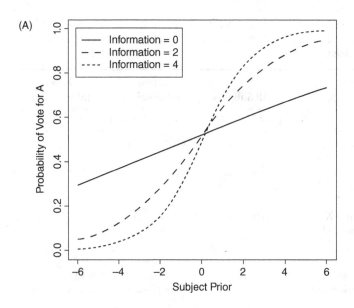

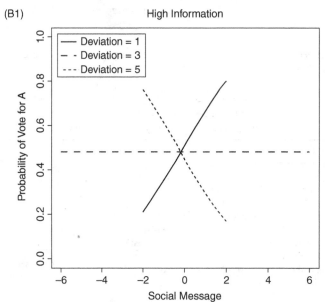

FIGURE 5.1. Voting, social messages, and priors.

A. Estimated vote probabilities by subject's prior contingent on information level, for all subjects. Other variables held at mean values.

B. Estimated vote probabilities by low-information and high-information heuristics for low- and high-information subjects. Other variables held at mean values.

Note: priors are held constant at zero among high-information subjects, and hence the range of possible messages varies across fixed deviation levels.

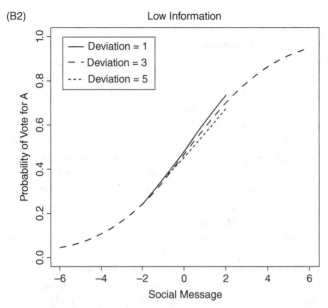

FIGURE 5.1. (cont.)

message and the divergence between the message and the prior (the credible message contingency).

As the note to Table 5.4 indicates, the combined messages and combined priors regarding the two candidates are measured as the differences of the distances separating the subject's ideal point from the priors and the messages regarding the two candidates. The divergence between the priors and the messages are measured as the average mean squared difference between the prior and message for each candidate. In both models, the priors and the messages demonstrate discernible effects on the vote. Among the highly informed, the message is discounted both to the extent that it deviates from the subject's prior, as well as the extent to which the messenger's preference diverges from the preference of the recipient. In contrast, among the less-informed, neither heuristic is employed.[13]

The magnitudes of effects among the well-informed are displayed in the first panel of Figure 5.1B, where we see the predicted probability that a highly informed subject will vote for Candidate A as a function of the message received from the informant. The figure shows that the effect of the message is contingent on its deviation from the subject's own prior. The message is most influential when it lies closer to the subject's own prior, but the effect is actually reversed when it diverges most sharply from the subject's prior. The figure's final panel

---

[13] The experimental results shown in this chapter are based on a replication of an earlier study (Ahn, Huckfeldt, and Ryan 2010). In that analysis, the highly informed employed a credible message heuristic while the less informed employed the credible messenger heuristic.

(B2) shows the same probability for the less informed. In this instance the effect of the message is highly comparable across levels of disagreement between the informant's message and the subject's prior.

Thus, not only do well-informed subjects weight their own priors more heavily, but they use different criteria in evaluating incoming messages from potential informants. In particular, the well-informed subjects dismiss messages that do not agree with their own preconceptions, they are skeptical regarding messages from informants with divergent preferences, and hence we see an irony imbedded in the communication process. Subjects clearly value expertise more than shared preferences in selecting informants, but communication is not the same as influence. While subjects are ready and willing to communicate with experts who hold divergent preferences, the better-informed subjects appear to be particularly skeptical regarding the information that is communicated.[14]

The use of such heuristics constitutes substantial limits on the influence of political communication, and the well-informed are the most difficult to influence (Lodge and Taber 2000). While they choose individuals with divergent preferences as informants, they are unlikely to be persuaded by messages that conflict with their own priors. This naturally leads to the issue of whether these well-informed subjects are being *too* cautious. That is, how likely are they to be misled?

CROSS-PRESSURES AND THE IMPLICATIONS FOR CORRECT VOTING

The analysis now turns to a counterfactual consideration of the consequences due to social communication for correct and incorrect voting. This analysis is counterfactual because we are not interested in how the subjects *actually* voted, but rather how they *would have* voted if they had based their votes on informant messages versus their own priors, in situations where the messages and priors lead to different votes.

When subjects face a choice between expertise and compatibility in the selection of an informant, they often turn to experts with divergent perspectives. This creates a situation in which the interest of the subject potentially conflicts with the interest of the messenger, and many subjects thus confront the dilemma of (biased) messages that conflict with their own priors. We focus on this problem in the analyses that follow. What are the implications for voting correctly – for voting in line with their own underlying preferences?

Both the subject priors and the informant messages come as a set of two-point estimates, one for each of the two candidates' respective positions. Each set of point estimates translates into three possible vote cues: vote for Candidate A, indifference between A and B, and vote for Candidate B. Thus, for the purposes of this analysis, these point estimates are translated into the correspondingly appro-priate vote cues. We employ an ordered logit model in Part A of Table 5.5 to

---

[14] For complementary arguments, see Calvert 1985a on communication as confirmation, as well as Ross et al. (1976) on attribution and the limits of persuasion.

TABLE 5.5. *Correct votes, subject priors, and informant messages. Standard errors for coefficients are corrected for clustering (ordered logit models).*
A. *Correct vote by subject prior and informant message.*

| | All Subjects | | Information Purchased | | | |
| | | | 0 or 1 piece | | 2 to 4 pieces | |
	Coef.	T-Ratio	Coef.	T-Ratio	Coef.	T-Ratio
Messages	0.621	6.46	0.532	3.10	0.639	5.70
Prior	0.980	10.77	0.658	4.87	1.194	10.32
Cut 1	−0.554 s=0.086		−0.380 s=0.121		−0.711 s=0.108	
Cut 2	0.638 s=0.071		0.568 s=0.097		0.679 s=0.107	
N	903		321		582	
χ^2, d.f., p	151, 2, 0.00		31, 2, 0.00		147, 2, 0.00	

B. *Predicted probability that priors and messages lead to correct vote with which they agree.*

| p the correct vote is: | All Subjects | | Low Information | | High Information | |
	Prior=A Message=A	Prior=B Message=B	Prior=A Message=A	Prior=B Message=B	Prior=A Message=A	Prior=B Message=B
A	0.74	0.10	0.69	0.17	0.75	0.07
B	0.10	0.72	0.15	0.65	0.08	0.76

C. *Predicted probability that priors and messages lead to correct vote with which they conflict.*

| p the correct vote is: | All Subjects | | Low Information | | High Information | |
	Prior=A Message=B	Prior=B Message=A	Prior=A Message=B	Prior=B Message=A	Prior=A Message=B	Prior=B Message=A
A	0.45	0.29	0.44	0.38	0.46	0.22
B	0.27	0.43	0.33	0.39	0.23	0.47

regress the "correct vote" for the subject on the message cue and the prior cue within the same three groups. In this context, a "correct vote" is defined as a vote for the candidate with a true position that lies closest to the subject's own position: −1=Candidate A is closer to the subject's own position; 0=the candidates are equally distant; and 1=Candidate B is closer. (This coding accounts for the fact that some subjects should be indifferent between candidates even though they are not allowed to abstain.) The logit models show that both the subject priors and the informant messages consistently point toward the correct vote, with positive coefficients that generate substantial t-values and discernible effects.

Based on these model estimates, Part B of Table 5.5 shows the predicted probabilities of voting correctly based on subject priors and informant messages, when the subject's prior and the informant's message are consistent in their implications. The lesson is that, when the message coincides with the prior, the subjects are highly likely to vote correctly. (Note that the column probabilities do not sum to 1 because indifference is excluded.) This is *especially* true among well-informed subjects, but both groups demonstrate high probabilities of correct voting when individuals vote on the basis of a prior and a message that coincide.

In contrast, Part C of Table 5.5 shows the predicted probabilities of voting correctly when the subject's prior and the informant's message point toward opposite candidates. In this situation the subjects are always more likely to vote correctly if they follow their own instincts. This is particularly true among the well-informed, but even the poorly informed do not improve the probability of voting correctly when they disregard their own prior. In these circumstances, the probability of voting correctly is greatly reduced as well. This is primarily due to the particular cases where priors are most likely to conflict with messages – situations where candidates converge and getting it right becomes a more formidable task.

Why does the prior generate more reliable guidance than the message in these instances? First, as we have seen, even a relatively meager amount of privately consumed information can go a long way toward improving the ability to vote correctly. Moreover, when messages are biased, they typically run contrary to the interests of the recipient. Finally, messages and priors are most likely to conflict in situations where the two candidates hold positions that converge. In these circumstances, even a relatively minor bias in the message can produce a message that conflicts with a subject's prior. In short, the downside risk of messages taken from informants with divergent preferences is greatest at the point where individuals face their most difficult political decisions.

The experiment is constructed to ensure that the prior is based on unbiased information, but in the real world this is unlikely to be the case. At the same time, an individual is more likely to control the bias of the information that she takes from the media and the political environment – that is, both the liberals who watch MSNBC and the conservatives who watch FOX are choosing biased information that presumably coincides with their own view of the world. The challenge arising from socially supplied messages is that they are likely to carry biases that the recipient may neither control nor embrace. That is, of course, both the problem and the virtue of social communication in politics.

In summary, the subjects who receive conflicting guidance from informant messages and their own priors typically lie within uncertain terrain. When the subject's prior provides the same guidance as the informant's message (N=415), either voting cue provides correct guidance 74 percent of the time. When the two provide divergent guidance (N=488), the prior provides correct guidance 42 percent of the time, and the message provides correct guidance 35 percent of the time.

TABLE 5.6. *Correct vote by subject and informant information levels and the distance between subject and informant. Logit model with standard errors corrected for clustering on subjects.*

	Coefficient	Z-Ratio
Subject info. level	0.277	3.31
Informant info. level	0.058	0.66
Subject/informant distance	−0.146	−2.23
Extreme subject	0.205	1.82
Period	0.013	0.66
Constant	0.477	0.99
N (subjects)	903 (70)	
χ^2, df, p	19.13, 5, 0.00	

In short, the subjects typically face a complex decision-making task when their own priors conflict with the messages they receive from others. Not surprisingly, such conflicts are more likely to arise when the distance separating the candidates is minimized, the distance between the candidates and the subject is minimized, and the subject's preference lies nearly equally distant between candidate positions.

In Table 5.6, we once again consider the correct vote, but in this instance it is estimated as a consequence of the information levels of the subject and the informant, the distance between the preferences of the subject and the informant, the extremity of the subject's preference, and the period during the experimental session in which the particular election took place.[15] While subject information levels enhance the likelihood of correct voting, informant information levels do not, and the likelihood of a correct vote declines as a function of the distance between informant and discussant preferences. Neither the extremity of the subject's preference nor the election period generate discernible effects, although subject extremity lies in a borderline range.

These effects, graphically demonstrated in Figure 5.2, lie at the core of the problem. They suggest that political communication is a political exercise, not an exercise in objectively defined civic virtue. That is, political communication is aimed at achieving political purposes, and those purposes are defined by the originator of the message. Hence, the information level of the informant is irrelevant to the likelihood that the recipient will vote correctly when correct voting is defined in terms of the recipient's own goals and preferences. Again, the informants' messages are not aimed at improving the quality of decision-making, but rather at convincing other individuals to vote in ways that further the informants' own goals.

[15] In this analysis, all subjects who are indifferent between candidates are coded as having made a correct vote regardless of their choice.

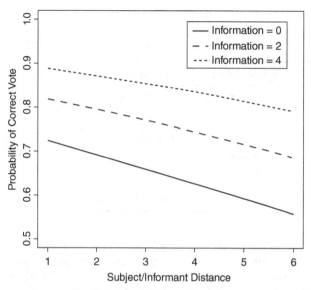

FIGURE 5.2. Predicted probability of a correct vote by subject information level and distance between subject and informant. Values calculated based on model in Table 5.6 with all other variables held constant at their means.

Several primary implications arise from these results. First, the subjects are not gullible. While they are willing to consider messages from experts with divergent preferences, the well-informed demonstrate their own defenses rooted in caution and skepticism. Second, the implications of the messages are not wildly at variance with the implications of the subjects' priors, particularly among the less-informed. The participants are both conveyers and recipients of information. Hence, informants should be aware of the concerns facing the recipients, and the recipients should be aware of the informant's temptation to send a self-serving message. Also, we see some indirect evidence to support the speculation that the communication process may be self-policing.

Finally, the practice of democracy occurs at its most basic level in the conversations among individuals who must consider how they will vote. In this context, it comes as no surprise that the message reflects the interests of the messenger. To expect otherwise is to ignore the reality of democratic politics as the interplay among individuals motivated by their own beliefs, passions, and interests (Madison, 1961).

THE EXPERIMENT AND THE REAL WORLD

Our experiment involves an abstract rendering of reality, and hence it is important to consider what the experiment fails to take into account. First, many real life citizens are, quite fortunately, not limited to a single informant, and hence they consider messages not only in the context of their own beliefs, but also in the context of other messages communicated by other informants. If you are well-informed and hold a strong belief, you may very well discount the message from a friend suggesting your belief is wrong. In contrast, if *all* your friends say you are wrong, you may be more likely to change your mind (Huckfeldt, Johnson, and Sprague 2004). In subsequent chapters, our experimental subjects will receive messages from multiple messengers – sometimes sending homogenous signals and sometimes sending heterogeneous signals.

Second, the value of socially mediated information is not simply as a source of persuasion and influence, but also as a stimulus to pay attention. Political communication networks are at least as important with respect to activation as they are with respect to influence, and the implications of activation are not simply about creating agreement within communication networks. Rather, political communication creates awareness and appreciation of divergent preferences, and hence collectively more sophisticated and reasoned judgments, regardless of whether influence occurs. In short, educated public opinion does not necessitate homogeneity, and this paper points toward the importance of information, knowledge, and expertise in this educational process.

A final problem relates to the real-world interpretation of fixed preferences. While the subjects in this experiment are not omniscient, they do have complete information regarding their own immutable preferences, as well as the immutable preferences of others. Such circumstances are atypical in the real world. Not only do citizens lack precise information regarding the true preferences of others, they often also lack information regarding their own preferences. Many preferences need to be informed and negotiated, and persuasion is more than simply passing along information. In a world marked by negotiable preferences and higher levels of ambiguity, the impact of messages from politically divergent sources is only likely to increase.

IMPLICATIONS AND CONCLUSIONS

Lower information costs translate into higher levels of information consumption. More information, in turn, translates into higher-quality decisions, but additional information demonstrates steadily decreasing value – that is, minimal amounts of information go a long way toward informing judgments. This is not to say that ignorance is instrumental or beneficial. Some information is necessary for the use of even the most basic cognitive shortcuts (see Kuklinski and Quirk 2000; Lau and Redlawsk 2006; Lupia and McCubbins 1998).

The value of minimal information may sometimes be underappreciated, not only in scholarly discussions, but also within the deliberations that occur among our subjects. Well-informed individuals may overestimate their own expertise, and individuals may overestimate the expertise among well-informed others. Given the bias attached to messages from politically divergent informants, potential recipients may be wise to consider the less biased messages sent by politically proximate informants, even when these messages are based on less information.

The important point is that even rational voters with well-defined goals face daunting challenges when they seek to become politically informed. In the face of steep information costs, it is sensible to rely on expert advice provided by politically like-minded associates. The problem is that the contextually available experts are not always like-minded, and the like-minded are not always expert, creating the potential for communication to transmit both bias and error.

When confronted with a contextually induced tradeoff between expert informants with divergent preferences and poorly informed informants with convergent preferences, our subjects regularly choose in favor of expertise, but they also demonstrate heuristic defenses with respect to misinformation. The well-informed are less likely to trust messages that diverge from their own judgments, as well as being less likely to trust messages that come from people with divergent preferences. As a consequence, these heuristics make it less likely that novel, well-informed viewpoints will penetrate strongly held pre-existent beliefs, thus generating a conservative bias within the communication process.

Is the electorate self-educating? Our preliminary answer is yes, with some important caveats. In combination with Chapter 3, this chapter suggests that the well-informed play a singularly important role in the communication process, but communication is not persuasion, and well-informed individuals resist messages that do not conform to their own judgments (Lodge and Taber 2000). In contrast, the less-informed are more amenable to influence, and hence they are also more vulnerable to informants who do not share their underlying preferences. Thus, while communication may be dominated by those who are well informed, their influence is often limited by the views and underlying preferences of information recipients. In this way, the tension between autonomy and influence sustains the vitality of political discussion and disagreement, even as it places political boundaries on the potential for a self-educating electorate (Jackman and Sniderman 2006).

None of this means that social communication is without political consequence, but rather that the consequences extend beyond persuasion and the creation of unanimity. Some individuals are located in homogeneous contexts where there is no forced tradeoff between expertise and shared preferences in the search for informants. Others are located in heterogeneous contexts where they are likely to form heterogeneous communication networks. In short, while individuals demonstrate significant levels of skepticism regarding divergent messages and divergent messengers, they are also willing to consider heterogeneous signals, and this willingness lies at the heart of democratic politics.

The next chapter explores the individual and aggregate consequences of the tradeoff between expertise and shared preferences in greater detail. In an experiment that builds on the analysis of this chapter, 14 subjects are divided into two groups. The distribution of information costs and preferences within the two groups is experimentally manipulated, and hence the individual's search for expert informants with shared preferences is contextually constrained. Based on this design, we address the contextual constraints operating on the formation of networks as well as the mobilization of bias through social communication.

CHAPTER 5 APPENDIX

I. DESCRIPTION OF SUBJECTS

Subjects were recruited from political science classes at the University of California, Davis. They were offered a $5.00 show-up fee and the opportunity to earn additional income depending on their success in the experiment. (Their actual earnings varied between $7.75 and $25.50.) In addition, some of their professors offered bonus points in their courses for participation.

The population of students at the university is relatively more liberal, more Democratic, and more ethnically diverse than the larger U.S. population, and these population characteristics are reflected in our subjects. (See Table A5.1.)

TABLE A5.1. *Subject demographics and political orientations.*

Age		Race		Gender	
18	24%	Asian	44%	Female	55%
19	38	White	35	Male	45
20	18	Hispanic	11		
21	12	Black	1		
22	6	Other	9		
23	1				
24	1				
27	1				
N=	119		119		119

Self-identified partisanship		Self-identified ideology	
Strong Democrat	13%	Extreme Liberal	8%
Not Strong Democrat	18	Liberal	20
Independent-leaning Democrat	24	Slightly Liberal	15
Independent	13	Moderate	28
Independent-leaning Republican	16	Slightly Conservative	10
Not Strong Republican	10	Conservative	14
Strong Republican	6	Extreme Conservative	1
		Haven't thought about it	3
N=	119		119

The particular political leanings of our subjects are irrelevant to the experiment because we have defined an abstract preference space that is not anchored in contemporary political issues. Moreover, we have no reason to believe that these college students are more or less trusting, cooperative, or self-seeking than the population at large. Perhaps their most distinctive characteristic is that they tend to be very bright and quick learners. While that makes the research easier to conduct, we have no reason to believe that it compromises the results.

2. EVIDENCE REGARDING STRATEGY EVOLUTION DURING THE EXPERIMENT

The subjects typically participated in 15 independent rounds during the experiment. While the experiment was not designed to foster a learning process, it is still conceivable that strategies evolved during the experiment. An analysis of the primary information and communication behaviors does not show any evolution, however. We consider several criteria: the amount of information purchased by subjects, the distance between subjects and their selected informants, the amount of information purchased by those selected as informants, and the levels of bias in the messages sent regarding each of the candidates. In Table A5.2, the means for each of these behaviors within a round (and for each session) are regressed on the number of the round (1 through 15) for all 17 sessions. This means that we are clustered by sessions, and hence we include a clustering correction.

Table A5.2 shows, at most, only modest effects. Only two of the t-values lie in the range of demonstrating discernible effects – the amount of information purchased and, correspondingly, the amount of information purchased by informants. In both instances, there is a very modest decline in the amount of information purchased that totals over 15 rounds. None of the other behaviors demonstrate any effect whatsoever.

TABLE A5.2. *Mean behaviors within a round regressed on the sequence number for the round, for all rounds and sessions. Each row in this table provides the slope coefficient, its t-value, and the predicted 15 round effect. Least squares models. N=251, corrected for clustering on 17 sessions.*

	Coefficient	t-value	15 round effect
Information purchased by subjects	−.016	1.95	−.234
Distance between subject and informant	.002	.31	.035
Information purchased by informants	−.02	1.82	.294
Bias in message regarding Candidate A	−.008	.51	−.124
Bias in message regarding Candidate B	.007	.44	.09

3. INSTRUCTIONS TO PARTICIPANTS

The following instructions were read to all subjects before the experiment began. These instructions reference screens that can be viewed at johnbarryryan.com.

Thank you for participating in today's experiment. I will be reading from a script to ensure that every session of this experiment receives the same instructions. At your computer, you should find this entire script as well as a single page that summarizes the experimental session. These instructions explain the nature of today's experiment as well as how to navigate the computer interface you will be working with. We ask that you please refrain from talking or looking at the monitors of other participants during the experiment. If you still have a question or problem, please raise your hand and one of us will come to you.

In today's experiment, all monetary amounts, earnings and costs are denominated in Experiment Currency Units or ECUs. At the end of the experiment, your earnings in ECUs will be translated into dollars at the rate of 1 ECU equals 1 cent. So, if you end with a balance of 1,500 ECUs, you would be paid $15 plus the $5 show up fee for a total of $20. We will pay you in cash at the end of the experiment.

Today's experiment consists of 16 time periods. Each period consists of a contest between two candidates. At the beginning of each period, you will be assigned a position from 1 to 7 which is the same as your participant number and you will be given an endowment of 100 ECUs. Your goal is to elect the candidate whose position is closer to your own. To accomplish this goal, you will both buy private information and ask other participants for information. Information will cost 25 ECUs, 5 ECUs or the information will be free. The cost of information is randomly assigned. If information costs you 25 ECUs, you can buy up to two pieces of information. Otherwise you can obtain up to 4 pieces of information.

At the end of each period, ECUs will be awarded based on the outcome of the election. If the candidate closer to you wins the election, you will earn 50 ECUs. If the candidate closer to you loses the election, you will lose 50 ECUs. If both candidates were equally appealing to you, you are awarded no ECUs and you have no ECUs deducted from your total.

Please turn to your computer screens. We have prepared several demonstration screens to help you get familiar with the actual screens you will see during the experiment.

(SCREEN ONE) This is the first screen you will see in each period. The top of each screen will display your position, the period, and the time remaining in each period. We suggest that you make your decisions for a screen within the time limit You should be careful in making your choices, but it is in your own best interest to make your choices as quickly as you are able.

As you can see, there are two candidates, A and B. Candidate A's position is equally likely to be any whole number between 1 and 6, and Candidate B's position is equally likely to be any whole number between 2 and 7. This screen also tells you how much information about the candidates will cost you. Enter the amount of information that you wish to buy and click OK.

(SCREEN TWO) This is the next screen you will see. Regardless of how much information you bought on the previous screen, this screen displays what it would look like if you had bought three pieces of information. Each piece of information is an independently drawn signal about the candidate's positions. On average these signals accurately represent the candidates' true positions, but any single piece of information may not. The table on the handout shows the possible signals that you will receive for all the different positions the candidates can hold. The signal for any candidate lies within three points on either side of the candidate's true position and you are equally likely to receive any of the seven possible signals within the interval. This means that even though the candidates' positions are between 1 and 7, the signals can fall out of those bounds. For example, if the candidate's position is a 1, you are equally likely to receive any signal that lies between −2 and 4.

Based on the signals you see, you are asked to estimate the candidates' positions. Enter estimates for the two candidates and click OK.

(SCREEN THREE) You also have the opportunity to obtain information from other participants. This screen displays a table of all of the participants; it provides you with their positions and the amount of information they bought. With this knowledge you may request information from one of the other participants. Enter the subject number from whom you want information and then press OK.

(SCREEN FOUR) If none of the other participants ask you for information, you must click OK to move on. If other participants do ask you for information, you will see a screen that looks like this. At this point, you have the opportunity to accept or reject the request for information. You are not penalized or rewarded for accepting requests and you are not penalized or rewarded for rejecting requests. Click the circle that says yes if you want to provide that participant with information and click the circle that says no if you want to reject the request for information. After you have done this for all of the participants who requested information, click OK.

(SCREEN FIVE) This is where you enter the information that you are going to provide to the other participants. You are reminded of the signals you received from the candidates. You do not need to provide identical information to each of the participants who requested information from you. Enter the candidate information that you want to provide, and then click OK.

(SCREEN SIX) On this screen, the election will take place. You are reminded of your position and the signals you received from the candidates. If another participant agreed to provide you with information, then you will see that information as well. Based on this information and the knowledge that Candidate A's position is between 1 and 6 and Candidate B's position is between 2 and 7, your goal is to figure out the candidates' positions and vote for the candidate closer to your position. There are examples on the handout. If your

position is 5 and you believe Candidate A's position is 6 and Candidate B's position is 3, then you should vote for Candidate A because 5 is closer to 6 than 3. If your position is 5 and you believe Candidate A's position is 1 and Candidate B's position is 3, you should vote for Candidate B because 5 is closer to 3 than 1. Please vote for one of the candidate's and then click OK.

(SCREEN SEVEN) This is the final screen. The two candidates' positions are revealed as is the outcome of the election. You will also learn for which candidate you should have voted, as well as the number of ECUs you earned in this period. That is calculated by starting with your 100 ECU endowment. From that the cost of the information you purchased is subtracted. If the candidate closer to your position won the election, you earn an additional 50 ECUs. If the candidate closer to your position lost, you lose 50 ECUs. If both candidates were equally close to your own position, you earn no ECUs but do not lose any either. The most ECUs you can earn in a single period is 150 ECUs, the fewest ECUs you can earn in a single period is zero. Beneath your earnings for this period, you will see the total number of ECUs earned up to this point in the experiment.

The experiment will consist of 16 periods just like this one – the first period will be a practice period and will not count to your experimental pay. At the end of the experiment, you will be asked for some demographic information and then a couple of questions about your general political leanings.

This concludes the demonstration screens. We are now ready to begin the actual experiment. We ask that you follow the rules of the experiment. Anyone who violates the rules may be asked to leave the experiment with only the $5 show up fee. Are there any questions before we start?

6

Expertise and bias in political communication networks

T. K. Ahn, Robert Huckfeldt, Alex Mayer, and John Barry Ryan

> All forms of political organization have a bias in favor of the exploitation of some kinds of conflict and the suppression of others because *organization is the mobilization of bias*. Some issues are organized into politics, while others are organized out.
>
> E. E. Schattschneider (1960: 71)

As we have seen, a primary obstacle to political participation lies in the individual costs of acquiring and processing political information. One way for citizens to minimize these costs is to obtain political information from other well-informed individuals, thereby giving rise to networks of political communication. These networks, in turn, produce their own complex and often unforeseen consequences, creating politically distinctive and consequential patterns of interdependence among citizens who communicate about politics. As a consequence, central issues in the analysis of political communication relate to the criteria for locating reliable sources of guidance, as well as the consequences of the resulting networks for the diffusion of information, patterns of influence, the organization of the electorate, and hence the creation and mobilization of political bias (Schattschneider 1960).

Ideal informants are typically characterized by the joint presence of political expertise and shared preferences (Crawford and Sobel 1982; Downs 1957; Lupia and McCubbins 1998), but the supply of these individuals quite often varies across groups and settings (Miller 1956; Mutz and Mondak 2006). Moreover, looking for informants beyond an individual's own setting adds to information costs, thereby negating the efficiencies of social communication. Readily available informants – those located in the same families, churches, workplaces, and so on – provide the least costly sources of socially supplied information.

The problem is that many people find themselves in situations where their own political predispositions and needs for information are at variance with their local surroundings. The liberal Democrat raised in a conservative religious group may not locate politically compatible views at church social functions, and the political activist who is a committed bridge player may find the level of political expertise within his bridge group to be disappointing. In these and similar ways, individuals are often located within groups and settings unlikely to support the creation of communication networks that are both politically reliable and informative.

This chapter builds on Chapter 5 to evaluate the consequences of contextual variation for the construction of communication networks. While people prefer to obtain political information from well-informed associates who share their own preferences, to what extent should we expect strategic individuals to invest resources in the creation of political networks reflecting these preferences? What are the resulting implications for the centrality of participants within communication networks, levels of political polarization between groups, the diffusion of expertise, and patterns of bias in communication?

The analysis is based on small group experiments involving two groups of seven participants who communicate with one another via networked computers. The experiments extend the experimental design of Chapter 5 with the purpose of taking into account variations in the contextual constraints operating on network formation. In a context of uncertainty regarding the positions of candidates, participants are rewarded with a cash incentive if the candidate closest to them wins the election. As before, participants may use three sources of information: free public information, private information with costs that vary across individuals, and information provided by other participants that also varies in cost.

EXPERTS, BIAS, AND OPINION LEADERS

The earliest empirical studies of individual voting behavior, conducted by Lazarsfeld and his Columbia University colleagues (Lazarsfeld et al. 1968; Berelson et al. 1954), revealed the importance of political communication among citizens. This led, in turn, to a focus on complex communication processes in which opinion leaders play a critical role, mediating both the flow and interpretation of information, and creating opinion homogeneity within primary social groupings (Katz 1957; Katz and Lazarsfeld 1955). These opinion leaders are not generalists – those influential in politics may not be similarly influential in fashion or finance. To the contrary, the influence of opinion leaders lies in their own areas of interest and expertise. Thus, in view of the many individuals who were poorly informed in the 1948 election, Berelson et al. (1954) argue that interdependence enhances the civic capacity of democratic electorates.

Downs (1957: chapter 12) revisits the results of these early voting studies with a primary focus on the *consumers* of information, arguing that the utility of socially communicated information lies in its potential to minimize recipients' information costs. Rather than collecting and analyzing political information on their own, individuals might rely on information provided by well-informed associates. Because recipients run the risk of being misled or misinformed by biased information from informants holding divergent preferences, Downs stresses the importance of selecting expert informants with politically compatible viewpoints.

This potential for individuals to be misled has led to a burgeoning literature on the difficulties inherent when both the senders and the receivers of political signals are motivated by their own goals (Austen-Smith 1990; Austen-Smith and Feddersen 2009; Crawford and Sobel 1982; Lupia and McCubbins 1998; Boudreau 2009). In particular, the potential arises for "cheap talk" – situations in which individuals are free to send misleading signals without any penalty, and hence the sender is unable to assure the receiver that the message being sent is valid (Crawford 1998). Indeed, in the absence of an institutional mechanism assuring the receiver that the sender's message can be trusted (Boudreau 2009), the potential for social communication to enhance collective outcomes is rendered problematic, and a "babbling equilibrium" (Lewis 1969) is generated in which no useful information is transmitted. As Crawford (1998) points out, however, not all talk is cheap talk. As the preferences of the sender and the receiver come into closer alignment, the incentive to mislead is increasingly diminished.

Hence, both the literature on opinion leadership and the literature on strategic communication point toward the political homogenization of social communication. The Columbia school suggests that the power of social influence produces homogeneity within primary groupings, while the political economy tradition points toward the difficulty of sending credible messages when preferences are heterogeneous. Moreover, literatures in social and political cognition point toward the personal discomfort that arises due to politically heterogeneous communication (Festinger 1957; Mutz 2006), with the potential to create self-selected patterns of association, conflict avoidance, self-censored political communication, and systematic biases in the recognition of politically divergent messages (Huckfeldt and Sprague 1995). The combined view thus portrays a world in which opinion heterogeneity within communication networks is personally disagreeable, potentially misleading, reduced due to the efforts of opinion leaders, and hence quite rare.[1]

THE COSTS OF COMMUNICATION

An implicit assumption underlying these conclusions is that social communication is free, with readily substitutable communication alternatives. That is, if you are a religiously conservative, politically liberal, pro-Keynesian voter, you should be able to locate, at little or no cost, a fellow traveler with similar

---

[1] A cheap talk analysis implies that listeners might simply ignore messages from politically divergent sources, but a boundedly rational listener may take them into account (Crawford 2003), and a strategic voter may use these signals as confirmatory evidence (Calvert 1985a).

preferences and beliefs from whom to extract useful political information and guidance. The problem with this view is that social communication is unlikely to be free if individuals wish to exercise strict control over the people who are included within their communication networks (Huckfeldt and Sprague 1995).

Observational studies confirm both that patterns of association tend to be clustered by shared preferences (Berelson et al. 1954) and that discussion is more likely to occur with associates judged to be politically expert (Mendez and Osborn 2010).[2] While seeming to support the capacity of individuals to control their own patterns of political communication, these studies also raise questions regarding the practical limits on the search for the perfect informant. First, the construction of communication networks is a two-way street, and it is less than obvious whether recipients select informants or informants select recipients. The individuals most likely to engage in political communication are those who are interested and informed – individuals who enjoy politics (Fiorina 1990). Hence, opinion leaders may be the instigators, and recipients may not be able to avoid the messages that they send (Huckfeldt and Mendez 2008).

Second, the path of least resistance is to select an informant readily at hand. From a collective action standpoint, the costs of an extended search for like-minded associates are likely to swamp the expected benefits, once these benefits are down-weighted by the minuscule probability that improved information will be politically decisive in achieving a desired outcome. Equally important, politics is not the only criterion of choice in selecting associates, and thus relatively few individuals are likely to structure their associational lives around the optimization of political communication. Likewise, individuals often reside in multiple environments – home, sports club, place of worship, workplace – making it even more difficult to control the political mix of the people with whom they come into regular contact (Mutz and Mondak 2006).

Finally, not only are distributions of preferences and expertise likely to vary across groups, but they are likely to be imperfectly correlated. Hence, an individual might find herself in a group that is full of political experts but lacking in like-minded individuals, or among fellow travelers lacking even a shred of useful political knowledge. In this general context, some individuals seem particularly fortunate in being surrounded by expert individuals with compatible preferences, but this scenario produces its own problems. An expert surrounded by other experts may make a redundant contribution to the political sophistication of the group. That is, informants may be easily replaceable within environments where (1) their particular preferences dominate and (2) collective levels of expertise are quite high. Hence, the environmental constraints surrounding the choice of political informants carry implications for the centrality of even highly expert informants within communication networks.

---

[2] Efforts show that perceptions of expertise are little affected by disagreement but are subject to perceptual biases based on cultural traits such as gender (Mendez and Osborn 2010).

In short, while individuals reduce their information costs by relying on politically expert associates with shared political preferences, the proximate supply of these informants is finite. Thus individuals face a series of implicit choices and tradeoffs – whether it makes sense to pay the costs of looking beyond their own groups to find ideal informants, the relative virtues of expert informants versus fellow travelers, and more. Indeed, communication networks are created at the intersection between associational preferences and the supply of potential informants. These intersections, in turn, affect the dissemination of information, the creation of consensus and polarization among groups, and the political bias introduced through communication. These issues, in turn, pose a series of important observational challenges.

THE EXPERIMENTAL FRAMEWORK

The analysis is based on an experimental framework similar to the one presented in Chapter 5, but with modifications designed to address the issues identified above. In the words of Vernon Smith (1982), our goal is not to construct a "nomothetic" experiment aimed at establishing laws of behavior, but rather a "heuristic or exploratory" experiment aimed at incorporating several theoretical traditions within the same analysis. Such an analysis would be impossible without an experiment, and even an experimental analysis makes it difficult to address all the issues identified. For example, our design creates a counterfactual world in which the formation of communication networks responds only to the choices of those motivated to receive messages, not to those who are motivated to send them.[3]

The revised design includes several important features. First, all individuals have an incentive to vote correctly, and information is central to their capacity to do so. Second, private information costs are experimentally manipulated. Some individuals have high costs and strong disincentives to invest, while others can invest at little or no cost. Third, free communication with other participants is restricted to the members of a participant's own immediate group, and communication beyond the group is costly. Fourth, the distributions of expertise and preference are experimentally manipulated within groups and across experimental sessions to assess the consequences of environmental constraints on network formation and communication.

Our experimental framework is designed to combine the advantages of small group dynamics with network representations of communication in the context of an experimental design. The experimental setting is based on a mock election with two "candidates" who are not real human subjects, but are represented as positions on a one-dimensional policy space. The preference space varies from 1 to 7, where each participant has an integer position that remains constant

---

[3] This is, in fact, a conservative counterfactual. Targeting by opinion leaders serves to *increase* the heterogeneity of communication (Huckfeldt and Mendez 2008).

across the rounds in an experimental session. In contrast, the candidate positions are represented on the same scale, but they are reset at each round.

The participant's goal is to elect the "candidate" most closely matching her own position on the same dimension, and she is rewarded with a cash incentive if the candidate closest to her wins the election at that round. The exact positions of the candidates are not known to the voters, thereby creating an incentive to obtain information. Obtaining information incurs costs, and these costs are varied randomly across participants. In order to minimize costs, participants have an opportunity to obtain information from other participants, and to employ public information that is free. Because both costs and preferences are applied randomly within groups, they are orthogonal to one another.

While individual preferences and information costs are randomly assigned within groups, the distributions of preferences and information costs across groups are manipulated experimentally. We conducted a total of 12 sessions, three in each of the four experimental conditions or *contexts*. Fourteen subjects participated in each of the 12 sessions.[4] All sessions were identical in terms of the aggregate distribution of preferences (or ideal points) and information costs among the 14 voters. Two subjects were assigned to each of the integer points from 1 to 7, such that there were two subjects with ideal point 1, two subjects with ideal point 2, and so on. In terms of information costs, each session had four low-cost voters who paid zero for information, four medium-cost voters who paid 5 ECUs for a piece of information, and six high-cost voters who paid 25 ECUs for each piece of information.

The four contexts differ in terms of how the preferences and information costs are distributed between two groups of seven subjects. In sessions where information costs are identical between the groups, two subjects pay nothing for information, two subjects pay 5 ECUs, and three subjects pay 25 ECUs within each group. When costs are distributed asymmetrically, one subject pays 5 ECUs for each piece of information in the high-cost group, and six subjects pay 25 ECUs. In the low-cost group, four subjects pay nothing and three subjects pay 5 ECUs.

In sessions where preferences are distributed identically within groups, one subject in each group holds each of the positions from 1 through 7. When preferences are distributed asymmetrically, two subjects in the first (or right-leaning) group are at position 7, 2 at position 6, 2 at position 5, and 1 at position 4. In the second (or left-leaning) group, 2 subjects are at position 1, 2 at position 2, 2 at position 3, and 1 at position 4.

---

[4] The experiments were run at UC Davis, and the subjects were paid student volunteers. The experiment was programmed using z-Tree (Fischbacher 2007). Each session lasted approximately one hour. Subjects were paid a $5.00 show-up fee plus additional earnings denoted in Experimental Currency Units (ECUs) during the experiment and converted to real dollars at an exchange rate of 100 ECUs = $1.00. The average earning was $14.40 including the show-up fee. 90% of the earnings fell in the range of $11.00 to $17.00.

TABLE 6.1. *Experimental design.*

| | | Distribution of preferences between groups 1 and 2 | |
		Asymmetric	Symmetric
Distribution of information costs between groups 1 and 2	Asymmetric	Context 1: AI-AP Group 1: (4,5,5,6,6,7,7) (*m, h, h h h h h*) Group 2: (1,1,2,2,3,3,4) (*l,l,l,l,m,m,m*)	Context 3: AI-SP Group 1: (1,2,3,4,5,6,7) (*m, h, h h h h h*) Group 2: (1,2,3,4,5,6,7) (*l,l,l,l,m,m,m*)
	Symmetric	Context 2: SI-AP Group 1: (4,5,5,6,6,7,7) (*l,l,m,m,h,h,h*) Group 2: (1,1,2,2,3,3,4) (*l,l,m,m,h,h,h*)	Context 4: SI-SP Group 1: (1,2,3,4,5,6,7) (*l,l,m,m,h,h,h*) Group 2: (1,2,3,4,5,6,7) (*l,l,m,m,h,h,h*)

Note: In the acronyms associated with the contexts, A refers to asymmetrical, S: symmetrical, I: information, and P: preference. For each group, the set of numbers show the ideal points distribution in the group and the set of symbols show the information cost distribution, where *l* means low, *m*: medium, and *h*: high.

Three experimental sessions are assigned to each of four distributional contexts. In the *first context*, information costs and preferences are distributed asymmetrically. The first group has right-leaning preferences and high information costs. The second group has left-leaning preferences and low information costs. In the *second context*, information costs are distributed identically within groups, but preferences are distributed asymmetrically. The first group has right-leaning preferences, and the second has left-leaning preferences. In the *third context*, preferences are distributed identically within the groups, but information costs are distributed asymmetrically. The first group has high information costs, and the second has low information costs. In the *fourth baseline context*, costs and preferences are symmetrical between groups.

Table 6.1 summarizes the distribution of preferences and information costs within and between groups. Note that within the context of each group, the distribution of preferences and information costs are random and independent of each other. Participants were identified by unique numbers ranging from 1 to 14. These numbers were confidential, thus maintaining anonymity. All interactions were made via networked computers based on the experimental procedures, and no other communications were allowed among the subjects during the experiment.

THE EXPERIMENTAL PROCEDURE

The experiment begins in the same manner as the experiment in Chapter 5. Before the experiment begins, participants are randomly assigned integer preferences, information costs, and group memberships that remain unchanged for the duration of the experiment. Additionally, all participants are informed that Candidate A's position is between 1 and 6, while Candidate B's position is between 2 and 7. Then, in each of the approximately 15 rounds per session, the following steps occur:

1. Participants receive 100 ECUs, of which 50 ECUs can be spent on information.
2. The two candidates' positions are drawn from the respective intervals.
3. Participants may purchase information at their assigned cost. A single "piece" of information arrives in the form (a, b) where a and b are integer estimates of the candidate positions. With α and β as true positions, the signals a and b are randomly and independently drawn from uniform intervals $[\alpha-3, \alpha+3]$ and $[\beta-3, \beta+3]$. Participants are informed how signals are drawn, reflecting on average the true candidate positions. (Participants are not told that a signal of -2 or 9 for Candidate A and -1 or 10 for Candidate B is thus definitive.)
4. After the subjects receive the information, they are asked to provide a prior judgment regarding each candidate's position. They are truthfully told that their judgments will not be communicated to other participants.
5. After being shown all other participants' preferences, group memberships, and information purchases, each participant is provided an opportunity to request information from two others. If an informant belongs to their own group, the information is free. If the informant belongs to the opposite group, the participant pays 10 ECUs. Potential informants are not required to comply with the request, and they are told that they need not provide the same information to all requestors. Participants almost always agree to provide information, consisting of a single message with their estimates regarding each candidate's position.
6. After communication is completed, participants are provided with a summary of all the information they have received, and they vote for one of the candidates.
7. The outcome of the election is revealed to the voters. If the winning candidate's position is closer to a voter than the losing candidate's position, the voter earns 50 extra ECUs. If the winning candidate's position is farther away from the voter's position than the losing candidate's position, 50 ECUs are subtracted from the voter's account. If candidates are equally distant from the voter or if the election ends in a tie, the voter neither gains nor loses. Thus, whether participants gain or lose ECUs is only indirectly related to the quality of their own judgments – they can, for example, fail to vote for the candidate closest to them and still benefit if that candidate wins. A voter could thus earn as much as 150 ECUs in a round, but only if they did not purchase any information. The minimum

payoff is 0 ECUs – when a voter spends 50 ECUs on purchasing information and her candidate loses the election.

8. Participants are informed of their net earnings within the round as well as
their accumulated earnings across rounds.

9. Candidate positions are reset, and participants proceed to the next round.
At the end of the experiment, subjects are paid the show-up fee plus their
total earnings in cash (100 ECUs = $1.00).

Thus, the voters have three potential sources of information on which to base
their votes. First, the public information that the two candidates' positions are
drawn from different intervals could potentially help a voter in the absence of
other forms of information, and this information should be particularly helpful
to voters with more extreme positions. Second, voters are allowed to purchase
unbiased but noisy information on candidates' true positions. Third, each participant has an opportunity to request information from two other participants –
information that is noisy and potentially biased. They not only depend on the
reliability of information that serves as the basis for *the informants'* judgments,
but also on the ability and willingness of the informant to compile and provide
the information in an unbiased manner.

Do participants understand the experiment? We pre-tested the experiment to
make experimental procedures comprehensible, and before every session we
provided instructions followed by a practice period (see the appendix). Finally,
we carefully monitored the experiment, and it became clear that the participants
understood the experimental procedure.

The proximate consequences of the experimental manipulations meet our
expectations. First, participants with higher costs obtain less private information: 12 percent of the low- (or no-) cost individuals make fewer than two
information purchases, compared to 28 percent of the medium-cost individuals,
and 70 percent of the high-cost individuals.

Second, out-group information costs constitute a formidable barrier to communication. Participants received, on average, 1.88 information requests per
round: 1.49 requests from their own group and .39 requests from the opposite
group.

Third, Part A of Table 6.2 shows that participants' prior judgments are more
likely to reflect the candidates' true positions accurately when they are based on
more information. Hence, expertise is defined in terms of political skills and
knowledge that are enhanced by information. Expertise is measured in terms of
the consumption of information – the socially visible indicator available to other
subjects for use in evaluating the expertise of potential informants.

Finally, as Parts B and C of Table 6.2 show, informants are more likely to
communicate biased information when their preferences diverge from the preferences of the recipient – the strength of the relationship between the informant's
message and the informant's prior is less likely to be compromised when the
informant and the recipient share preferences.

TABLE 6.2. *Expertise, priors, and biased messages.*
A. *Prior judgments regarding candidates' positions by information purchased, candidates' true positions, and their interaction. Standard errors are adjusted for clustering on subject.*

	Candidate A		Candidate B	
	Coef.	T-Value	Coef.	T-Value
Amount of information subject purchased	−0.47	−7.41	−0.94	−12.03
Candidate's true position	0.25	5.82	0.20	5.17
Amount of Information * true position	0.16	11.15	0.18	13.16
Constant	2.45	13.08	3.98	17.97
N =	1,736		1,736	
R^2, s.e. of estimate =	.36, 1.43		.35, 1.42	

B. *Informant messages by prior judgments and distance between dyad members. OLS with standard errors adjusted for clustering on subject.*

	Coefficient	T-value
Initial estimate	0.92	31.62
Distance between dyad members	0.54	8.31
Estimate * distance	−0.14	−8.40
Constant	0.28	2.42
N	5,328	
R^2, M.S.E.	.44, 1.44	

C. *Predicted informant messages based on estimates in Part B.*

Distance between dyad members	Informant's initial estimate of candidate's position						
	1	2	3	4	5	6	7
0	1.20	2.12	3.05	3.97	4.89	5.82	6.74
1	1.60	2.39	3.18	3.96	4.75	5.54	6.33
2	2.01	2.66	3.31	3.96	4.61	5.26	5.91
3	2.41	2.92	3.44	3.95	4.47	4.98	5.50
4	2.81	3.19	3.57	3.95	4.32	4.70	5.08
5	3.22	3.46	3.70	3.94	4.18	4.42	4.67
6	3.62	3.73	3.83	3.94	4.04	4.15	4.25

These first-order consequences set the stage for a recurrent tradeoff that confronts subjects as they select informants. An expert informant's true assessment more accurately reflects the candidates' actual positions, but when the positions of the subject and the informant diverge, informants are more likely to send biased messages. Hence, in the tradeoff between expert informants and informants with shared preferences, subjects expose themselves to biased information if they choose in favor of expertise. This tradeoff is once again central to our argument, with important consequences for both the flow of information and the mobilization of bias.

CONTEXTUAL CONTINGENCIES OPERATING ON POLITICAL CENTRALITY

What makes experts influential? Some arguments are influential because they are inherently compelling, based on sound logic and judgment. Others are influential because they are confirmatory and supportive, reinforcing viewpoints an individual has encountered in the past. The former model portrays a communication process that addresses the details and nuances of complex issues, but abundant evidence suggests that few are equipped to participate in such a process (Delli Carpini and Keeter 1996). Moreover, discussion with experts is not a substitute for individual expertise (Jackman and Sniderman 2006), and individuals may be skeptical, even of information taken from highly credible sources (Taber and Lodge 2006).

As a consequence, influence has less to do with the intrinsic qualities of the message or the messenger, and more to do with patterns of support for the message (Huckfeldt, Johnson, and Sprague 2004). In this context, individuals are more likely to be influential to the extent that (1) they discuss politics frequently, thereby filling the conversational air waves with messages supporting their favored positions, (2) they are positioned within networks to guarantee maximal exposure of their views to others, and (3) the messages they send are confirmed by other messages obtained by a recipient. Hence, the role of the opinion leader is seen relative to the centrality of their location within political communication networks.

In the analyses that follow, a subject's centrality is defined both in terms of the frequency with which other participants select them as informants, as well as their own distance from other participants relative to the established communication links in the network. As we will see, the achievement of centrality is not simply due to an individual informant's level of expertise – it also depends on the distribution of expertise among others within the relevant context.

WHO RECEIVES THE MOST REQUESTS FOR INFORMATION?

What are the characteristics and locations of the individuals who receive the most requests for information? In the language of social networks, this points to a measure of "degree centrality" – individuals are more central to their own groups and to the opposite groups when they receive more requests from the in-group and out-group respectively (Freeman 1979). Part A of Table 6.3

TABLE 6.3. *Centrality and expertise.*
A. *Information requests received by subjects from in-groups and out-groups, by group and individual characteristics. T-values in parentheses.*

	In-group requests	Out-group requests
Amount of information subject purchased	0.09 (0.98)	.05 (0.66)
Information subject purchased minus mean information purchased in group	0.62 (6.56)	0.08 (1.36)
Mean information cost in group	0.01 (1.38)	-0.02 (-3.84)
Absolute difference between subject's preference and mean preference in group	0.01 (0.27)	-0.04 (-2.24)
Constant	1.13 (3.77)	0.70 (3.42)
N	1736	1736
Subjects	168	168
R^2	.42	.09
SE of estimate	1.04	.60

B. *Logged betweenness by group and individual information costs, with controls for information purchased and extremity of preference.*

	Coefficient	T-Value
Low-cost subject	1.183	3.86
Medium-cost subject	0.769	2.51
Extreme preference	-0.109	-0.88
Asymmetric cost	0.712	2.6
Asymmetric preference	-0.185	-0.53
Low cost* asymmetric cost	-1.189	-2.72
Medium cost* asymmetric cost	-0.677	-1.56
Extreme* asymmetric preference	0.060	0.34
Constant	1.139	3.77
N		168
Subjects		168
R^2		0.10
S.E. of estimate		1.16

C. *Predicted betweenness*

	Information cost		
	0	5	25
Asymmetric cost	5.035	5.556	5.066
Symmetric cost	8.118	5.364	2.486

Note: The 84 subjects in low- and high-cost groups participated in sessions where the information costs were asymmetrically distributed between the groups. The 84 subjects in medium-cost groups attended sessions where the information costs were symmetrically distributed between the groups.

regresses out-group and in-group requests for information received by an individual on several explanatory variables – the amount of information purchased by the subject, the difference between the amount of information purchased by the subject and the mean amount purchased by the relevant group, the mean information cost in the group, and the absolute difference between individual preference and the mean preference in the group.

Several factors stand out as being particularly important. First, centrality within a participant's own group (the "in-group") is enhanced by the individual's information purchases relative to the mean level of purchases in the group. An abundance of experts creates a situation in which even relatively expert informants are less likely to become particularly central.

Second, out-group centrality is diminished by the mean information cost in the out-group. Not only is it more difficult for the high-cost individuals in these out-groups to obtain information on their own, but they also have fewer remaining resources to obtain information from another group. Hence, they realize the double penalty of both individual and group-based incapacities.

Finally, shared preferences do not appear to produce more in-group requests – the absolute difference between the subject's preference and the mean preference within the in-group produces a coefficient with a small t-value. Subjects do, however, receive somewhat more requests from the out-group if their preference lies closer to the mean preference in the out-group.

NON-DIRECTIONAL CENTRALITY

An alternative conception of centrality is based on social proximity to the entire network, without regard to whether an individual is requesting or receiving information. Individuals score higher on a "betweenness" measure to the extent that they lie along more of the shortest routes (the geodesic paths) connecting other pairs of subjects. Hence, these individuals are central because they are more likely to be located on the connecting paths along which information is communicated most efficiently (Freeman 1979).

In the analysis of Part B of Table 6.3, all rounds for a particular subject in a particular session are combined in a single observation, and hence we undertake the analysis in terms of information costs that are constant across rounds.[5] As the expected betweenness values in Part C show, information costs are directly related to centrality when costs are distributed *symmetrically* between the groups – lower costs translate into higher levels of centrality. When costs are distributed *asymmetrically* this relationship disappears. Why?

When information costs are distributed asymmetrically, there is an abundance of low-cost informants to choose from within one group, but none in the other group. Most communication occurs within groups, and hence no informant plays

---

[5] The model in Table 6.3B logs the dependent variable because it is positively skewed. For the values in Part C, we calculated the non-logged betweenness prediction.

a particularly central role. In contrast, when costs are distributed symmetrically, each group has several low-cost individuals who are likely to serve as the primary informants for the other members within the group. In short, we see once again that centrality depends not only on the characteristics of individuals, but the particular configurations of the contexts within which these individuals are located.

WHAT ARE THE CRITERIA THAT INDIVIDUALS USE IN SELECTING INFORMANTS?

In this analysis the focus shifts from the individuals being selected as informants to the individuals making the selection – whether or not participants request information from particular individuals. Hence, the analysis includes each possible dyad at every period of all the sessions, increasing the number of observations to 22,568 dyads.[6]

In the Table 6.4 logit model, we consider whether one subject requests information from another subject, as a function of several characteristics related to each subject in the potential dyad. A dyadic proximity measure indexes the absolute difference between the ideal points of the potential informants and requestors. In addition, several dummy variables are also included in the regression: (1) whether the potential informant and requestor belong to the same group; (2) whether the requestor pays the medium information cost (5 ECUs); (3) whether the requestor pays the high information cost (25 ECUs); and (4) the interaction between high information costs for the requestor and shared group membership for the potential dyad.

Magnitudes of effects are addressed in Table 6.4B, where the predicted probability of a request is shown to be contingent on factors included in Table 6.4A. The distance between the ideal points of subjects and potential informants is important, but its effect is much less pronounced than the information levels of potential informants. For example, the second and fourth rows of the table show that the potential informant's information purchases increase the probability from .11 to .45 and from .04 to .24 – approximately four- and six-fold increases. In contrast, reducing the distances between ideal points increases the probability from .04 to .11 and from .24 to .45 – approximately two-fold increases. The table also shows a negative effect for out-group communication that is enhanced among high information cost subjects. (Recall that high-cost individuals cannot purchase social information from the out-group if they have already purchased two pieces of information during the round.) In short, participants appear to weigh expertise more heavily than shared preferences in selecting informants.

---

[6] A clustering procedure avoids underestimating standard errors for the model coefficients, where the clusters are the 168 subjects who participated in the experiment (Rogers 1993).

TABLE 6.4. *Factors affecting the subjects' selection of informant.*
A. *Whether subject chooses a potential informant. Standard errors are adjusted for clustering on subject (logit model).*

	Coef.	T-Value
Potential informant's information level	0.48	11.47
Distance between subject and potential informant's ideal points	−0.16	−4.68
Subject and potential informant are in same group	1.36	5.22
Subject pays medium information cost	0.33	1.41
Medium information cost * same group	−0.42	−1.24
Subject pays high information cost	−0.70	−2.83
High information cost * same group	1.10	3.33
Constant	−3.38	−14.02
N (potential dyads)		22,568
Subjects		168
χ^2, df, p		270.06, 7, .00

B. *Predicted probabilities of selection based on estimates in Part A.*

Subject information cost	Distance between subject/informant ideal points	Same group?	Potential informant information level Low (0)	High (4)
low/medium	0	no	.05	.24
low/medium	0	yes	.11	.45
low/medium	6	no	.02	.11
low/medium	6	yes	.04	.24
high	0	no	.02	.10
high	0	yes	.17	.58
high	6	no	.01	.04
high	6	yes	.07	.35

In summary, our experimental results establish the relative importance of the criteria that participants impose on informant selection, as well as the implications for the communication of bias and the centrality of political experts. We turn, now, to the aggregate implications.

AGGREGATE CONSEQUENCES OF INDIVIDUAL CHOICE CRITERIA

Micro-motives play important roles in the formation of communication networks, but these networks also generate important macro-consequences (Schelling 1978) – aggregate implications that arise as a consequence of individual selection criteria. Interdependence holds the key to understanding the relationships between individuals and aggregates in this analysis. The aggregate is more than a simple summation of individuals, depending instead on the particular patterns of inter-dependence that exist among actors (Achen and Shively 1995).

In this context, the relative distributions of preferences and information within groups become particularly important for levels of communication between groups. We construct an agent-based model of network formation that extends the experimental results. Rather than two groups with seven subjects in each group, the model includes nine agents in each of four groups. Expanding the numbers of agents and groups makes it possible to consider higher levels of variance in group composition, as well as the attendant consequences for dominance, biased communication, and polarization among and between groups.

As Table 6.5 shows, agents are arranged in four quadrants, where each quadrant represents one of the four experimentally manipulated distributions

TABLE 6.5. *Symmetrical and asymmetrical preference and information distributions across groups for agent-based model.*
A. *Symmetrical preference distributions across groups*

Group 1			Group 2		
0	1	2	0	1	2
3	4	5	3	4	5
6	7	8	6	7	8

Group 3			Group 4		
0	1	2	0	1	2
3	4	5	3	4	6
6	7	8	6	7	8

B. *Asymmetrical preference distributions across groups*

Group 1			Group 2		
0	0	0	2	2	2
0	1	1	3	3	3
1	1	2	3	4	4

Group 3			Group 4		
4	4	5	6	7	7
5	5	5	7	7	8
6	6	6	8	8	8

TABLE 6.5. *(cont.)*

C. *Symmetrical information distributions across groups*

Group 1				Group 2		
0	1	1		0	1	1
2	2	2		2	2	2
3	4	4		3	4	4

Group 3				Group 4		
0	1	1		0	1	1
2	2	2		2	2	2
3	4	4		3	4	4

D. *Asymmetrical information distributions across groups*

Group 1				Group 2		
0	0	0		1	1	1
0	1	1		2	2	2
1	1	1		2	2	2

Group 3				Group 4		
2	2	2		3	4	4
2	2	2		4	4	4
3	3	3		4	4	4

of preferences and information. Within each quadrant, 36 agents are assigned to four groups. Four contextual distributions are thus established across the groups: (1) asymmetrical preferences and information, (2) asymmetrical preferences and symmetrical information, (3) symmetrical preferences and asymmetrical information, and (4) the baseline condition of symmetric preferences and information.

SYMMETRIC DISTRIBUTIONS

In symmetric distributions, each group's composition is identical with respect to the characteristic in question. Each agent within each group is randomly assigned a unique preference on a scale of 0 to 8, and distributions of information within groups approximate the marginal distribution of information among experimental subjects {0, 1, 1, 2, 2, 2, 3, 4, 4}. Thus, the distributions are symmetrical across groups and random within groups.

ASYMMETRIC PREFERENCES

In two alternative contexts, preferences are assigned asymmetrically: {0, 0, 0, 0, 1, 1, 1, 1, 2}, {2, 2, 2, 3, 3, 3, 3, 4, 4}, {4, 4, 5, 5, 5, 5, 6, 6, 6}, {6, 7, 7, 7, 7, 8, 8, 8, 8}. While the aggregate distribution corresponds to the baseline, preferences are highly skewed across the groups.

ASYMMETRIC INFORMATION

Similarly, information is also assigned asymmetrically in two contexts: {0, 0, 0, 0, 1, 1, 1, 1, 1}, {1, 1, 1, 2, 2, 2, 2, 2, 2}, {2, 2, 2, 2, 2, 2, 3, 3, 3}, {3, 4, 4, 4, 4, 4, 4, 4, 4}. As before, information is independent from preferences within groups, and the aggregate distribution corresponds to the baseline.

All agents select two other agents as informants, and each of the other 35 agents is assigned a probability of being selected that is proportional to the probability set by the logit model of Table 6.4. Hence, based on the empirical results, preference is given to agents in the same group with similar preferences and more information. In the first formulation, the agents are not restricted in their ability to acquire information through communication regardless of their own information level, thereby omitting the high cost factors from the model. This is equivalent to assuming that all the agents have low and moderate information costs. (The appendix provides a parallel analysis showing that the implications of omitting the high-cost individuals are not consequential.) The model is run for 100 iterations, for each contextual distribution, with each agent making two selections at each iteration. Hence, agents for a particular nine-agent group make a total of 1,800 selections.

PATTERNS OF COMMUNICATION AMONG THE AGENTS

Table 6.6 shows the proportion of requests directed from agents within groups on the rows, to agents within groups on the columns. The main diagonals within *each* part of the table show that agents are likely to select informants within their own groups. As expected, little variation occurs along the diagonal entries in the baseline distribution of Part D – in-group selection probabilities vary from .761 to .776, and all the other selection probabilities vary within very tight bounds of .068 to .087. In short, when the expertise and preference distributions are symmetrical within the groups, all agents face the same selection task using the same criteria.

In Part B of the table, when information is distributed symmetrically but preferences are distributed asymmetrically, the values in the main diagonal are even larger, varying from .803 to .863. In this instance, there is even less likelihood that an agent would reach beyond the group for an informant. Every group has the same information distribution, but preferences are highly clustered. Hence, it is a particularly straightforward task for agents to select an

TABLE 6.6. *Agent-based simulations of cross-group communication for low- and medium-cost subjects: group transition rates with implied equilibria.*
A. *Distributions: asymmetrical preferences; asymmetrical information*

Source of request	Source of information				
	Group 1	Group 2	Group 3	Group 4	Σ
Group 1	0.742	0.068	0.077	0.113	1.00
Group 2	0.027	0.763	0.077	0.132	1.00
Group 3	0.008	0.048	0.812	0.132	1.00
Group 4	0	0.019	0.043	0.937	1.00
Equilibrium	0.017	0.102	0.205	0.676	

B. *Distributions: asymmetrical preferences; symmetrical information*

Source of request	Source of information				
	Group 1	Group 2	Group 3	Group 4	Σ
Group 1	0.852	0.074	0.048	0.026	1.00
Group 2	0.078	0.818	0.064	0.041	1.00
Group 3	0.049	0.083	0.803	0.064	1.00
Group 4	0.032	0.037	0.068	0.863	1.00
Equilibrium	0.266	0.263	0.232	0.238	

C. *Distributions: symmetrical preferences; asymmetrical information*

Source of request	Source of information				
	Group 1	Group 2	Group 3	Group 4	Σ
Group 1	0.583	0.073	0.109	0.235	1.00
Group 2	0.027	0.697	0.081	0.194	1.00
Group 3	0.019	0.046	0.766	0.168	1.00
Group 4	0.016	0.037	0.045	0.902	1.00
Equilibrium	0.041	0.119	0.186	0.654	

D. *Distributions: symmetrical preferences; symmetrical information*

Source of request	Source of information				
	Group 1	Group 2	Group 3	Group 4	Σ
Group 1	0.763	0.073	0.077	0.087	1.00
Group 2	0.085	0.772	0.075	0.068	1.00
Group 3	0.079	0.081	0.761	0.079	1.00
Group 4	0.081	0.071	0.073	0.776	1.00
Equilibrium	0.256	0.246	0.239	0.258	

expert informant with a compatible preference. Part B does, however, show slight but systematic variation in the out-group selection probabilities across out-groups. As the preferences of the out-group grow more distant from the in-group, the corresponding selection probabilities grow smaller.

In contrast, Parts A and C display significant variation in the size of the in-group selection probabilities. In Part A, where preferences and information levels are both distributed asymmetrically, the in-group selection probability increases from .742 to .937 as the level of information within the group increases. The agents in group 1 confront a challenging task – they are located in a low-information group with distinctive preferences. If they choose informants in group 4 to maximize expertise, they pay the price of selecting an informant with highly divergent preferences. Alternatively, if they make informant selections that maximize shared preferences by choosing an in-group agent from group 1, they select from among the least expert agents.

In Part C, with preferences distributed symmetrically across groups but expertise levels distributed asymmetrically, agents confront a choice that is in some ways easier. All agents in every group are able to find an expert informant in group 4 with preferences that approximate their own. Not surprisingly, the in-group selection probability for group 4 is relatively high: .902. The agents in group 1 – the group with the lowest information level – demonstrate the lowest in-group selection probability in the table: .583. And they show a correspondingly high probability (.235) of selecting an informant from the politically expert fourth group.

Finally, it is important to emphasize that these selection probabilities are all based on the Table 6.4A model. Hence the differences are not based on idiosyncratic individual-level traits of the agents, but rather on differences in the contextually imbedded sets of choices they confront.

DYNAMICAL IMPLICATIONS OF CONTEXTUAL VARIATION

Contextual variations in the distributions of preferences and expertise produce dynamic consequences for information flows, with advantages and disadvantages for particular groups. Each of the four sets of group-based selection proportions can be treated as a transition matrix for a fixed arbitrary unit of time, providing the probability that information from groups on the columns will be communicated to groups on the rows (each row thus sums to unity). We treat this as a Markov process, and the transition matrix is defined as C, where

c_{ij} = the probability that someone from group i will obtain information from group j at any particular opportunity.

At some initial time-point before a particular subject is a topic for communication, information is held individually but not communicated. As initial conditions, we treat information sources as being distributed proportionally across the four groups {.25, .25, .25, .25}. Hence, we define:

$g_{jt}=$ a four column row vector with the cumulative proportions of information in the population taken from groups 1 through 4 at time t.[7]

The dominance of a politically expert group is based on the group members' increased access to information, but dominance is only realized through the communication process – and not simply realized, but actually enhanced. While communication increases the volume of information available throughout a population, all information originates from a particular source, and as we have seen in Table 6.2, the information (with bias) is distinctive to its source.

This process produces an equilibrium distribution of information g* that is wholly a function of the transition probabilities, independent of the initial distribution of information. The only behavioral information needed to identify the equilibrium vector is the matrix of transition probabilities, and these equilibria are shown in the bottom row of each part of Table 6.6.

When information is distributed symmetrically across groups, the behavioral responses of the agents create communication networks with an egalitarian equilibrium vector for the population that is balanced across the groups. When information is distributed asymmetrically, the communication networks generate an equilibrium vector that *dramatically magnifies* the initial informational inequalities, and expert groups achieve informational hegemony.

HOW ACCURATE IS THE COMMUNICATED INFORMATION?

Information and preference distributions affect group dominance relative to information flows, and hence they also create the potential for disparities in the quality of information communicated between groups. We examine message quality by once again using estimates obtained from the experimental setting and extending them based on an agent-based model. The Table 6.2A estimates are used to predict agent priors according to the amount of information they have purchased, the candidate's position, and their multiplicative interaction. Here we consider two candidate configurations: polarized candidates with Candidate A positioned at 1 and Candidate B at 7; and convergent candidates with Candidate A at 3 and Candidate B at 5.

We use these agent priors to estimate the message sent by informants to requesters, based on the model in Table 6.2B, where the message is defined in terms of the distance between the informant and the requester, the informant's initial estimate, and an interaction. Using these estimates, the noise attached to messages communicated between agents is defined as:

$$noise = \sqrt{(message - prior)^2}$$

[7] Selection probabilities are assumed to be constant in time, and the experimentally generated selection probabilities support this assumption (see the appendix). The equilibria are independent of initial conditions (Kemeny and Snell 1960; Jackson 2008: chapter 8).

Agents receive information about the two candidates, based on calculated priors and messages for each. Our estimate of the noise received by a particular agent requester from a particular agent informant is then the average of the noise estimates associated with each candidate.

These noise estimates allow us to investigate the quality of information communicated between groups, contingent on the four configurations of preference and information distributions described above. Biased communication between groups becomes particularly relevant when preferences are distributed asymmetrically across groups, and hence *we restrict ourselves to considering the two contexts with asymmetric preference distributions.* To estimate the quality of information sent between groups, we simply average the noise calculations for all messages received by each group, according to the group where the messages originate. For example, if the agents in group 1 made 5 requests to agents in group 4, we estimate the noise associated with each of the 5 requests and average these to obtain a final estimate of information quality sent by group 4 to group 1. The noise estimates for communication among low and medium-cost agents are presented in Parts A and B of Table 6.7 for polarized candidates, positioned at 1 and 7, and in Parts C and D for convergent candidates, positioned at 3 and 5. (Very similar results occur when the analysis includes high-cost subjects; see Table A6.2 in the appendix.)

Polarized candidates clearly increase the noise communicated between groups. Within each table, however, it is also clear that the information and preference distributions produce strong effects on the accuracy of information transmitted between groups. For both symmetrical and asymmetrical information distributions, individuals receiving information from outside their own groups receive less accurate information compared to information originating within their own group. The volume of communication between groups is much higher when information is also distributed asymmetrically. Hence, the strongest aggregate effect depends on the joint presence of asymmetrical distributions for both information and preference.

IMPLICATIONS AND CONCLUSIONS

Our analysis supports an expectation that individuals seek out expert informants with shared preferences, but this is only part of the story. Network formation occurs within a social context that introduces opportunities and constraints on patterns of association. Problems thus arise when the range of available options is constrained – when an individual's own preferences are rare, when the supply of experts is low, and especially when these two circumstances coincide. When forced to choose, experimental participants look primarily for expert informants, and only secondarily for informants with preferences similar to their own – a result that coincides with observational studies of network formation (see Chapter 3).

TABLE 6.7. *Agent-based simulations of noise in cross-group communication, for low- and medium-cost subjects, in contexts with asymmetrically distributed preferences.*
A. *Polarized candidates with asymmetrical preferences and asymmetrical information*

Source of request	Source of information			
	Group 1	Group 2	Group 3	Group 4
Group 1	0.19	0.55	1.29	2.6
Group 2	0.45	0.31	0.72	1.85
Group 3	0.77	0.58	0.38	0.95
Group 4	*	1.16	0.73	0.48

B. *Polarized candidates with asymmetrical preferences and symmetrical information*

Source of request	Source of information			
	Group 1	Group 2	Group 3	Group 4
Group 1	0.37	0.88	1.52	2.25
Group 2	0.84	0.4	0.86	1.53
Group 3	1.51	0.81	0.41	0.77
Group 4	2.21	1.52	0.78	0.38

C. *Convergent candidates with asymmetrical preferences and asymmetrical information*

Source of request	Source of information			
	Group 1	Group 2	Group 3	Group 4
Group 1	0.06	0.18	0.43	0.87
Group 2	0.15	0.1	0.24	0.62
Group 3	0.26	0.19	0.13	0.32
Group 4	*	0.39	0.24	0.16

D. *Convergent candidates with asymmetrical preferences and symmetrical information*

Source of request	Source of information			
	Group 1	Group 2	Group 3	Group 4
Group 1	0.12	0.29	0.51	0.75
Group 2	0.28	0.14	0.29	0.51
Group 3	0.5	0.27	0.14	0.26
Group 4	0.74	0.51	0.26	0.13

Note: * = insufficient information to calculate noise.

We should not be surprised that experimental participants are hesitant to invest heavily in an extended search for the ideal political informants. Given sufficient time and resources, individuals might carry out extended searches for associates, but time and resources are typically scarce, and hence individuals often carry out truncated searches within the pool of readily available individuals, constrained as a matter of cost and convenience.[8] There are, of course, exceptions to this pattern – internet dating services provide one example – but the exceptions are typically exceptional, and observational studies affirm the importance of availability in network construction (Huckfeldt and Sprague 1995). Distributions of preferences and information levels within groups thus carry important implications for individuals, with important aggregate consequences as well (Achen and Shively 1995). First, group boundaries on communication redefine political expertise relative to particular settings, and centrality in the flow of information is thus affected by distributions of expertise. Second, when information is distributed asymmetrically across groups, the likelihood of communication between groups is enhanced, and the primacy of expertise over shared preferences as a selection criterion fosters heterogeneous streams of information.

The primacy of expertise is accelerated in the real world by the intrinsic nature of experts who invest in political information because they value being informed (Fiorina 1990). Many of the same experts also realize value in talking about politics, thus creating heterogeneous streams of information. It is not that people necessarily prefer the experience of diverse preferences. Rather, heterogeneous information is a byproduct of the activist individuals who value information – both acquired and communicated – as an end in itself (see Chapter 4).

Correspondingly, the potential for polarized groups is greatest when information is distributed symmetrically and preferences are distributed asymmetrically across groups. In this context, the contextual distributions of preferences and expertise create self-contained camps of like-minded individuals who are readily able to locate politically astute informants with shared preferences. Conversely, individuals are more likely to encounter divergent views and biased messages when expert informants with shared preferences are scarce – when information and preference distributions produce a disadvantage for their particular viewpoints, thereby creating a social dimension to the mobilization of political bias (Schattschneider 1960).

In these and other ways, particular patterns of interdependence among individual actors, fostered by contextual distributions of preferences and expertise, carry important consequences for aggregate realities. An important element of the solution to ecological fallacies, both theoretically and empirically, thus lies in a concentrated investment in understanding the nature of interdependence among individual citizens.

---

[8] An analysis of costs and benefits for the experimental subject's information search is provided in the appendix.

The design of these experiments is not motivated by the goal of determining whether or not experimental participants act rationally. To the contrary, our primary goal is to create an experimental platform that provides an abstract yet realistic representation of the communication networks through which individuals send and receive political messages with uncertain informational content. Hence, the experiments are far too complex for a complete analysis as non-cooperative games. At the same time, the basic design – which builds on a spatial model – makes it possible to undertake a partial analysis of the strategic challenges facing the experimental participants. Hence, in the next chapter, we will examine the extent to which subjects' vote choices are "correct," the circumstances under which social communication yields efficiency gains, and the settings in which social information is likely to yield improved decisions.

CHAPTER 6 APPENDIX

INSTRUCTIONS TO PARTICIPANTS

The following instructions were read to all subjects before the experiment began. These instructions reference screens that can be viewed at johnbarryryan.com.

Thank you for participating in today's experiment. I will be reading from a script to ensure that every session of this experiment receives the same instructions. These instructions explain the nature of today's experiment as well as how to navigate the computer interface you will be working with. We ask that you please refrain from talking or looking at the monitors of other participants during the experiment. If you still have a question or problem, please raise your hand and one of us will come to you.

In today's experiment, all monetary amounts, earnings and costs are denominated in Experiment Currency Units or ECUs. At the end of the experiment, your earnings in ECUs will be translated into dollars at the rate of 1 ECU equals 1 cent. So, if you end with a balance of 1,500 ECUs, you would be paid $15 plus the $5 show up fee for a total of $20. We will pay you in cash at the end of the experiment.

Today's experiment consists of up to 15 time periods. Each period consists of a contest between two candidates. At the beginning of each period, you will be assigned a position from 1 to 7 and you will be given an endowment of 100 ECUs. Your goal is to elect the candidate whose position is closer to your own. To accomplish this goal, you will both buy private information and ask other participants for information. Information will cost 25 ECUs, 5 ECUs or the information will be free. The cost of information is randomly assigned. If information costs you 25 ECUs, you can buy up to 2 pieces of information. Otherwise you can obtain up to 4 pieces of information.

At the end of each period, ECUs will be awarded based on the outcome of the election. If the candidate closer to you wins the election, you will earn 50 ECUs. If the candidate closer to you loses the election, you will lose 50 ECUs. If both candidates were equally appealing to you, you are awarded no ECUs and you have no ECUs deducted from your total.

Please turn to your computer screens. We have prepared several demonstration screens to help you get familiar with the actual screens you will see during the experiment.

(SCREEN ONE) This is the first screen you will see in each period. The top of each screen will display your position, the period, and the time remaining in each period. We suggest that you make your decisions for a screen within the time limit. You should be careful in making your choices, but it is in your own best interest to make your choices as quickly as you are able.

As you can see, there are two candidates, A and B. Candidate A's position is equally likely to be any whole number between 1 and 6, and Candidate B's position is equally likely to be any whole number between 2 and 7. This screen also tells you how much information about the candidates will cost you. Enter the amount of information that you wish to buy and click OK.

(SCREEN TWO) This is the next screen you will see. Regardless of how much information you bought on the previous screen, this screen displays what it would look like if you had bought three pieces of information. Each piece of information is an independently drawn signal about the candidate's positions. On average these signals accurately represent the candidates' true positions, but any single piece of information may not. The table on the handout shows the possible signals that you will receive for all the different positions the candidates can hold. The signal for any candidate lies within three points on either side of the candidate's true position and you are equally likely to receive any of the seven possible signals within the interval. This means that even though the candidates' positions are between 1 and 7, the signals can fall out of those bounds. For example, if the candidate's position is a 1, you are equally likely to receive any signal that lies between -2 and 4.

Based on the signals you see, you are asked to estimate the candidates' positions. Enter estimates for the two candidates and click OK.

(SCREEN THREE) You also have the opportunity to obtain information from other participants. This screen displays a table of all of the participants, it provides you with their positions and the amount of information they bought. With this knowledge you may request information from two of the other participants.

Participants 1 through 7 are in one group; participants 8 through 14 are in another group. Information from members in your group is free; information from members of the other group costs 10 cents.

You are to enter the subject numbers from whom you want information and then press OK.

(SCREEN FOUR) If none of the other participants ask you for information, you must click OK to move on. If other participants do ask you for information, you will see a screen that looks like this. At this point, you have the opportunity to accept or reject the request for information. You are not penalized or rewarded for accepting requests and you are not penalized nor rewarded for rejecting requests. Click the circle that says yes if you want to provide that participant with information and click the circle that says no if you want to reject the request for information. After you have done this for all of the participants who requested information, click OK.

(SCREEN FIVE) This is where you enter the information that you are going to provide to the other participants. You are reminded of the signals you received from the candidates. You do not need to provide identical information to each of the participants who requested information from you. Enter the candidate information that you want to provide, and then click OK.

(SCREEN SIX) On this screen, the election will take place. You are reminded of your position and the signals you received from the candidates. If another participant agreed to provide you with information, then you will see that information as well. Based on this information and the knowledge that Candidate A's position is between 1 and 6 and Candidate B's position is between 2 and 7, your goal is to figure out the candidates' positions and vote for the candidate closer to your position. There are examples on the handout. If your position is 5 and you believe Candidate A's position is 6 and Candidate B's position is 3, then you should vote for Candidate A because 5 is closer to 6 than 3. If your position is 5 and you believe Candidate A's position is 1 and Candidate B's position is 3, you should vote for Candidate B because 5 is closer to 3 than 1. Please vote for one of the candidate's and then click OK.

(SCREEN SEVEN) This is the final screen. The two candidate's positions are revealed as is the outcome of the election. You will also learn for which candidate you should have voted, as well as the number of ECUs you earned in this period. That is calculated by starting with your 100 ECU endowment. From that the cost of the information you purchased is subtracted. If the candidate closer to your position won the election, you earn an additional 50 ECUs. If the candidate closer to your position lost, you lose 50 ECUs. If both candidates were equally close to your own position, you earn no ECUs but do not lose any either. The most ECUs you can earn in a single period is 150 ECUs, the fewest ECUs you can earn in a single period is zero. Beneath your earnings for this period, you will see the total number of ECUs earned up to this point in the experiment.

The experiment will consist of up to 15 periods just like this one. At the end of the experiment, you will be asked for some demographic information and then a couple of questions about your general political leanings.

This concludes the demonstration screens. We are now ready to begin the actual experiment. We ask that you follow the rules of the experiment. Anyone *who violates the rules may be asked to leave the experiment with only the $5 show up fee. Are there any questions before we start?*

2. HIGH-COST SUBJECTS IN THE AGENT-BASED MODEL

What are the implications of including the high-cost subjects in the analysis? We do this in Table A6.1 by assigning agents holding 0, 1, and 2 pieces of information to the high-cost category, proportionate to the distribution in the experimental results. These agents then select informants according to the full logic of Table 6.3, including the decreased likelihood of selecting a member of an out-group. Including the high-cost agents drives up the entries in the main diagonal of the transition matrix, particularly for entries that represent higher cost groups. Once again, the high-cost groups that need additional information the most are least able to take advantage of expertise located in groups other than their own. At the same time, the equilibrium vectors are little changed from Parts A and C of Table 6.6. The highest cost groups in the asymmetric information distributions account for very little of the aggregate information, and the dominance of the lowest cost group is only modestly reduced.

TABLE A6.1. *Agent-based simulations of cross-group communication for all subjects: group transition rates with implied equilibria.*
A. *Distributions: asymmetrical preferences; asymmetrical information*

Source of request	Source of information				
	Group 1	Group 2	Group 3	Group 4	Σ
Group 1	0.86	0.032	0.041	0.068	1.00
Group 2	0.013	0.853	0.055	0.079	1.00
Group 3	0.004	0.033	0.852	0.111	1.00
Group 4	0	0.018	0.034	0.948	1.00
Equilibrium	0.017	0.128	0.204	0.65	

B. *Distributions: asymmetrical preferences; symmetrical information*

Source of request	Source of information				
	Group 1	Group 2	Group 3	Group 4	Σ
Group 1	0.916	0.042	0.027	0.016	1.00
Group 2	0.05	0.865	0.054	0.031	1.00
Group 3	0.04	0.054	0.857	0.048	1.00
Group 4	0.018	0.034	0.044	0.903	1.00
Equilibrium	0.301	0.241	0.221	0.237	

TABLE A6.1. *(cont.)*

C. *Distributions: symmetrical preferences; asymmetrical information*

Source of request	Source of information				
	Group 1	Group 2	Group 3	Group 4	Σ
Group 1	0.754	0.024	0.063	0.159	1.00
Group 2	0.011	0.812	0.054	0.123	1.00
Group 3	0.009	0.035	0.838	0.118	1.00
Group 4	0.01	0.032	0.06	0.898	1.00
Equilibrium	0.038	0.148	0.267	0.546	

D. *Distributions: symmetrical preferences; symmetrical information*

Source of request	Source of information				
	Group 1	Group 2	Group 3	Group 4	Σ
Group 1	0.843	0.043	0.053	0.06	1.00
Group 2	0.057	0.824	0.06	0.058	1.00
Group 3	0.058	0.059	0.821	0.063	1.00
Group 4	0.057	0.051	0.067	0.825	1.00
Equilibrium	0.268	0.225	0.25	0.257	

Table A6.2 replicates the analysis and noise estimates of Table 6.7 with *high-cost agents included*, and it produces highly comparable results.

3. PATTERNS OF CHANGE ACROSS THE PERIODS

The analyses presented in the text do not consider the possibility of a learning process that produces changes in behavior across periods. We address these issues in this section. First, Table A6.3 replicates the analysis of Table 6.2A for subjects in the first five periods, as well as for subjects in later rounds. The coefficient estimates are nearly identical across early and later rounds, suggesting that subject information levels had the same effects on the accuracy of their estimates in the early periods as in the late periods. Subjects with less information did not learn some way to improve their estimates of the candidate positions as the experiment proceeded.

Table A6.4 and Figure A6.1 evaluate the subjects' choice of informants across the periods. In these analyses, periods 11 and 12 are dropped as only four sessions completed 11 periods and only one session completed 12 periods. Table A6.4 shows the mean number of in-group and out-group requests that subjects receive by period. There is a slight tendency for in-group requests to increase and out-group requests to decline across rounds, but these differences are small and not statistically significant.

TABLE A6.2. *Agent-based simulations of noise in cross-group communication, for low-, medium-, and high-cost subjects, in contexts with asymmetrically distributed preferences.*
A. *Polarized candidates with asymmetrical preferences and asymmetrical information*

Source of request	Source of Information			
	Group 1	Group 2	Group 3	Group 4
Group 1	0.2	0.56	1.36	2.65
Group 2	0.41	0.31	0.64	1.86
Group 3	0.71	0.56	0.38	0.97
Group 4	*	1.04	0.64	0.49

B. *Polarized candidates with asymmetrical preferences and symmetrical information*

Source of request	Source of information			
	Group 1	Group 2	Group 3	Group 4
Group 1	0.37	0.84	1.43	2.31
Group 2	0.84	0.39	0.78	1.62
Group 3	1.53	0.74	0.4	0.78
Group 4	2.28	1.52	0.88	0.37

C. *Convergent candidates with asymmetrical preferences and asymmetrical information*

Source of request	Source of information			
	Group 1	Group 2	Group 3	Group 4
Group 1	0.07	0.19	0.45	0.88
Group 2	0.14	0.1	0.21	0.62
Group 3	0.24	0.19	0.13	0.32
Group 4	*	0.35	0.21	0.16

D. *Convergent candidates with asymmetrical preferences and symmetrical information*

Source of request	Source of information			
	Group 1	Group 2	Group 3	Group 4
Group 1	0.12	0.28	0.48	0.77
Group 2	0.28	0.13	0.26	0.54
Group 3	0.51	0.25	0.13	0.26
Group 4	0.76	0.51	0.29	0.12

TABLE A6.3. *Replicating Table 6.2A with data split between early and late periods. Prior judgments regarding candidates' positions by information purchased, candidates' true positions, and their interaction. Standard errors are adjusted for clustering on subject.*
Candidate A

	First 5 periods		Later periods	
	Coef.	T-value	Coef.	T-value
Amount of information subject purchased	−0.44	−5.54	−.49	−6.31
Candidate's true position	0.30	5.65	.20	3.48
Amount of information * true position	0.16	8.08	.17	9.02
Constant	2.32	10.34	2.55	10.44
N =	840		896	
R^2, s.e. of estimate =	.39, 1.38		.33, 1.48	

Candidate B

	First 5 periods		Later periods	
	Coef.	T-value	Coef.	T-value
Amount of information subject purchased	−0.94	−9.21	−0.95	−9.54
Candidate's true position	0.18	3.45	0.21	3.99
Amount of information * true position	0.18	9.83	0.18	9.72
Constant	4.01	13.88	3.94	13.66
N =	840		896	
R^2, s.e. of estimate =	.36, 1.41		.34, 1.43	

TABLE A6.4. *Mean number of in-group and out-group requests subjects received by period. Periods 11 and 12 dropped due to the small number of sessions that completed that many periods.*

Period	1	2	3	4	5	6	7	8	9	10
In-group requests	1.43	1.46	1.42	1.43	1.44	1.51	1.55	1.51	1.53	1.51
Out-group requests	.46	.42	.45	.45	.42	.35	.34	.36	.35	.36
Subjects	168	168	168	168	168	168	168	168	168	154
# of Sessions	12	12	12	12	12	12	12	12	12	11

Figure A6.1A summarizes the characteristics of the chosen informants. We have seen that subjects place a large emphasis on the expertise of the potential informants and are less concerned about the difference in their ideal points. One might expect that subjects would learn to be wary of choosing informants with

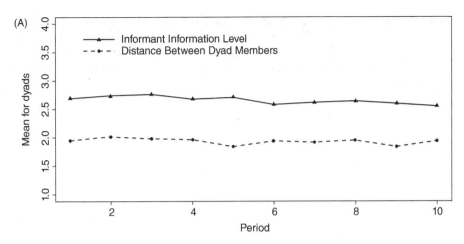

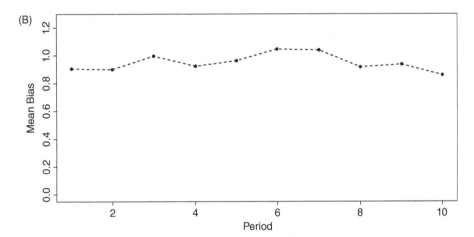

FIGURE A6.1. Social information exchange over time.

A. Characteristics of subjects' chosen informant by period.

B. Mean bias in messages sent by period. Bias is equal to the absolute difference between a subject's prior judgment about the candidate's position and the message they send about that candidate's position.

divergent preferences. As Figure A6.1A shows, however, this is not the case. The mean information level of the chosen informants is unchanged over the periods, and the typical distance between the preferences of the subject-informant dyad also does not vary.

Finally, Part B of Figure A6.1 displays the levels of bias in the messages regarding each candidate, defined as the absolute difference between a subject's prior judgment regarding each candidate's position and the message they send about that candidate's position. This figure also shows remarkably little change across the periods. Subjects do not appear to send more biased messages in later rounds than they do in early rounds. Taken together, these analyses suggest that the behavior of the subjects was relatively stable across the periods.

7

Interdependence, communication, and calculation

Costs, benefits, and opinion leadership

T. K. Ahn, Robert Huckfeldt, and John Barry Ryan

> In an information-rich world, the wealth of information means a dearth of something else: a scarcity of whatever it is that information consumes. What information consumes is rather obvious: it consumes the attention of its recipients. Hence a wealth of information creates a poverty of attention and a need to allocate that attention efficiently among the overabundance of information sources that might consume it.
>
> Herbert A. Simon (1971:40–41).

The previous two chapters addressed political communication and interdependent actors, based on an experimental framework designed around purposeful, goal-seeking individuals. This experimental framework is informed by a spatial model of elections, as well as game-theoretic work on committee decisions and "cheap talk." While the experimental setup thus resembles a game, the purpose was not to design an experiment that is analytically tractable, but rather to make the interaction structure explicit. While the experiments might be criticized for their highly abstract nature, they are also too complex to derive game-theoretic equilibria.

Indeed, game-theoretic efforts on related issues typically analyze a small substage of our experimental setting with many simplifying assumptions. For example, some studies assume voters have identical preferences so as to analyze how voting rules and communication protocols affect the incentives to invest in private information (Gerardi and Yariv 2008; Gershkov and Szentes 2009; Persico 2004). Indeed, the "surprisingly subtle interaction" (Austen-Smith and Feddersen 2009, 763) among multiple factors (numbers of voters, voting rules, preference distributions, communication protocols, etc.) make it imperative to fix most other factors in order to derive analytical results relative to one or two variables.[1]

---

[1] Many studies take this approach. Helpful reviews on that research include Farrell and Rabin (1996) on strategic communication in general, Austen-Smith and Feddersen (2009) on strategic communication in committee settings, and Gerling et al. (2005) on costly information acquisition.

In contrast, the voters in our experimental setting not only have diverse preferences, but they may also choose to acquire costly information from other voters who may or may not share their own preferences. As suggested earlier, the complexity of our experimental setup thus puts this effort in the category of what Vernon Smith (1982: 940–942) calls "heuristic" or "exploratory" experiments as opposed to the "nomothetic" experiments aimed at establishing laws of behavior by testing a completely articulated theory. A heuristic or exploratory experiment relies less on mathematically complete theory, focusing instead on the consequences of experimental treatments that are previously unexplored. However, our experiment is not devoid of an underlying theoretical framework, and hence partial analyses on some aspects of the strategic incentives are possible based on the explicit assumptions of the experimental design.

THE USE OF ANALYTIC BENCHMARKS

Even the relatively simple experimental setting in Chapter 5 is too complex for a full analysis as a non-cooperative game, but it is possible to provide some benchmarks to help understand the contours of the decision-making task faced by the subjects. These benchmarks provide guidance in the assessment of whether privately obtained and socially obtained information increase the probability of voting correctly. The analysis in this section is based on the experimental framework outlined in Chapter 5, but most of the conclusions hold for the experiment in Chapter 6. Later in this chapter, we will directly address the "rationality" of information acquisition across groups in Chapter 6's experiment.

THE VALUE OF PUBLIC SIGNALS

The subjects have access to three types of information: public, private, and social. Public information is available to all at no cost and is common knowledge: Candidate A's position is an integer between 1 and 6, Candidate B's position is an integer between 2 and 7, and the candidates' positions are randomly and independently drawn from uniform distributions.

Thus, there are 36 possible and equally likely configurations of the two candidates' positions. The two candidates' positions are identical in 5 of these 36 configurations. Voter 1(7) would vote for Candidate A(B) in 21 cases, for B(A) in 10 cases, and would be indifferent in 5 cases. If voter 1(7) cast her vote based on the public information only, she should vote for Candidate A(B) and the probability that the vote is cast correctly is 26/36 or about 0.72, counting the

---

Crawford and Sobel (1982) is the seminal work on strategic information transmission via cheap talk. Austen-Smith (1990) is an influential early work on strategic communication in committees from a game-theoretic perspective. Landa and Meirowitz (2009) discuss the implications of game theoretic works on cheap talk on deliberative democracy.

votes in indifferent cases as correct. Similar calculations show that the ex ante probability of voting correctly is 25/36 (about 0.69) for voters 2 and 6, 24/36 (about 0.67) for voters 3 and 5, and 23/36 (about 0.64) for voter 4.[2] This analysis implies that if the cost of purchasing private information is the same, the middle voter (voter 4) has the largest incentive to purchase private information and the extreme voters (voter 1 and voter 7) have the smallest incentive.[3]

BELIEF UPDATE WITH PRIVATE SIGNALS

Recall that the private signals which voters purchase are integer numbers randomly drawn from a uniform distribution plus and minus three of the true candidate position. This element of the design has several implications including (1) the correct Bayesian belief update with private signals is different from simply taking the algebraic mean of the signals, (2) some signals (extreme values) are more informative than other signals, and (3) some candidate positions are easier (in the probabilistic sense) to estimate than other candidates' positions. This is not unlike the differing value of certain statements in a campaign. One could reasonably assume that a candidate who calls for the "death of capitalism" is highly unlikely to be a conservative. Moreover, candidates who stake out a middle position on any particular issue may be more or less conservative on the other issues.

Given time, knowledge, and energy, the subjects should use a Bayesian method to update their beliefs regarding candidate positions by using available information to shrink the variance around privately obtained signals. We pursue this strategy in Table 7.1, where the probabilities of the possible positions for Candidate A are shown, contingent on signals. These probabilities are derived as Bayesian posteriors, based on a simple tree reversal illustrated in Figure 7.1, and the first step in constructing this table is to identify the positions that each signal eliminates: the signal of –2 for Candidate A eliminates all positions except 1, the signal of –1 eliminates positions 3 to 6, etc.

Some signals are thus less informative – signals 3 and 4 do not allow elimination of any positions, and any position included within a column is equally

---

[2] In these calculations, a subject votes correctly when the two candidates are equally distanced from a voter regardless of which candidate the subject chooses. Hence, voter 4 is ex ante indifferent between the two candidates, but would vote correctly at a rate higher than .5 because of the situations when the candidates are equally distanced from voter 4.

[3] Also note that none of the voters are unconditionally in favor of one or the other candidate. In the real elections with two major candidates or parties, one can imagine a significant proportion of the electorate having their mind fixed on one party without any realistic chance of voting for the other. Thus, one way to understand our experimental setup is that we consider only those voters who can be persuaded one way or the other depending on the information they obtain. The underlying preference dimension, which varies from 1 to 7, can thus be viewed as truncated. This is also realistic for the candidates given the incentives for moderation in two-party elections (but see Stone and Simas 2010).

TABLE 7.1. *Probability of Candidate A's position, contingent on value of privately purchased signals.*[a]

Candidate Position	Privately purchased signal											
	−2	−1	0	1	2	3	4	5	6	7	8	9
6						0.167	0.167	0.2	0.25	0.333	0.5	1
5					0.2	0.167	0.167	0.2	0.25	0.333	0.5	
4				0.25	0.2	0.167	0.167	0.2	0.25	0.333		
3			0.333	0.25	0.2	0.167	0.167	0.2	0.25			
2		0.5	0.333	0.25	0.2	0.167	0.167	0.2				
1	1	0.5	0.333	0.25	0.2	0.167	0.167					
Expected value[b]	1	1.5	2	2.5	3	3.5	3.5	4	4.5	5	5.5	6
Standard deviation[b]		0.71	0.82	1.12	1.26	1.71	1.71	1.26	1.12	0.82	0.71	

[a] The probability of a candidate position (P) based on a signal (S) is defined as the Bayesian posterior: $\mathrm{pr}(P|S)=[\mathrm{pr}(P)\mathrm{pr}(S|P)]/\mathrm{pr}(S) = \mathrm{pr}(P,S)/\mathrm{pr}(S)$.

[b] Both the expected value and the standard deviation are defined, contingent on a particular signal, within the columns.

Recall that Candidate A can only hold one of the six positions between 1 and 6, and that signals are drawn from a uniform distribution of the seven positions centered at the candidate's true position.

Let: P = candidate's true position
      S = private signal regarding candidate

Then: pr(P=1)=1/6
       pr(P=2)=1/6
       .
       .
       etc.

       pr (S=-1)|(P=1)=1/7
       pr(S=-1)|(P=2)=1/7
       pr(S=-1)|(P>2)=0

Using a Bayesian tree reversal, we want to know the probability that Pr(P=1)|(S=-1)=.5

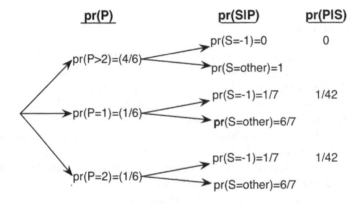

Hence, the Bayesian posterior   pr(P|S) = [pr(P)pr(S|P)]/pr(S)
                                Pr(1|-1) = [(1/6)(1/7)]/(1/42+1/42)=.5
                                Pr(2|-1) = [(1/6)(1/7)]/(1/42+1/42)=.5
                                Pr(3|-1) = [(1/6)(0)]/(1/42+1/42)=0
                                .
                                .
                                etc.

FIGURE 7.1. Deriving the Bayesian posterior for the probability that Candidate A holds position 1, given that a subject receives a signal that Candidate A holds position -1.

probable, contingent on the signal. It is, of course, still possible to calculate the expected values for the true candidate positions within each column, contingent on the particular signal. Hence, for the populations that receive any particular signal, we show the standard deviation as well as the expected value. While the expected values of the true positions track the signal quite closely, the variances around the expected values are quite high at the middle range of the signals (3 through 5). For a subject who receives one or two signals equal to 4, neither the expected value nor the central limit theorem is likely to be of much consolation, even though these scenarios produce straightforward sampling problems.

In contrast, some candidate positions are easier to ascertain than other candidates' positions. For example, a position of 4 for Candidate A can generate signals ranging from 1 to 7. Among them, the most informative signals are 7 (which eliminates positions 1 through 3), and 1 (which eliminates positions 5 through 7). Indeed, if an individual receives two private signals regarding the same candidate – a 1 and a 7 – the candidate's position can only be a 4. The *most* informative single signal possible for Candidate A's true position of 1 is –2, which eliminates all but the true position. Indeed, one of the chief virtues of purchasing additional signals is that it increases the likelihood of further narrowing the range of possible positions held by a candidate.

THE VALUE OF PRIVATE SIGNALS

More information increases a voter's likelihood of voting correctly and the probability of one's preferred candidate to win – but information is costly for the majority of the voters in our experimental setting. How much should one pay for information? We determine upper limits on the value of information assuming that one's vote is pivotal instead of a full equilibrium analysis. Recall that a subject gains 50 ECUs if the correct candidate wins, loses 50 ECUs if the wrong candidate wins, and do not gain or lose ECUs if the two candidates are equally distanced. Also recall that in each session, 2 voters are low-cost voters who can obtain up to four pieces of information for free, 2 are medium-cost voters who pay 5 ECUs per piece and could buy up to four pieces of information, and 3 are high-cost voters who pay 25 ECUs per piece and could buy up to 2 pieces of information.

In order to assess values, we ran one million iterations of a computer simulation. The simulation follows the experimental procedure, but omits the social exchange of information. First, two candidates' positions are generated from the respective interval. Second, once the positions are fixed, four signals are generated for each of the two candidates. Then, for each voter, the belief update and voting decisions are made incrementally from one piece to four pieces of information. Due to the symmetry of the simulations for voters 5, 6, and 7, they are not run separately, but rather imputed from the simulations for voters 1, 2, and 3.

The marginal expected value of the first piece of information is about 11 ECUs, the second about 6 ECUs, the third about 4 ECUs, and the fourth about 2 ECUs – but note that these are the maximum values assuming that a voter uses the private information fully and correctly and the voter is pivotal in determining the electoral outcome. The actual values would thus be smaller than these when voters do not use the correct ianian update method and/or when one's vote is not pivotal.

TABLE 7.2. *Subject information purchases by information costs for subjects in the experiments in Chapters 5 and 6.*
A. *Chapter 5*

	0	5	25	N
0	1.33%	7.00%	26.89%	146
1	8.00%	22.67%	36.89%	258
2	9.00%	35.33%	36.22%	296
3	3.00%	13.67%	–	50
4	78.67%	21.33%	–	300
N	300	300	450	1050

$\chi^2=686.5$ p=0.000

B. *Chapter 6*

	0	5	25	N
0	4.84%	13.91%	31.99%	331
1	7.66%	14.11%	38.17%	392
2	14.72%	24.60%	29.84%	417
3	11.90%	23.19%	–	174
4	60.89%	24.19%	–	422
N	496	496	744	1736

$\chi^2=913.8$ p=0.000

Hence, the analysis suggests that, for the high-cost voters, it is not worth buying even a single piece of information. Medium-cost voters should expect to increase the probability of a correct vote from buying the first piece of information, but the value of the second piece is doubtful. The low-cost voters, if strategically optimizing, would want to obtain all four pieces because this information is free, ignoring for these purposes the cognitive costs of processing the information.

Do subjects consider these costs in their information purchases? While information costs are clearly important, we see considerable variation in the subjects' levels of attentiveness to the cost factor. Table 7.2 presents the amount of information a subject purchases by the subject's information costs. Part A of the table displays the results for the experiment in Chapter 5, while Part B of the table displays the results for the experiment in Chapter 6.

The results show that as information costs increase, subjects are generally less willing to purchase information, but financial costs alone do not wholly explain information acquisition. While the majority of subjects for whom information is free choose to receive all the information to which they are entitled, a sizeable proportion (21 percent in Chapter 5 and 39 percent in Chapter 6) choose to receive less than the maximum amount even though the information is free. At the other extreme, about one-third of high-cost subjects purchase two pieces of information even though the 50 ECU cost is prohibitively expensive.

In short, the participants' behavior cannot be wholly explained in terms of tangible information costs alone. Some of those who incur no *financial* cost may not be willing to pay the *cognitive* costs of processing multiple pieces of information. Conversely, we have seen that, from a cost-benefit perspective, a single piece of information is unlikely to warrant an expenditure of 25 ECUs, but people who are personally invested in choosing the correct candidate may be willing to pay these outsized costs.

Hence, while information costs are clearly related to information acquisition, the relationship is noisy in the laboratory, just as it is in real-world elections. Some well-educated individuals are bored or put off by newspaper articles on election campaigns. Other people, with lower levels of education, are politically engaged consumers of any and all information that is available. These latter individuals, like the high-cost information consumers in our experiments, are motivated by concerns other than the minimization of information costs, and hence they are likely to join the ranks of experts and activists with disproportional levels of influence in politics.

CONFLICT OF INTEREST AND INCENTIVES FOR STRATEGIC COMMUNICATION

As the distance between a pair of voters' ideal points gets longer, the probability that the two voters would want to vote for different candidates increases. If this conflict of interest leads to an attempt to mislead by providing false information then voters have reasons to worry about obtaining socially communicated information from someone whose ideal point is far away from one's own. Distance, defined as the absolute difference between the positions of a pair of voters, is a good heuristic measure of the ex ante conflict of interests, but there is non-linearity between distance and conflict of interest. The probability that two voters in each of the 21 undirected dyads will strictly prefer different candidates can be viewed as an index of the ex ante conflict of interest probability.

Indeed, the probability increases as a function of the distance between a pair of voters, but this increase is non-linear. Table 7.3 displays the ex ante probabilities that two voters will have strictly opposite preferences. For example, pair (1,3) and pair (3,5) are both 2 points apart on the unidimensional scale, but the latter pair has a greater probability of conflict (5/36 vs. 15/36). Given the same distance, therefore, the probability of conflict is greater when the two voters are on different sides of the midpoint.

To what extent do subjects behave strategically in the signals they send? That is, are informants more likely to send truthful signals to recipients whose preferences lie on their own side of the preference midpoint than to recipients whose preferences lie on the opposite side of the midpoint? The dependent variable in Figure 7.2 measures the truthfulness of the messages conveyed by

TABLE 7.3. *Ex ante conflict of interest probability – the probability that two voters will have strictly opposite candidate preference.*[a]

Sender	Receiver					
	2	3	4	5	6	7
1	1/36	5/36	13/36	23/36	29/36	31/36
2		3/36	11/36	21/36	27/36	29/36
3			5/36	15/36	21/36	23/36
4				5/36	11/36	13/36

[a] Cases in which one or both individuals are indifferent are not considered as cases of conflicting interest. The corresponding probabilities for the pairs not shown can be inferred from the table.

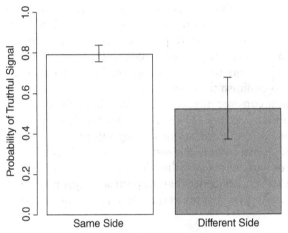

FIGURE 7.2. Truthful signals sent by informants when subject–informant pairs are on the same side or different sides of the midpoint. Error bars show 95% confidence intervals with standard errors corrected for clustering on informants.

comparing the informants' initial estimates of candidate positions to the signals that they send. The variable is constructed in three steps.

1) Using the recipient's ideal point and the informant's estimates of candidate positions, we determine the informant's likely belief regarding the candidate for whom the recipient *should* vote.

2) Using the recipient's ideal point and the informant's messages to the recipient, we determine for which candidate the informant's signals suggest the recipient *should* vote.

3) The dependent variable is coded 1 if the vote based on the informant's estimates and the vote based on the informant's signals are the same – if

the informant appears to be candidly and accurately representing his or her beliefs. The dependent variable is coded 0 if the two votes are different – if the informant appears to be misrepresenting his or her beliefs.

Based on this analysis, informants appear to send candid signals 67.6 percent of the time. Figure 7.2 splits the subject–informant pairs into two types: (1) both subject and informant are on the same side of the midpoint; (2) subject and informant are on different sides of the midpoint. As expected, subjects are more likely to send truthful signals if they are on the same side of the midpoint. When the informant is on the same side of the midpoint as the subject, the informant sends a candid signal 79.3 percent of the time. And the probability of a candid signal drops 27 points if the subject and informant are on opposite sides of the midpoint.

It should be noted, however, that informants send candid signals to subjects on the opposite side of the midpoint about 50 percent of the time, even though those subject-informant pairs were in conflict 68 percent of the time. Hence, not all subjects behaved as self-interested, strategic players. Either because of an aversion to misrepresentation (Gneezy 2005) or to concerns about fairness (Fehr and Schmidt 1999), some informants sent truthful signals even though such candor carried the potential to diminish their own payoffs.

Once again, simple economic considerations do not fully explain the behavior of our subjects. For some subjects, the urge to see their own candidate win the election overpowers any hesitance to provide misleading information. Other subjects are able to control their own competitive instincts, perhaps because they are less willing to dissemble, or perhaps because they do not care as deeply about the outcome. Once again, we see clear evidence that the partisan motivations and competitive instincts of the activist play an important role in the communication process.

TRADE OFF BETWEEN EXPERTISE AND PREFERENCE SIMILARITY

In almost all cases, it is better to weight preference similarity above expertise when choosing an informant. The trade off is a function of (1) the voter's information level (i.e., the probability of a correct vote based on the private signals he or she receives) and (2) the configuration of potential informants in terms of the preference similarity and the information level. The necessary condition is that by getting information from an informant, the probability of correct voting should increase. The sufficient condition is that the informant is the best among the worthy informants (who pass the necessary condition).

The analyses thus far have shown that the marginal value of additional information decreases rapidly and that voters would vote correctly two-thirds of the time even without private signals due to the availability of the public information and the cases in which two candidates are equally distanced. On the other hand, the probability of conflict rapidly increases as the distance between a

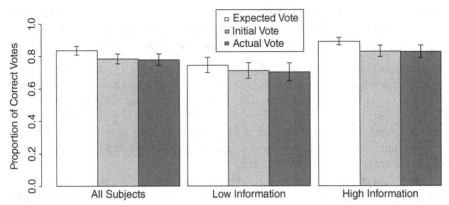

FIGURE 7.3. Percent of correct votes using Bayesian elimination, votes implied by the initial estimates of candidates' positions, and the actual percent of correct votes. Error bars show 95% confidence intervals with standard errors corrected for clustering on subjects and sessions.

pair of voters gets longer. In almost all cases, therefore, a strategically optimizing voter would choose one of their immediate neighbors as the source of information. Alternatively, a strategic voter might conceivably choose an informant who is *not* an immediate neighbor when neither the potential requestor nor her immediate neighbors have purchased any private signals. Among our subjects, only 8 percent experienced such a situation. Thus, the choice of an informant who is not an immediate neighbor is typically a non-optimal choice which, in turn, increases the potential danger of getting misled.

To evaluate how well subjects use private and social information, we compare the proportion of correct votes for subjects in Chapter 5, assuming that the subjects estimate candidate positions based on three alternative methods: (1) Bayesian elimination of possible candidate positions following the private information stage – the procedure described in detail below; (2) the subjects' initial estimates of the candidates' positions; (3) the subjects' actual votes as revealed in the experiment. Thus, in Figure 7.3, we can compare the votes *implied* by Bayesian elimination to the votes *implied* by the subjects' own estimates without social communication, to the subjects' *actual* votes that were contingent on both their *own* estimates *and* social communication.

To determine the candidate estimates via Bayesian elimination, the following steps were employed for each subject.

1. We determine what candidate positions were possible given the signals the subject received. For example, if a subject received a signal of 1 for Candidate A, we eliminated positions 5 and 6 as possibilities.
2. We assume that the subject chooses the midpoint of the remaining range of possible candidate positions as a point estimate for each of the candidates – a strategy that is consistent with Table 7.1.

3. We use these resulting Bayesian estimates of candidate positions to arrive at a predicted vote in the same way as we use the subject's actual estimates to predict a vote in the absence of social communication.

Figure 7.3 illustrates the utility of all three methods. For all subjects – regardless of information level – the best estimate is the Bayesian method described above and the worst is the actual vote. Thus, the calculation of the appropriate vote based on private information falls short of the Bayesian calculation, and social communication has the net effect of reducing the probability of a correct vote based on private information. Most importantly, however, the differences across the three criteria are relatively minor.

Our subjects are unlikely or unable to apply either Bayesian reasoning or computer simulations to the challenges they confront in the experiment. None of them have the time and few of them have the background to apply these principles. Moreover, and quite reasonably, they would be unlikely to believe that the payoff is worth the investment. In much the same way that (1) very few penny-ante blackjack players attempt to count cards and (2) very few voters comprehensively prepare for their votes in a city council election, the subjects in our experiments employ a variety of useful shortcuts in approaching the challenges they confront.

In addition, Figure 7.3 presents net results for the population as a whole. In fact, these net outcomes fail to reveal much difference in the probability of correct voting. Some subjects would improve the probability of a correct vote by adopting a Bayesian strategy, but others would not. Some subjects would improve the probability of a correct vote by ignoring socially communicated messages, but others would benefit by taking account of socially communicated messages.

INCENTIVES FOR CROSS-BOUNDARY INFORMATION ACQUISITION

Finally, we focus on the problem addressed in the previous chapter – on the contextually contingent incentives for acquiring costly information from an out-group informant. We do this indirectly by calculating the values of private information – that is, if an expert informant communicates undistorted information to a subject, the recipient becomes as well-informed as the informant. Hence, the value of the socially acquired information is the same as the value of the informant's private information. The recipient might compare the value of the informant's privately obtained information against the social acquisition costs, which is 10 ECUs if the subject and the informant belong to different groups. The primary problem that arises, however, is that the recipient cannot assume that the informant is providing unbiased information.

We will see that, if a voter thinks her vote is pivotal, she might find it worth paying the cost of acquiring information from a member of the opposite group. For example, if a subject with a high information cost locates an expert informant with the same preference in the out-group, she might be willing to pay the 10 ECUs, particularly if suitable informants are not available within her own group. At the same time, the analysis will also show that a purely strategic calculation of costs and benefits frequently leads to a conclusion that these costs are too high. In short, the 10 ECU cost creates a zone of ambiguity that it is neither always too small relative to the expected gain nor so large as to keep all voters from considering the possibility of acquiring out-group information.

The analyses of Chapters 5 and 6 suggest that, from a strategic standpoint, individuals tend to overinvest in the acquisition of information. This over-investment might be due to limited strategic sophistication (Crawford 2003). Alternatively, it might also be the result of an urge to perform well in competitive contests (Ahn, Isaac, and Salmon, 2011). That is, the activist impulse on the part of participants might be a consequence of their own moth-and-flame urges to become more fully involved, irrespective of cost. Finally, overinvestment may arise due to the recognition that informants often provide meaningful information to others when, from a strategic standpoint, they would be expected to engage in cheap talk (Cai and Wang 2006).

With these factors in the background, what *should* be a rare event, i.e., paying 10 ECUs for information from another group, might happen with greater frequency. That is, if the innate desire to vote correctly and thereby win an election plays a role in the information acquisition decision, and if an information seeker either rightly or wrongly believes that the experts with different preferences would provide useful information (Calvert 1985a), then we will see the cross-boundary information seeking more often than can be expected from narrowly strategic, payoff maximizing calculations.

The value of information is a function of (1) the size of payoff at stake in an election, (2) the increased probability of voting correctly due to the information, and (3) the probability that the voter will be pivotal. In the analysis we assume that the voter is pivotal to calculate the upper limit of the value of information. A voter receives 50 ECUs if the candidate with a position closer to his own wins the election, loses 50 ECUs if the candidate with the position farther from his own wins the election, and neither gains nor loses if the two candidates are equally distant from his own position. Hence, the payoff swing for a voter as a result of an election is 100, but the value of voting correctly is at most 50 ECUs due to the even number of voters – that is, a pivotal vote can either change the election result from losing to a tie, or from a tie to winning. In either case, the maximum possible payoff consequence is 50.

Publicly available information sets the baseline probabilities of voting correctly for voters with different ideal points. Additional information, either privately purchased or socially acquired, has the potential of further improving the probability of voting correctly. As explained in the text, the individually purchased information consists of signals about candidate positions in the form of integer numbers drawn randomly from a uniform distribution, bounded above and below (±3) the candidate's true position. The most effective strategy is to use the information to rule out the possibility of particular candidate positions, thereby corresponding to an application of the Bayes' Rule to this setting.

For example, voters know, based on the public information, that Candidate B cannot be located at position 1. If a voter obtains a privately purchased signal that Candidate B holds position 3, this means that the candidate's position must lie in the interval bounded by 2 and 6 inclusively. As additional information is obtained, the voter might be able to narrow the range of possible positions further, thereby arriving at a progressively more precise estimate. The simple algebraic mean of the signals produces similar outcomes in many cases, but such a strategy will result in more incorrect votes over time. A strategic voter using the elimination method, and choosing a candidate based on private signals only, would calculate the average distance of the remaining possible positions for each of the two candidates to the voter's own ideal point. By choosing the candidate whose possible positions are on average closer to the voter's own ideal point, the voter maximizes the probability of voting correctly.

We determine the values of the private information by running one million computer simulations, assuming that (1) the subjects use Bayesian elimination to estimate candidate positions, and (2) that the voters are pivotal. The second assumption likely overestimates the value of the information, as voters are *not* always pivotal. The first row of Table 7.4A shows the probability that a subject votes correctly if she relies solely on the publicly available information. Subsequent rows in the table set these probabilities for corresponding amounts of privately purchased information. Hence, subjects with positions 1 and 7 improve their probabilities of voting correctly from .72 to .94 as a consequence of buying four pieces of information.

Table 7.4B translates these probabilities of voting correctly into objectively defined benefit in ECUs. For example, the expected value of four pieces of information for a voter at position 1 is 10.8 ECUs.[4] This value is only slightly different from the value obtained by multiplying the improved probability of voting correctly (.22) by the size of the electoral payoff (50). The difference is due to the fact that a voter is considered to be voting correctly whenever the two candidates are equally distant from the voter. Table 7.4B shows that there are a total of 7 out of 12 cases in which purchasing the specified amount of information increases the expected payoff by more than 10 ECUs.

With this analysis as a backdrop, we can assess the costs and benefits of acquiring information from a member of the out-group. The most optimistic scenario in support of paying 10 ECUs to get information from a member of the

---

[4] Note that the value of information is less in the experiment described in Chapter 6 than the experiment in Chapter 5. Information is worth more when the number of voters is odd – as in Chapter 5 – because a single subject can swing the election from a payoff loss to a payoff gain. Chapter 6's experiment has an even number of voters which results only in a swing from a payoff loss to break even or breaking even to a payoff gain.

TABLE 7.4. *Determining the value of private information. Results from one million simulations by candidate positions and private information signals.*
A. *Probability of voting correctly by voter positions and private information acquired.*

Private information purchased	Voter positions			
	1 and 7	2 and 6	3 and 5	4
0	0.72	0.7	0.67	0.64
1	0.82	0.81	0.77	0.73
2	0.88	0.87	0.84	0.8
3	0.91	0.91	0.88	0.85
4	0.94	0.93	0.91	0.89

B. *Upper limits on the value of information for different voter positions.*

Pieces of information	Voter positions			
	1 and 7	2 and 6	3 and 5	4
1	4.9	6	6.4	6
2	7.9	9.1	9.4	9.3
3	7.7	10.9	11.3	11.5
4	10.8	12	12.6	13.1

other group is the case in which a high-cost voter with position 4 who purchased no information finds another subject in the other group with the same ideal point of 4 who purchased 4 pieces of privately obtained information. The informant should not mislead the voter in this case because their interests are perfectly aligned. By following the direction of the expert informant, the subject votes as if she has four pieces of information. Voting based on what the informant says, indicated by the messages received, will increase the expected electoral payoff by 13.1 ECUs. After paying the 10 ECU cost the net gain is 3.1 ECUs.

Even with this increase in expected earnings, the strategic value of a request for out-group information is contingent on the potential informants available within the requestor's own group – that is, it makes sense only if no one in the in-group is sufficiently expert with similar preferences to provide high-quality, reliable information. Hence, these analyses establish the fact that obtaining information from someone in the other group is often not strategically rational from a narrow earnings-maximization perspective.

The willingness of our subjects to obtain out-group information, as well as their willingness to emphasize expertise rather than shared preferences in the selection of informants, is difficult to explain in the absence of other explanatory devices – the difficulty of carrying out the analysis we have just provided; bounded rationality; the activist's competitive urge to contribute to a winning cause; trust of experts with divergent preferences; and so on. Our argument is *not* that subjects are irrational, but only that strategic calculation regarding the direct costs and benefits connected with the experiment do not provide an entirely satisfactory account of their actions. At the same time, the experiment also makes it clear that the high cost of cross-boundary information acquisition encourages subjects to think carefully about the contextual factors as well as to compare the distribution of preferences and expertise within one's own group relative to those in the other group.

IMPLICATIONS AND CONCLUSIONS

In conclusion, while we might see a slight increase in the level of "correct voting" if our subjects acted as socially isolated Bayesian decision-makers, the gains would be marginal, and the individual and social costs would increase. Moreover, while some individuals are misled by socially communicated information, others benefit.

The implications for citizenship and democratic politics are straightforward. It is, in the abstract, conceivable that citizens could participate as socially independent decision-makers who use sophisticated decision-making strategies. As an empirical reality, this will not happen except in the most exceptional cases. Just as important, such an outcome would impose costs that would be injurious to the political and social well-being of the whole. In general, a democratic society is likely to be better off if there *is* a division of labor with respect to politics. Some people need to be the activists and experts who occupy central roles as opinion leaders. Others need to spend their time at other important social and political pursuits: coaching little league baseball, practicing violin, working at the local food pantry, organizing neighborhood associations, and much, much more.[5]

None of this means that voters are irrational. To the contrary, our analysis suggests that the effort and resources required to pursue optimal information-gathering and voting strategies are unlikely to pay dividends – *either* at the level of individuals *or* at the level of the society. Not only is the task complex, but the information-processing strategies of individuals are complex as well.

In the next chapter, we introduce a new experiment in which networks are fixed and experimental participants receive multiple social messages. To cope with this added complexity, subjects develop partisan shortcuts for interpreting these social messages. Perhaps surprisingly, these shortcuts prove to be effective for some uninformed subjects, but lead to poor decisions for some informed subjects.

---

[5] For the classic statement of this position, see Berelson et al. (1954: chapter 14).

8

Partisanship and the efficacy of social communication in constrained environments

John Barry Ryan

> It should be stated flatly at the outset that this volume is devoted to the thesis that the political parties created democracy and that modern democracy is unthinkable save in terms of parties. As a matter of fact, the condition of the parties is the best possible evidence of the nature of any regime.
>
> E. E. Schattschneider (1942: 1)

The experimental design employed in this chapter diverges from those in the previous chapters in several important ways. First, these experiments reintroduce the role of parties and partisanship relative to social communication and opinion leadership. Our argument is that partisanship plays an important yet frequently maligned and under-utilized role in the communication process. In particular, it provides the recipient of communication with an important device to use in sifting and evaluating the bias of an incoming message based on its partisan origin.

Second, the experiment in this chapter assumes that individuals have limited ability to control the social flow of political messages. In contrast, the experiments in the previous chapters are based on a very different view of the communication process. Subjects were seeking information from their fellow subjects, and selecting discussion partners whom they believed were most likely to provide useful information. Hence, they exercised control over both the sources of information as well as their own responses to that information. The alternative view entertained in this chapter is that people often receive political messages from acquaintances independently of their own preferences. There is, for example, little that one can do to avoid a grouchy uncle's rants at holiday gatherings regarding the President or Congress. Such a view of the social communication process inspires the experimental design of this chapter. The experimental participants cannot choose from *whom* they receive messages, but only how they will incorporate these messages in formulating their judgments.

Finally, the experiments utilized in the previous chapters, as well as most of the formal literature on political communication, view discussion as a predominantly dyadic process involving one individual receiving information from one inform-ant. The decision to model discussion as dyadic assumes that receivers evaluate the credibility of messages in a particular manner – judging the credibility of each messenger separately and determining whether or not to accept the message. In this way, even if the listener receives messages from multiple people, each of those conversations can be viewed as a separate dyadic interaction.

In the real world, however, voters seldom experience conversational effects in dyadic isolation – as though the dyads are separate and apart from an interpre-tively significant social context. According to an autoregressive influence model (Huckfeldt, Johnson, and Sprague 2004), informants are influential to the extent that their messages are confirmed by the other messages an individual receives. One consequence of this is that voters might be persuaded by politically biased messages that are socially reinforced, even though these messages benefit the messenger rather than the recipient. The poorly informed may be particularly vulnerable, and hence while political discussion might be an effective informational shortcut for the informed, it may result in poorer decisions among the uninformed.

This chapter uses an experimental framework to expand the social commu-nication process beyond simple dyads. Moving to larger discussion networks has several implications for social communication and "correct voting" (Lau and Redlawsk 1997). First, it allows us to address questions regarding how individuals evaluate incoming messages. For example, do individuals judge the credibility of the messengers (as choice theoretic models suggest) or do they evaluate the content of the messages (as an autoregressive model suggests)? Second, it helps specify the conditions under which social communication and opinion leaders will lead to correct and incorrect voting.

In the experiment, subjects choose between computer-generated candidates who offer two types of payoffs: (1) a *global* benefit that all subjects receive, and (2) a *partisan* payoff that is a bonus if the candidate from the subject's party wins but a penalty if the candidate from the subject's party loses. Subjects do not know the true magnitude of a candidate's global benefit, but they receive private signals that aid them in estimating the payoff. In a control group, each subject receives these private signals and then votes without communicating with other subjects. In a treatment group, subjects receive the same private signals but then share information with each other regarding the size of the global benefit before voting. The value of social communication is evaluated by comparing the decisions of the treatment group subjects before and after communication, as well as comparing the votes of the treatment group to those of the control group.

DYADIC SOCIAL COMMUNICATION

Given the myriad political contests and complex issues in politics, it comes as no surprise that many individuals minimize information costs by using information taken from their more politically engaged associates. Indeed, even the politically engaged rely on information taken from others (Katz 1957). Individuals also receive information from the media and reach conclusions about the state of the economy, the competency of candidates, and all of the other factors that influence vote decisions. These evaluations serve as their judgmental priors, which are then updated based on the messages they receive through their discussion networks (McPhee 1963). The final judgment is thus a combination of the messages individuals receive both from the media and from their discussion partners (Barabas 2004).

Several models are helpful for understanding how individuals incorporate socially acquired information (e.g., Lupia and McCubbins 1998; Jackman and Sniderman 2006). Political discussion often conveys information that is either intentionally or unintentionally biased, and hence it can be seen as a form of cheap talk (Crawford and Sobel 1982). Such information is most reliable and trustworthy when both members of a discussion dyad share preferences (Crawford 1998), thereby eliminating the incentive to mislead and obfuscate (Boudreau 2009). Even if they are not purposefully dissembling to gain a strategic advantage, information from partisan discussion partners may reflect their own partisan biases (Bartels 2002). Hence, these models imply a proposition about the source of information to which individuals might be expected to be most receptive. According to an ***in-party message acceptance hypothesis*** (**H₁**): *When an individual makes a vote choice, she only incorporates information sent by a member of her own party.*

At the same time, the manner in which these biases affect an individual recipient will depend on the expertise of the listener. An informed recipient should be less dependent on social information to make a correct decision – they should have enough information to vote correctly and hence the additional, potentially biased information is more likely to be misleading (Lupia and McCubbins 1998). The truly uninformed are most in need of social information, but they are also most vulnerable to voting against their own interests (Jackman and Sniderman 2006). It is thus paramount that the uninformed identify a speaker's biases and incorporate only information from those with similar biases.[1] This leads, in turn, to a second proposition. The ***contingent benefit for the uninformed hypothesis*** (**H₂**) suggests that: *A poorly informed individual only benefits from social information if it is taken from a member of his own party, or in the case of an independent, from another independent.*

MOVING BEYOND THE DYAD: THE AUTOREGRESSIVE INFLUENCE MODEL

While previously discussed models often treat political discussion as a purely dyadic process, socially obtained information is not typically communicated in

---

[1] One might question whether individuals discuss politics with people with opposing preferences, but as earlier chapters suggest, the evidence is quite clear that individuals often communicate with others who do not share their own political instincts (also see Huckfeldt, Ikeda, and Pappi 2005).

isolation – that is, recipients often receive information from multiple messengers. From a strict choice theoretic perspective, this should not matter as each message could be evaluated on a case-by-case basis, with the recipient rejecting messages sent by someone with different political viewpoints. This further assumes, however, that a listener chooses which messages to accept or reject based on who sent the messages.

Alternatively, the recipients may not evaluate incoming messages based solely on the messenger's biases and incentives. Instead, they may accept messages based on the relative frequency with which a particular message is reinforced by other messengers. Hence, this chapter's argument makes an important distinction between dyadic interactions and discussion with a larger social network. According to an autoregressive influence model (Huckfeldt, Johnson, and Sprague 2004), individuals are more likely to accept messages when they are in accord with other messages previously received. Individuals, therefore, should be most likely to support the candidate favored by the majority of the people with whom they discuss politics, independent of partisan loyalties.

Why would subjects accept messages from multiple opposing partisans and ignore messages from a single member of their own party? Many individuals will view two or more people sending similar messages to be verification of those messages. If information sources are largely unbiased, then this would be a rational strategy. In contrast, if social messages are biased and both discussion partners have the same preferences, then a biased message is "verified" by a source with the same bias.[2] Thus, it is not really verified at all, but it may be incorporated into the posterior judgments because it has been corroborated by another source – albeit an untrustworthy one. Viewed objectively, the individual should ignore this social information, but may believe the messages because they all suggest the same vote. This suggests a proposition that is contrary to the *in-party message acceptance hypothesis*. The ***autoregressive influence hypothesis*** (H$_3$) suggests that *an individual is more likely to vote incorrectly when she receives social information primarily from members of a different party than when she receives information primarily from fellow partisans.*

WHAT DOES IT MEAN TO VOTE CORRECTLY?

Research related to discussion and "correct" voting has been limited in part because of the method typically used to study voting behavior – the analysis of survey data. In this context, it is often difficult to determine whether someone made a "correct vote" choice because an objective determination of whom the voter should have supported is difficult to obtain. Lau and Redlawsk (1997) develop a creative means for using surveys to determine correct voting based

---

[2] Calvert (1985a) notes that there are situations where individuals use information from advisors with different biases effectively. In the Calvert model, however, it is the *content* of the advisor's message that is especially important.

on the following three factors: (1) whether the voter chose the candidate with similar issue positions, (2) whether the voter chose the candidate who is more closely linked to the voter's social group, and (3) the mean job performance rating of the incumbent, if an incumbent exists (see also Lau, Andersen, and Redlawsk 2008.)

Using Lau and Redlawsk's (1997) method, Sokhey and McClurg (2012) conclude that people are more likely to vote correctly if they speak exclusively with like-minded individuals.[3] The cross-sectional nature of their data, however, makes it difficult for them to show the persuasion process (Kenny 1998). They do not observe who the voters would have chosen in the absence of discussion, and they cannot evaluate whom the discussion helped and whom it hurt.

When voting correctly is defined as voting for the candidate with similar issue positions, partisans should almost always vote for the candidate from their party. Stokes (1963) recognizes, however, that candidates provide two types of benefits to voters: *global* benefits on *valence* issues, and *partisan* benefits on *positional* issues. Valence issues are consensual issues in which all voters desire the same outcome – e.g., a government that is not corrupt and provides peace and prosperity.[4] *Positional issues* are divisive issues for which voters have different preferred policies. If a candidate lacks the competency to provide for the general social welfare (i.e., offers low global benefits), even a strong partisan with very similar issue positions might vote for the candidate from the other party.

We will define *correct voting* as voting for the candidate that offers the greater *total* benefit, taking into account both valence and position issues. This definition of correct voting rests on several simplifying assumptions. First, it assumes that a candidate provides an objective valence benefit. In fact, it may be that the valence benefit is based on voter values and is subjective as well (Gerber and Green 1999). For example, one voter may value providing the best average welfare, while another may care more about raising the lowest level of welfare experienced in their society. These differences in values, however, should be captured by differences in position benefits.

Second, this definition of correct voting assumes that voters have true, fixed issue positions – potentially including indifference. In reality, voters may change their opinion during the course of a campaign. Even if they hold the same issue positions throughout the campaign, they may reevaluate which issues are important, which may change the value of the benefits offered on positional issues.

---

[3] Richey (2008) found that individuals who speak more frequently with political experts were more likely to vote correctly, but he did not include a measure of network heterogeneity in his analysis.

[4] Lau and Redlawsk's (1997) measure places more emphasis on position issues, but it does attempt to account for valence benefits by including a measure of incumbent job performance. For all of its strengths, this part of the measure is flawed. A poor performing incumbent provides a lower valence benefit than a well-performing incumbent, but this is not the comparison that matters. What is important is the performance of the incumbent relative to the potential performance of the challenger – which is never observed in the real world.

This also could change which members of the social network have preferences that are similar to the voter's own preferences (Baldassarri and Bearman 2007). Such an assumption, however, is necessary to evaluate a correct vote. Without this assumption, it is impossible to tell whether a voter was duped into voting in favor of someone else's interests instead of her own or whether she rationally updated her opinions.

RESEARCH DESIGN

These issues are best tested through an experimental research design. First, there is no way to objectively measure the valence benefit that candidates will offer in real-world politics. Second, one has to see whom a voter would have chosen in the *absence* of discussion to determine whether and how discussion influenced the vote. Third, the analyst needs to observe what social information the voter received and who sent those messages. Fourth, an experiment allows for assignment to social networks answering the well-founded concern that contextual effects are simply due to the consequences of self-selection (Achen and Shively 1995).

To test the effects of interpersonal communication on correct voting, we employ a small group experiment in which subjects in a *treatment group* receive private information about two computer-generated "candidates" and then share information with other subjects before voting for one of the two. The subjects – 135 in all – were recruited from undergraduate political science courses at the University of California, Davis. A follow-up experiment – to be described later – yields a *control group* by giving 81 subjects private information but not allowing any communication among them. Subjects in both experiments received a $10.00 show-up fee plus whatever earnings they accrued during the experiment. The experiments were programmed using z-Tree (Fischbacher 2007).[5]

THE TREATMENT GROUP

Parties and candidates

The experimental design randomly assigns subjects their partisan affiliation: party A, party B, or independent. Subjects attempt to determine the benefits offered by computer-generated "candidates" of the parties – candidates named Adams and Bates, respectively – in a mock election. There are nine subjects participating in each experimental session: three in A, three in B, and three independents. In each session, subjects participate in multiple periods, each of which is a unique election with different global benefits and partisan payoffs.

---

[5] Nine of the subjects in the control group were undergraduates at Florida State University. Separate analyses demonstrate that recruiting students from two different universities does not invalidate the conclusions reached in this chapter.

The subjects' characteristics – their partisanship and information levels – do not change.

At the end of every experimental period, each subject is told to vote for the candidate he believes will provide him with the larger payoff. Typically, this will be a candidate from the subject's party, but on occasion a subject will receive a larger payoff from the other party's candidate.

GLOBAL BENEFITS

Much like candidates in a real election, the candidates offer subjects two types of benefits. First, candidates provide a global benefit that is the same for all subjects and can be conceived as the benefit a candidate provides on valence issues. The global benefit provided by each candidate is independently and randomly drawn from a uniform distribution with a lower bound of 20 Experimental Currency Units (ECUs) and an upper bound of 100 ECUs. Subjects receive the global benefit offered by the candidate who received the most votes from the nine subjects.

PARTISAN PAYOFFS

In addition to the global benefits, subjects in parties A and B receive either a party bonus or a penalty depending on the outcome of the election. These are akin to the benefits candidates provide on positional issues. If Adams wins the election, members of party A receive a bonus while B partisans receive a penalty. To the contrary, the B partisans benefit if Bates wins the election, and the A partisans are penalized. The magnitude of both an individual's partisan bonus and her partisan penalty is randomly drawn from a uniform distribution with a minimum of 10 ECUs and a maximum of 20 ECUs. On average, subjects in party A are better off if Adams is elected, subjects in party B are better off if Bates is elected, and independents are indifferent between Adams and Bates.[6]

TIMELINE OF THE EXPERIMENT

Each subject is aware of the distribution from which each candidate's global benefit is drawn and of her individual party payoff, but she does not know any candidate's global benefit in a particular election.[7] The subjects must use private

---

[6] In expectation, the weakest partisans – those with a partisan pay of 10 ECUs – would receive a greater benefit from their party's candidate 71.2% of the time; partisans with the mean partisan pay – 15 ECUs – would receive a greater benefit from their party's candidate 79.8% of the time; the strongest partisans – those with a partisan pay of 20 ECUs – would receive a greater benefit from their party's candidate 86.9% of the time. At the end of the experiment subjects are paid at a rate of 1 cent per ECU. Subjects received between $14.00 and $21.00, with a median pay of $17.00.

[7] The exact instructions provided to subjects are available in the appendix.

and social information to estimate the candidates' global benefits. The experiment proceeds over the following four stages.

STAGE 1: PRIVATE INFORMATION STAGE

Subjects receive private information about each candidate's global benefit, and then make their own initial estimates for each candidate.

As displayed in Table 8.1A, subjects are randomly assigned to one of five different information conditions, each defined by the number of signals (or pieces of information) subjects receive about the candidates, where a signal consists of information about both candidates. Therefore, if a subject receives two signals, that means the subject sees two signals about Adams' benefit and two signals about Bates' benefit. The subjects remain in the same information condition throughout the experiment.

TABLE 8.1. *Subject information levels and networks.*
A. *Subject's private information levels*

	Number of signals received by subject								
Condition	A1	A2	A3	I4	I5	I6	B7	B8	B9
#1	1	0	0	2	1	3	4	3	2
#2	4	0	3	2	3	1	1	2	0
#3	0	4	1	3	1	2	2	0	3
#4	1	3	3	0	4	0	2	1	2
#5	3	2	2	4	0	0	1	3	1

B. *Network providing social information*

	Sender			
Recipient	Alter 1	Alter 2	Alter 3	Network Type
A1	A2	I4	B9	Heterogeneous
A2	A1	A3	I5	Homogeneous A (in-group)
A3	I6	B7	B8	Homogeneous B (out-group)
I4	A2	A3	I5	Homogeneous A (out-group)
I5	I6	B7	B9	Homogeneous B (out-group)
I6	A1	I4	B8	Heterogeneous
B7	I4	B8	B9	Homogeneous B (in-group)
B8	A1	A3	I5	Homogeneous A (out-group)
B9	A2	I6	B7	Heterogeneous

Note: The three subjects from Party A are denoted A1, A2, and A3; the three independents are denoted I4, I5, and I6; and the three subjects from Party B are denoted B7, B8, and B9.

In each condition, one subject receives four signals, and the other eight subjects are evenly divided over the four remaining information levels: three signals, two signals, one signal, or zero. The top row of the table identifies the subjects by their partisan status – A, B, or independent (I) – and a unique participant identification number (1 though 9). Each column displays the number of signals a participant receives in each of the information conditions.

For each signal, the computer screen displays "Candidate Adams/Bates says his benefit is:" and then an integer value. The integer values are randomly drawn from a uniform distribution centered on the candidate's true benefit and extending 25 ECUs above and below that benefit.[8] Thus, on average, the private information received by subjects reflects candidates' true global benefits, but the information is *noisy*.

After receiving private information, each subject is asked to estimate the global benefit that each candidate provides. These estimates measure subjects' beliefs prior to social communication.

STAGE 2: FIRST SOCIAL INFORMATION STAGE

Subjects send messages about the size of candidates' global benefits to one another, and they update their estimates of the candidates' global benefits.

Each subject sends a message conveying information about the candidates to three other subjects: one from party A, one from party B, and one independent. Once again, the messages are integer values asserting the size of the global benefit each candidate offers. No other communication is allowed. Subjects are told that they do not have to make identical assertions to each subject, but they are not encouraged to misrepresent their beliefs. Subjects may make assertions strategically, however, because they know the private information level and partisanship of each subject.[9]

Subjects receive social information from the networks listed in Table 8.1B. Networks in this experiment take on one of three types: heterogeneous, homogeneous A, and homogeneous B. In heterogeneous networks, there is one member of each party and one independent. In homogeneous networks, there are

---

[8] This means that subjects can receive assertions that a candidate offers a benefit that is impossible. For example, if a candidate offers the lowest possible benefit of 20 ECUs, subjects may receive signals that say that the candidate offers a benefit of –5 ECUs. This is a necessary aspect of the design allowing subjects to easily calculate expected payoffs based on the private information they receive.

[9] Survey evidence suggests that individuals can accurately identify the preferences of their political discussion partners, but they do have an easier time recalling the preferences and opinions of stronger partisans and those with whom they discuss politics most frequently (Huckfeldt 2007b). As Chapter 3 shows, individuals are also able to differentiate between political expert and inexpert individuals, even though these perceptions are imperfect and can be biased by gender and levels of political engagement.

two members of either party A or party B and an independent. Partisan subjects, therefore, may receive messages from a majority of like-minded subjects (an in-group network), a heterogeneous network, or a network without any subjects who share their biases (an out-group network).

After receiving social information, subjects again estimate the candidates' benefits. They are reminded of their previous estimates of Adams' and Bates' global benefits, thus permitting subjects to update their estimates based on the new information they received.

STAGE 3: SECOND SOCIAL INFORMATION STAGE

Subjects again send messages about the size of candidates' global benefits to one another. They again update their estimates of the candidates' global benefits.

Subjects convey new assertions about candidates' global benefits to the same three subjects to whom they previously provided information. This allows individuals to incorporate information they received through social communication in addition to the private information they initially received. Subjects are reminded of their previous estimates of global benefits and asked to make a final estimate of the benefit each candidate provides.

STAGE 4: VOTING AND PAYOFFS

Each of the nine subjects then votes for a candidate, the candidate with the most votes is declared the winner, and the true global benefit of each candidate is revealed.

Subjects are then paid based on the benefits offered by the candidate who receives the most votes. In calculating the payments, the global benefit of the winning candidate is awarded to each subject (partisan or independent). In addition, each member of the winning candidate's party is awarded her partisan bonus and, similarly, each member of the losing candidate's party is docked his penalty amount. Although subjects are not paid based on whether they voted correctly, a correct vote increases the probability that a subject will be paid more.

Subjects then participate in a new campaign with new, randomly drawn, candidate benefits. The subjects' parties, partisan pay, information levels, and networks remain the same throughout the experiment. Subjects participate in as many elections as they can complete within one hour.[10]

---

[10] All subjects participate in one practice period. After the practice period, one experimental session involved five periods, one session involved six, two involved seven, one involved eight, one involved nine, four involved ten, one involved eleven, and four involved twelve periods. The analyses that follow use data from the first seven elections of each experimental session. Capping the number of elections at seven allows for balance across all fifteen sessions. Including all elections in computations does not change the paper's substantive conclusions.

THE CONTROL GROUP

After completing the main treatment, a follow-up experiment was conducted to create a control group. The experimental software was programmed based on the randomly drawn benefits and signals from the treatment session. Therefore, subjects in this control group participate in elections with candidates offering the same benefits and sending the exact same signals as in the initial experiment.[11] The subjects in the control group, however, receive private information, estimate the candidates' benefits, and then vote without ever exchanging messages with their fellow subjects. Hence, for each of the treatment subjects, there is a control subject who received the exact same private information and then voted based solely on that information. The votes of these treatment and control subjects can be directly compared to assess the value of the social information.

WHAT HAVE WE LEARNED?

Treatment subjects vary on two main dimensions: the amount of private information they possess and the partisanship of the network that provides social information. For simplification, we divide subjects into the uninformed (those who receive no signals) and the informed (those who receive at least one signal) because the marginal value of additional information after the first signal is small. Subjects' networks can be characterized as in-group, out-group, or heterogeneous based on the partisanship of the subject and the network.

The design allows for both *between-subjects* and *within-subjects* tests of the hypotheses. The between-subjects tests compare the votes of the main treatment group to the votes of the control group. The subjects in the control and the treatment groups have the same private information. Hence, differences in vote decisions between the control and the treatment groups should capture the effect of social communication.

The within-subjects tests involve the treatment subjects' initial estimates of the global benefits. We assume that if subjects had voted after receiving private information but before receiving any social information, each subject would have chosen the candidate that maximized her payoff based on her known party pay and her beliefs about the global benefits. This yields an *implied vote* in the absence of social information for each subject, which can be compared to

---

[11] Each treatment session was paired with a control session, but some control sessions were paired with two treatment sessions. Hence, the participants in some control sessions first participated in the elections corresponding to one treatment session and then participated in the elections corresponding to a second treatment session. This means, for example, that some control subjects participating in their eighth election are being compared to treatment subjects participating in their first election. While it is conceivable that this might affect the comparisons, other analyses show no behavioral changes across rounds.

the subject's actual vote to determine the effect of social information on her decision.[12]

THE IN-PARTY MESSAGE ACCEPTANCE HYPOTHESIS (H_1)

If this hypothesis is supported, then control and treatment subjects should vote for the same candidates except when the treatment subject receives messages from someone in their party. In the within-subjects analyses, the only subjects who should have final votes different from implied votes are those who received messages from someone in their party.

THE CONTINGENT BENEFIT FOR THE UNINFORMED HYPOTHESIS (H_2)

Based on this hypothesis, uninformed treatment subjects who receive social information predominantly from members of their own party should vote correctly more often than uninformed control subjects. In within-subjects analyses of those who are uninformed and receive social information from a member of their own party, the percentage of actual votes that are correct should be greater than the percentage of implied votes that are correct.

THE AUTOREGRESSIVE INFLUENCE HYPOTHESIS (H_3)

This hypothesis implies that treatment subjects in heterogeneous and out-group networks should vote correctly less often than control subjects. Also, these treatment subjects' implied votes should be correct more frequently than their actual votes.

THE BETWEEN-SUBJECT RESULTS

If social information serves as a useful information shortcut, then subjects in the treatment group (those who received social information) should vote correctly more frequently than subjects in the control group (those who did not receive social information). One might expect that uninformed subjects would benefit the most from social information. Informed subjects should already be voting

---

[12] It is possible to evaluate the extent to which the implied vote would have reflected what subjects actually would have done by observing the frequency with which the control group's votes matched the vote implied by their initial estimates. Remember, the control group subjects voted immediately after making their initial estimates. If their implied votes and actual votes are similar, this is evidence that the implied votes do measure the behavior that would have occurred. In the control group, implied votes and actual votes were the same 85.4% of the time, but they were a better predictor for independents (who needed to consider only global benefit) than partisans (who needed to consider both the global benefit and the partisan payoff). Implied votes predicted actual votes 94.6% of the time for independents and 80.1% of the time for partisans.

correctly at high levels, making it less likely that they would improve their level of correct voting.

Figure 8.1 compares the percentage of correct votes in the control and treatment groups by information level and network partisanship. The lighter bars in Figure 8.1 show the proportion of correct votes in the control group. The darker bars show the percentage of correct votes in the treatment group. Control group subjects are not located in networks as they did not receive social information. Thus, for control groups, the networks refer to the network of the paired treatment subject who received the same private information.

The results support *the contingent benefit for the uninformed hypothesis* (H_2), but only for independents. As the left panel in Figure 8.1B shows, 46 percent of uninformed independents vote correctly in the control group. The percent of uninformed independents who vote correctly rises to 69 percent in the treatment group. A *t*-test comparing those percentages shows a statistically significant difference ($t=3.45$; $p=.002$).[13]

(A1)

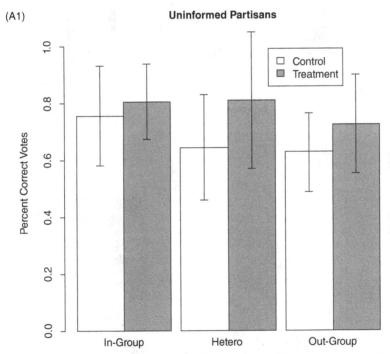

FIGURE 8.1. Percentage of correct votes for control and treatment groups by information level and network partisanship. Error bars display 95% confidence intervals with standard errors corrected for clustering on subjects.

---

[13] In all analyses, standard errors are corrected for clustering on subjects.

Informed Partisans

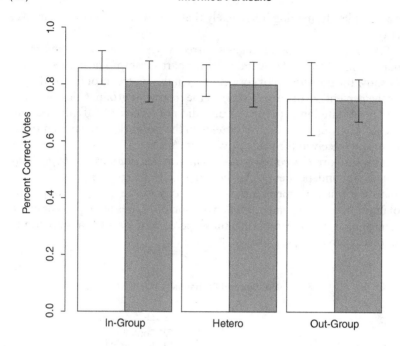

Independents

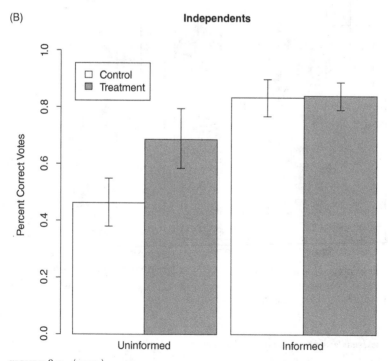

FIGURE 8.1. (cont.)

There is no statistically significant improvement for uninformed partisans overall or for uninformed partisans in particular networks. Overall, uninformed partisans voted correctly more frequently in the treatment group – 78 percent compared to 67 percent in the control group – but this difference is not statistically significant ($t=1.56$; $p=.129$). Uninformed partisans had more information to help them choose between the candidates than uninformed independents. Uninformed partisans could always vote for the candidate from their party and be correct most of the time.

Interestingly, informed partisans and independents voted correctly at very similar rates in both the treatment and control groups. Informed subjects voted correctly about 80 percent of the time in all cases except for partisans in out-group networks. About 75 percent of votes cast by both treatment partisans in out-group networks and their control group counterparts were correct. Yet this percentage of correct votes among out-group subjects is not statistically different from informed subjects in the other groups.

The results in Figure 8.1 suggest that social information has little effect on how individuals voted, with the exception of uninformed independents. However, the results in Table 8.2 – in which the unit of analysis is a subject pair – convey a different story. Recall that each treatment group subject is paired with a control group subject who had the same party, same party benefit, and received the same private information about the candidates. The dependent variable takes on one of four categories: (1) if both subjects voted for the same candidate and that was a correct vote; (2) if both subjects voted for the same candidate and that was an incorrect vote; (3) if the subjects voted for different candidates and the treatment subject voted correctly and thus was helped by social communication; (4) if the subjects voted for different candidates and the control group subject voted correctly and thus social information hurt the treatment subject.

As Table 8.2 shows, most of the time the treatment and control group subjects chose the same candidate. When social information influenced a treatment subject, however, it had different effects for uninformed and informed subjects. The uninformed are aided because, when the treatment and control subjects vote for different candidates, the social information tended to be helpful. This table shows that many partisans who lacked information benefited from the social communication. For informed subjects, however, the social information was often helpful, but just as frequently the social information led the subject to make an incorrect vote.

The *in-party message acceptance hypothesis* (H_1) would suggest that treatment and control subjects should vote for the same candidates unless the treatment subject is located in an in-group network. The results in Table 8.2 show that this is clearly not the case. Treatment and control partisans vote for different candidates more than one-third of the time when the treatment partisans receive social information from out-partisans. Clearly, the treatment subjects were updating their evaluations of the candidates based on social information even if that information came from informants with conflicting preferences. Hence,

TABLE 8.2. *Comparing correct votes in control and treatment groups by information level and network partisanship. Standard errors corrected for clustering on subject pairs.*
A. *Partisans*

Uninformed	In-group	Hetero.	Out-group	Informed	In-group	Hetero.	Out-group
Both right	63.4%	50.0%	50.0%	Both right	71.8%	68.9%	55.9%
Both wrong	7.3%	4.8%	15.0%	Both wrong	4.9%	7.5%	6.2%
Social helps	17.1%	31.0%	22.5%	Social helps	14.1%	11.1%	18.6%
Social hurts	12.2%	14.3%	12.5%	Social hurts	9.2%	12.4%	19.3%
N	41	42	40	N			
F=0.786; p= 0.526				F=2.144; p=0.058			

B. *Independents*

Uninformed	Hetero.	Out-group	Informed	Hetero.	Out-group
Both right	37.5%	32.5%	Both right	70.5%	74.0%
Both wrong	20.0%	20.0%	Both wrong	4.9%	6.2%
Social helps	30.0%	37.5%	Social helps	14.8%	9.4%
Social hurts	12.5%	10.0%	Social hurts	9.8%	10.5%
N	33	33	N	61	155
F=0.257; p=0.788			F=0.391; p=0.749		

the treatment subjects were not evaluating the incoming messages in the manner that the formal models would predict.

Informed partisans deserve special attention. These subjects should do the least updating based on social information. As partisans, they have strong ex ante reasons to prefer a particular candidate. As informed subjects, they do not need social information and have reasons to be skeptical about any social information that contradicts their previous beliefs. And yet, the subjects behaved differently based on who was providing the information according to the F statistic, which is statistically significant at the .10 level. Another way of evaluating this is to examine the frequency with which the control and treatment subjects voted for different candidates. When the treatment subject received information from in-partisans or a heterogeneous network, then the treatment and control subjects chose different candidates 23 percent of the time. When the treatment subject received information from out-partisans, then the treatment and control subject chose different candidates a statistically different 38 percent of the time (t=3.04; p=.003).

These results lend partial support to *the autoregressive influence hypothesis* (H_3), with treatment subjects being persuaded by members of the out-group. In the aggregate, however, this did not have a negative effect on correct voting because the information was just as likely to be helpful as harmful.

THE WITHIN-SUBJECTS RESULTS

Another way of testing the hypotheses is to look at how treatment subjects updated their voting decisions based on social information. The analysis in Figure 8.2 does this by comparing the implied votes based on the subjects' initial estimates to their actual votes. Remember, the initial estimates are based solely on private information. Hence, they can be used to determine how the subjects would have voted without social information.

Once again, these results support *the uninformed are aided hypothesis* (H_2), but only for independents. This time the difference between uninformed partisans and independents is even more striking. Uninformed independents were

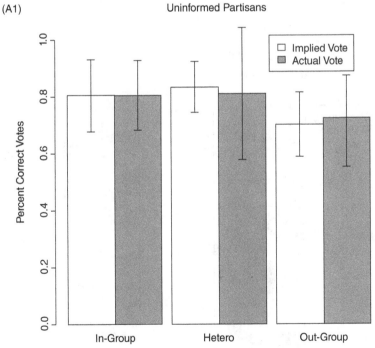

FIGURE 8.2. Comparing the percentage of actual correct votes to the percentage of initial, implied votes that were correct. Error bars display 95% confidence intervals with standard errors corrected for clustering on subjects.

Informed Partisans

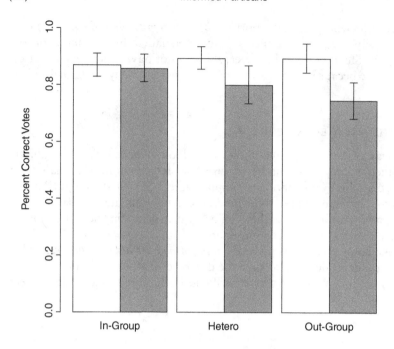

(B) Independents

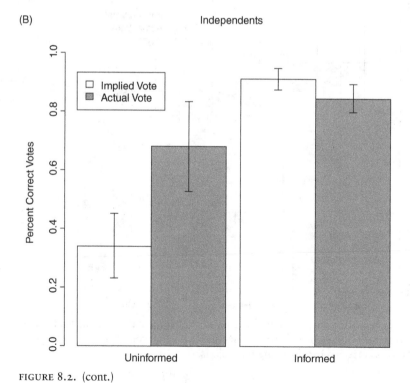

FIGURE 8.2. (cont.)

twice as likely to vote correctly following social information.[14] For uninformed partisans, social information appears to have made little difference on average; they were just as likely to vote correctly prior to social information as they were after receiving social information.

The within-subjects analysis makes the strongest statements about *the in-party message acceptance hypothesis* (H_1) and *the autoregressive influence hypothesis* (H_3). The *in-party message acceptance hypothesis* is clearly rejected as informed subjects updated their vote decisions based on social information regardless of the partisanship of the subjects providing information. The in-group networks actually showed the least amount of updating. These subjects planned on voting for their party's candidate prior to social information and the messages they received only confirmed that decision.

These results, on other hand, offer strong support for *the autoregressive influence hypothesis* (H_3). The implied vote of informed partisans in heterogeneous networks was correct 89 percent of the time. These subjects' actual vote was correct only 80 percent of the time, a statistically significant difference at the .10 level $(t=2.04; p=.053)$. The difference is even more striking for informed partisans in out-group networks as they vote correctly only 74 percent of the time $(t=3.52; p=.002)$. Uninformed independents were helped by social information, but informed independents were slightly hurt.[15] The implied vote of informed independents was correct 91 percent of the time. There was a statistically significant 7 percentage point drop in correct votes following social information $(t=2.81; p=.008)$. Hence, all types of informed subjects were harmed by social information, with the exception of those who received messages predominantly from members of their own party.

Taken together, the within-subjects results cast doubt on the benefits of political discussion. A small segment of the subjects – uninformed independents – were aided by social information. Informed subjects, on the other hand, were hurt by social information. This was especially the case for partisans who spoke with members of the other party.

Social networks reduced correct voting among the informed because the subjects sent biased social messages. This is shown by the OLS models in Table 8.3A. They regress the bias in the messages sent by subjects on the partisanship of the

[14] In Figure 8.2, subjects who estimated that Adams and Bates offered them the exact same total payoff have missing implied votes. This occurred in less than 5% of the cases. In all but one of the cases, the subjects with missing implied votes are independents. This missing data problem is especially serious for uninformed independents because they would have been flipping a coin if they voted without social information. The analysis was also performed by randomly assigning votes to these cases and the substantive conclusions are unchanged.

[15] In expectation, uninformed independents are indifferent between the two candidates. In the realized candidate benefits, uninformed independents should have voted for Adams 60% of the time. For this reason, the implied votes of uninformed independents are correct less than 50% of the time.

TABLE 8.3. *Bias in first messages sent about global benefits provided by candidates Adams and Bates by partisanship of sender and receiver. The dependent variable is the message minus the sender's initial estimate.*
A. *OLS models with standard errors corrected for clustering on subjects.*

	Adams		Bates	
	Coef.	Std. Err.	Coef.	Std. Err.
Sender: Party A/Receiver: Party A	4.830	1.289	−1.101	1.438
Sender: Party A/Receiver: Party B	5.052	1.544	−2.765	1.757
Sender: Party A/Receiver: Independent	3.912	1.483	−4.049	1.743
Sender: Party B/Receiver: Party A	−4.814	2.097	3.663	1.872
Sender: Party B/Receiver: Party B	−6.451	2.170	5.569	1.823
Sender: Party B/Receiver: Independent	−6.859	2.110	3.007	1.840
Sender: Independent/Receiver: Party A	2.268	1.079	−1.118	1.254
Sender: Independent/Receiver: Party B	−.6830	1.445	1.791	1.062
Constant	−1.941	0.952	−1.846	1.021
N (Subjects)	2754 (135)		2754 (135)	
R^2	0.059		0.030	

B. *Predicted values from Part A*

Adams		Sender			Bates		Sender		
		A	B	Ind.			A	B	Ind.
	A	2.89*	−6.75*	0.33		A	−2.95*	1.82	−2.96*
Receiver	B	3.11*	−8.39*	−2.62*	Receiver	B	−4.61*	3.72*	−0.06
	Ind.	1.97	−8.80*	−1.94*		Ind.	−5.90*	1.16	−1.85

* 95% confidence interval does not contain zero.

message sender and receiver. Bias here is measured by subtracting the message sent from the sender's initial estimate of the candidate's global benefit. Therefore, a positive value would indicate that the sender was saying that the candidate provides a larger benefit than the sender believes and the opposite for a negative value. As the predicted values in Table 8.3B show, partisans send messages that assert that the other party's candidate will offer a smaller benefit than the sender believes. Partisans also exaggerate the benefit offered by their candidate, but this effect is not as pronounced. The typical bias is less than 5 ECUs, meaning that the assertions reflect the sender's true beliefs to some extent. Subjects may have believed they were more likely to persuade others by slanting the truth rather than through complete distortion.

Partisans in out-group networks tend to vote incorrectly because the messages they receive are biased in favor of the other party's candidate. This increases the number of situations in which that candidate appears as a plausible choice and increases the probability that the subject will defect – i.e., vote for the candidate from the other party. In expectation, defection is a correct decision for partisans only 20 percent of the time. In this experiment, half of the subjects who defected were making a mistake. Subjects in out-group networks were more likely to defect, and hence they were more likely to vote incorrectly.[16]

IMPLICATIONS AND CONCLUSIONS

This chapter uses an experimental design to test three hypotheses about social information and correct voting. Both the between-subjects and within-subjects analysis showed that social communication is an effective information shortcut for uninformed independents, but is less useful for uninformed partisans. Many uninformed partisans benefited from social information, but the effect was too small to be statistically discernible. The between-subjects results showed that informed subjects used social information even when the messages came from a member of another party. Economic models of discussion suggest that this is a mistake (Downs 1957), an argument supported by the within-subjects analysis. Informed subjects voted incorrectly more often following social information when they received messages from members of another party.

These results call into question standard communication theories that view discussion as a dyadic process (e.g., Crawford and Sobel 1982; Lupia and McCubbins 1998). In this experiment, out-group subjects changed their votes because they received several messages from members of another party. In another experiment, subjects did not take into account the message sent from a single subject with conflicting preferences (Lupia and McCubbins 1998). From a rational choice standpoint, subjects should not have viewed messages from two biased sources as more compelling than a message from a single biased source. It appears, however, that subjects were often persuaded to vote as their social network was voting. This suggests that analysts need to take account of imitation (Boyd and Richerson 1985; Schlag 1999) conformity (Asch 1963), persuasion thresholds (Granovetter 1978), and socially sustained disagreement (Huckfeldt, Johnson, and Sprague 2004) when attempting to understand the effects of social communication.

The experimental results also speak to the ongoing debate about the efficacy and benefits of deliberation and group decision-making. Deliberation is often promoted because it exposes individuals to other points of view and helps inform their judgments (e.g., Fishkin 1991; Chambers 2003). At the same time, others have noted that deliberation may result in certain individuals or groups dominating discussion (e.g., Sanders 1997). Other critiques suggest that it can lead individuals to become ambivalent and withdraw from politics (Mutz 2006). The

---

[16] 40% of subject votes in out-group networks were defections compared to less than 30% in the other networks.

students of "cheap talk," in turn, point toward the dangers of people being duped and thus voting against their own interests (Crawford 1998).

These results reinforce our own argument that the social conversations of democracy are best seen as being first and foremost political rather than civic – that is, the participants in political conversations are not involved as dispassionate seekers after civic truth, but neither are they simply self-interested. They have positions and beliefs, and they attempt to convince others to agree. At the same time, they are also persuadable. Perhaps they are best seen, in the words of Tocqueville (2000), as practitioners of self-interest "rightly understood."

We have also seen that the participants in our experiments are regularly convinced to vote in ways that conflict with their narrowly defined self-interest, but should we see this as a problem or as an advantage due to social influence in politics? In the experiments of this chapter, the net effect of social communication in politics among the informed tends to cancel out – just as many are convinced to vote against their interests as are convinced to vote in ways that are consonant with their interests. In contrast, we see a net increase in correct voting among the uninformed. In short, social communication in these experiments produces flexible political boundaries and a net improvement in self-interested voting among the uninformed. Few would be disappointed if we could say the same regarding the implications for social communication among citizens in politics.

Finally, this chapter adds weight to the argument that the influence of opinion leaders is often contingent on factors lying beyond their own capacities, depending instead on the particular configuration of relations within the context where their leadership efforts are imbedded. While the experts and activists in our midst are most likely to play outsized roles as opinion leaders, the contexts in which they are imbedded serve to circumscribe their opportunities for success. As Warren Miller (1956) demonstrated, members of the political majority realize a significant advantage in their ability to mobilize their own ranks. Miller's results were at the level of counties, and our own argument is that the aggregate consequences of majority and minority status are tied to the stochastic implications of network formation and configuration. Moving the discussion to Miller's own analysis, Democrats in Democratic counties, as well as Republicans in Republican counties, realize a profound advantage – their efforts at mobilization and persuasion benefit due to their relative dominance within the social networks where the targets of their efforts are located.

In the next two chapters our attention turns to the cognitive and dynamic sources of complexity that underlie opinion leadership and social communication in politics. The influence of opinion leaders depends not only on the persuasive power of the messages they send, but also on the temporal durability of their own views. In order to address these issues, it becomes necessary for experimental participants to engage in a process of formulating prior judgments based on privately obtained information and updating those priors based on socially communicated information. The central issues become the variable rates of survival for those priors and the implications for opinion leadership.

CHAPTER 8 APPENDIX

INSTRUCTIONS TO PARTICIPANTS

The following instructions were read to all subjects before the experiment began. These instructions reference screens that can be viewed at johnbarryryan.com.

Thank you for participating in today's experiment. I will be reading from a script to ensure that every session of this experiment receives the same instruction. Feel free to ask questions if you require clarification. This instruction explains the nature of today's experiment as well as how to navigate the computer interface you will be working with. We ask that you please refrain from talking or looking at the monitors of other participants during the experiment. If you have a question or problem please raise your hand and one of us will come to you.

In the instructions that follow, all earnings are denominated in Experimental Currency Units or ECUs. At the end of the experiment, your earnings in ECUs will be translated into dollars at the rate of 1 ECU equals 1 cent. So, if you end with a balance of 1,500 ECUs, you would be paid $15 plus the $10 show up fee for a total of $25. We will pay you in cash at the end of the experiment.

Today's experiment consists of up to 12 periods. Each period consists of a contest between two candidates, Adams and Bates. If elected, each candidate will provide a benefit to all participants. Your goal is to use private information and information from your fellow participants as you figure out the benefits and then elect the candidate that will earn you more money. Each candidate's benefit is randomly drawn. The smallest benefit is 20 ECUs and the largest is 100 ECUs.

Additionally, some participants are assigned to a party called A or B, while some participants are independents. If you are in party A, you receive a bonus if Adams wins and receive a penalty if Bates wins. If you are in party B, you receive a bonus if Bates wins and a penalty if Adams wins. If you are an independent, you do not receive a bonus or a penalty regardless of the election outcome. For those participants in party A or B, your party bonus or penalty ranges from 10 ECUs to 20 ECUs.

Please turn to your computer screens. We have prepared several demonstration screens to help you get familiar with the actual screens you will see during the experiment.

(SCREEN ONE) This is the first screen you will see in each period. The top of each screen displays the period and the time remaining for this screen. We suggest that you make your decisions for a screen within the time limit, but you will not be forced to make decisions in that time.

In the upper left hand corner, you will see your participant number, your party, and the bonus or penalty you will receive depending on the outcome of the election. Remember, for members of party A, this is a bonus if Adams wins and a penalty if Bates wins. For members of party B, this is a bonus if Bates wins and penalty if Adams wins. This information will be in the upper left hand corner on every screen.

On this screen, you will receive private information about the candidates. The amount of private information you receive is randomly assigned. You may receive no information or as many as 4 pieces of information. Regardless of how much information you are assigned, this displays what it would look like if you were assigned 3 pieces of information. On average private information accurately represents the candidates' true benefit, but any single piece of information could be inaccurate.

Each piece of information is a number randomly drawn from an interval centered on the candidate's true benefit and extending 25 ECUs above and below that true position. So, while the candidate's proposals are bound between 20 and 100, the information you receive can fall outside of those bounds. There are examples on the handout. If the candidate proposes 20 ECUs, then the information can range from -5 and 45. If the candidate proposes 50 ECUs, the information can range from 25 to 75.

Based on the information you see, you are asked to estimate the candidate's proposals. Enter estimates for the two candidates and click OK.

(SCREEN TWO) You will also provide information to three other participants. You are accurately told the other participants' number and party as well as the amount of private information the other participant received on the previous screen.

You do not need to provide identical information to each of the participants. You are reminded of the private information you received on the previous screen. Enter the information about the candidates that you want to provide to the other participants and then click OK.

(SCREEN THREE) On this screen, you receive information from three other participants. These participants may be different from the participants that you provided with information. You are accurately told the other participants' number and party as well as the amount of private information the other participant received on the first screen.

Once again, you are asked to estimate the candidate's benefit. You are reminded of your previous estimate. Enter estimates for the two candidates and click OK.

(SCREEN FOUR) You will again provide information to three other participants. You are reminded of the information you received from the other participants on the previous screen. Enter the information about the candidates that you want to provide to the other participants and then click OK.

(SCREEN FIVE/SIX) On this screen, you receive information from three other participants. Once again, you are asked to estimate the candidate's benefit. You are reminded of your previous estimate. After entering your estimates, you will be asked to vote. You should vote for the candidate that will provide you with the better payoff. Your payoff is calculated by adding the candidate's benefit to the bonus or penalty you receive from that candidate winning. There is an example on the handout. In the example a member of party A has a party bonus of 15 ECUs. Adams has a benefit of 50 and Bates has a benefit of 75

ECUs. *In this case the participant should vote for Adams even though Adams' proposal is much lower. The participant will receive a payoff of 65 from Adams and only 60 from Bates once the party bonus or penalty is considered. However, if there is a large enough difference between the candidate proposals, you may want to vote for a candidate that isn't a member of your party.*

Enter estimates for the two candidates and click OK. Then vote for one of the two candidates and click OK.

(SCREEN SEVEN) This is the final screen. The two candidate's benefits are revealed as is the outcome of the election. You will also learn the number of ECUs you earned in this period as well as the number of ECUs you have earned up to this point in the experiment.

The experiment will consist of 12 periods like this one. At the end of these 12 periods, you will be asked a couple of questions about the experiment, asked to provide some demographic information, and a couple of questions about your general political leanings. All of your responses are anonymous.

This concludes the demonstration screens. We are now ready to begin the actual experiment. We ask that you follow the rules of the experiment. Anyone who violates the rules may be asked to leave the experiment with only the $10 show up fee. Are there any questions before we start?

9

Noise, bias, and expertise: the dynamics of becoming informed

Robert Huckfeldt, Matthew T. Pietryka, and Jack Reilly

> Not only in research, but also in the everyday world of politics and economics, we would all be better off if more people realised that simple nonlinear systems do not necessarily possess simple dynamical properties.
>
> Robert M. May (1976: 467)

The dynamics of diffusion and persuasion, as well as the manner in which these processes are affected by expert opinion leaders, play key issues in democratic politics. Moreover, the roles of experts and activists are particularly important in communication processes characterized by noisy and biased information, playing central roles in processes where people with variable levels of expertise and preference strength select informants, as well as being influenced by them. This chapter and the next are based on an experimental approach that addresses these problems at multiple levels of observation in a highly dynamic context – small groups of individuals communicating with one another in real time. The role of opinion leaders within the communication process is further heightened by two factors: (1) the higher value placed by participants on expert informants, which in turn exposes recipients to heterogeneous and potentially influential streams of information, and (2) the temporal persistence of judgments and opinions among those individuals who have invested more heavily in the acquisition of information.

Our argument is based on a model of electorates in which complex networks give rise to communication among interdependent individuals with heterogeneous preferences and levels of expertise. These individuals, in turn, both produce and encounter streams of information that are frequently noisy and biased. Such a model raises important questions regarding the dynamics of becoming informed. How do individuals balance their own individually acquired information with information they receive from others? Do individuals evaluate new information in the context of old information (Lodge and Taber 2000; Huckfeldt, Johnson, and Sprague 2004), or do they discard the old in favor of the new? Is the time-dependence of information and communication affected by individual expertise, by the reliance on socially mediated information, and/or by the heterogeneity of incoming information streams? What are the consequences of such temporal dependence for the social diffusion of information?

This chapter addresses these questions based on a small group experiment that implements variations in information costs across individuals, as well as making it possible to obtain information from others through a sequential series of social exchanges. The experiment provides incentives for individuals to become informed, but these incentives must be assessed relative not only to information costs, but also to the noise and bias attached to the information. On this basis we gain new insight regarding the influence of opinion leaders, as well as the dynamics of opinion leadership.

EXPERTISE, INFORMATION COSTS, AND INTERDEPENDENT CITIZENS

Due to the individually variable costs of becoming informed, one might expect democratic politics to be driven by a cadre of self-appointed experts within the electorate – individuals for whom the problem of information costs is greatly reduced, or for whom these costs do not apply. These experts are self-appointed because their roles are self-defined by their own interests and preferences in relationship to the value of political information. Having already paid the costs of becoming informed, the well-informed are more likely to be politically engaged across a range of political activities, including the process of communicating their views to others (Huckfeldt and Mendez 2008).

Such a view is premature for several reasons, and it runs the risk of exaggerating the net influence of single experts. First, many individuals receive multiple conflicting messages from experts with divergent viewpoints, and hence it is not that experts are necessarily lacking in influence, but rather that their messages must compete with other conflicting messages. Second, the recipients of messages are active participants in the communication process even when their supply of information is quite limited, and hence it becomes important to take into account the role of both the senders and the recipients of information in the communication process. In particular, individual information-processing strategies play a central role within communication networks, making it important to focus on the "nodes" as well as the "edges" – to address the role of individual recipients and communicators, as well the relationships that tie them to one another. This becomes particularly important relative to the value that recipients place on the information provided by alternative informants.

Downs' (1957) analysis assumes the importance of politically expert associates with compatible political orientations, but important problems relate to the identification and verification of an informant's expertise and trustworthiness (Boudreau 2009; Lupia and McCubbins 1998). Snowball surveys of naturally occurring communication networks show that individuals *do* communicate about politics more frequently with individuals whom they judge to be politically knowledgeable. Just as important, their perceptions of expertise among others are driven by the objectively verified expertise of potential informants – that is, they are typically quite accurate in recognizing the political preferences of those who are politically expert and engaged. These snowball surveys also show that the perceptions of expertise held by others, as well as the reported frequencies of political discussion, are only modestly affected by political agreement (Huckfeldt 2001; Huckfeldt, Sprague, and Levine 2000).

Moreover, when subjects in laboratory experiments are given the opportunity to obtain political information from other subjects, they place a greater emphasis on the expertise of other subjects rather than the presence of shared political preferences (see Chapters 7, 8, and 9). Similarly, in field experiments that address the natural formation of communication networks, both Lazer et al. (2010) and Levitan and Visser (2009) identify the minor role played by compatible political views in the formation of associational networks. In short, there is scant evidence to suggest that individuals exercise lock-grip control to avoid association with individuals holding preferences that are different from their own (see Huckfeldt and Sprague 1995; Huckfeldt, Johnson, and Sprague 2004). Thus, we turn to the role of the communication process itself to understand the manner in which noise and bias are filtered by the communication process within associational networks.

MEMORY CONSTRAINTS ON THE PROCESS OF BECOMING INFORMED

Time and the organization of human memory produce their own constraints on political communication and the process of becoming informed. Limitations on the capacity of working memory mean that individuals are continually storing and retrieving information in long-term memory, and information that is seldom retrieved becomes increasingly more difficult to recall. Time is certainly not the only factor affecting the accessibility of information from long-term memory. Some information is more compelling (and hence retrievable) than other information, due to both the inherent characteristics of the information and the correspondence between information characteristics and the cognitive map of the individual (Fazio 1995; Berent and Krosnick 1995). While time might play a potentially important and systematic role in the process, expectations diverge regarding the exact nature of the role, as well as the direction, of temporal effects.

First, as a counterfactual baseline, to the extent that individuals engage in memory-based processing with infinitely accurate recall, the first piece of information obtained in reaching a judgment should be as important as the last piece of information. More realistically, to the extent that individuals engage in memory-based processing with finite recall, we would expect a recency effect in which more recent information should have the greatest consequence.

Second, if the process of becoming informed is autoregressive (Huckfeldt, Johnson, and Sprague 2004), new information is processed in the context of old information. Hence, new information is less likely to be influential to the extent that it diverges from old information. In the context of memory decay, however, a persistent shift in the message being communicated ultimately swamps earlier signals in favor of more recent ones. In this way, an autoregressive process in the context of memory decay produces a complex moving average of messages, autoregressively upweighting earlier messages but simultaneously downweighting due to decay.

Finally, an on-line processing model employs an autoregressive framework in which new information is judged in the context of old information (Lodge and Taber 2000), but in this instance the effect of old information is summarized and consolidated in the form of a tally – an attitude or judgment that the individual brings to the interpretation of new information. When an individual receives new information in the on-line model, it is judged relative to prior judgments based on earlier information. In this case we see a primacy effect in which new information is less likely to be influential to the extent that (1) the pre-existent judgment is held more confidently and (2) the new information diverges from the old information. Here again, the primacy effect of earlier messages must compete with memory decay.

We rely on the early insights of McPhee's (1963) analysis in addressing the implications of social communication, political expertise, and memory decay for the political communication process. In his computer simulation, agents take information from sources in the environment, such as the news media. They form prior judgments on the basis of that information and share their opinions with others. Based on these communications, they update these priors and communicate again, in a repeated series of communications and updates. We pursue McPhee's contributions in the context of an experimental design and analysis that is inspired by a continuing stream of work in the study of social dilemmas (Ostrom, Gardiner, and Walker 1992; Fehr and Gächter 2002; Ahn, Isaac, and Salmon 2009).

THE EXPERIMENTAL DESIGN

Studies of political communication through social networks are beset by two related problems. First, social networks involve explicitly endogenous processes. You choose your associates subject to contextually constrained supply, and then your associates influence you. Hence, it is difficult to separate the influence of network construction from the influence of information transmission within and through networks.[1] Second, communication is not an isolated event, but rather a series of interdependent events best understood as a process that unfolds in time.

---

[1] Not all networks are endogenous to the choices of the participants, and indeed important experimental work has focused on the implications of exogenously imposed networks (see Kearns et al.

In this chapter and the next, we modify the design of our experimental framework to accommodate repeated interaction and communication, as well as their effects on participant judgments in real time. Our goal is to approximate the repeated and influential social interactions underlying the complex communication processes and individual interdependence occurring within social networks.

The experimental setting is once again based on a mock election with two "candidates" who are not real human subjects, but are represented as positions on a one-dimensional policy space. The preference space varies from 1 to 7, where each participant has a unique integer position that remains constant across the periods in an experimental session, but candidate positions are reset at each period. The participant's goal in each period is to elect the "candidate" most closely matching her own position on the same dimension, and she is rewarded with a cash incentive if the closest candidate to her wins the election at that period. The exact positions of the candidates are not known to the voters, thereby creating an incentive to obtain information. Privately obtained information incurs costs, and these costs are also assigned randomly to participants. In order to minimize costs, participants have an opportunity to obtain free information from other participants, and to employ public information that is also free.

Seven subjects participate in each experimental session, where one subject in each session holds each of the positions from 1 through 7. Two subjects pay nothing for privately purchased information, two subjects pay 5 Experimental Currency Units (ECUs), and three subjects pay 20 ECUs. Verbal communication was not allowed during the experiment, and all decisions and information exchanges were made using desktop computers. All participants were identified by their unique participant numbers, and thus they are not able to match these numbers to the true identities of the other participants in the experimental lab.

THE EXPERIMENTAL PROCEDURE

Each experimental session lasts for approximately one hour, and includes an average of 9 periods. A new election with new candidate positions occurs at each period, but the subjects' randomly assigned information costs and preferences are held constant for the entire session. Before an experimental session begins, participants are randomly assigned integer preferences and information costs that remain unchanged for the duration of the experiment.[2] Additionally, all participants are informed that Candidate A's position is between 1 and 6, while

---

2009; and Chapter 8 of this book). Most work in political communication has addressed networks that are endogenous to individual choice, and that is the literature we address here. Our argument is that, even when individuals are given control over network construction, their choices often are constrained by larger social contexts and their own competing priorities.

[2] The relationship between information costs and preferences is established randomly as well, but it is held constant across experimental sessions. Hence every session has the following cost, preference pairings: 1, 20; 2, 5; 3, 20; 4, 0; 5, 5; 6, 20; 7, 0.

Candidate B's position is between 2 and 7. Then, in each of the approximately 9 periods per session, the following steps occur:

1. Participants receive 100 ECUs, of which 50 ECUs can be spent on information. (Hence, subjects with an information cost of 20 ECUs can purchase only two "pieces" of information.)
2. The two candidates' positions are drawn from the respective intervals.
3. Participants may purchase *private information* at their assigned cost.
4. After the subjects receive the information, they are asked to provide a prior judgment regarding each candidate's position, and they are truthfully told that their judgments will not be communicated to other participants.
5. A new computer screen shows each participant the preferences and the amounts of private information that each of the participants has purchased. Based on this information, subjects are allowed to make a first request for *social information* from one other subject. This request for social information is free to the sender and receiver. Potential informants are not required to comply with the request, and they are told that they need not provide the same information to all requestors. Participants almost always agree to provide information, consisting of a single message with information regarding each candidate position.
6. After receiving the information, subjects are asked to update their prior judgments – to offer a new judgment regarding the position of the candidate.
7. Steps 5 and 6 are repeated two more times. Hence, subjects have the opportunity to make three information requests from other subjects, and they update their priors at each step. This produces a series of four judgments regarding the candidates' positions: a prior judgment after purchasing private information but before communication, as well as three updates after each of three communications with other participants. It is important to emphasize that *the subjects are never provided with a summary of the information they have received.* To the contrary, they assess and evaluate the information as it becomes available and they never have subsequent access. All information is thus provided sequentially and incrementally, and the subject's challenge is to integrate and assess the information.
8. After communication is completed, the participants record their last updated prior, and they are provided with an opportunity to purchase a single piece of information at a cost of 10 ECUs.
9. The participants cast their votes, and the outcome of the election is revealed. If the winning candidate's position is closer to a voter than the losing candidate's position, the voter earns 50 extra ECUs. If the winning candidate's position is farther away from the voter's position than the losing candidate's position, 50 ECUs are subtracted from the voter's

account. If candidates are equally distant from the voter, the voter neither gains nor loses. A voter could thus earn as much as 150 ECUs in a period, but only if she did not purchase any information (or if her information cost was zero). The minimum payoff is 0 ECUs – when a voter spends 50 ECUs on purchasing information and her candidate loses the election.

10. Participants are informed of their net earnings, which accumulate across periods.

11. Candidate positions are reset, and participants proceed to the next period. At the end of the experimental session, subjects are paid the show-up fee plus their total earnings in cash, where 100 ECUs equals U.S.$1.00. The range of total earnings, including the show-up fee, is from $8.00 to $17.00, and the mean earning is $12.00.

In summary, the participants thus have three potential sources of information on which to base their judgments regarding the candidates. First, the public information that the two candidates' positions are drawn from different intervals could potentially help a voter in the absence of other forms of information.[3] Second, voters are allowed to purchase unbiased but noisy private information on candidates' true positions. Third, each participant has an opportunity to request social information from other participants – information that is both noisy and potentially biased. That is, the requestor depends not only on the reliability of information that serves as the basis for *the informants'* judgments, but also on the ability and willingness of the informant to compile and provide the information in an unbiased manner.

The proximate consequences of the experimental manipulations meet our expectations. Participants with higher costs obtain less private information, and participants who purchase more private information are better able to make informed choices. Mean information purchases are 2.8, 1.9, and 1.2 for subjects with costs of 0, 5, and 20 ECUs. Simple regressions of subjects' *final judgments* regarding Candidate A's position on the candidate's *true* positions produce slope coefficients of .64 ($t=13.6$) for those who purchased 3 or 4 pieces of information, .54 ($t=9.4$) for those who purchased 2, and .25 ($t=4.7$) for those who purchased 0 or 1.

Our interests reach beyond these first-order consequences, however. The communication process is complex, based on interdependent actors, and participants cannot assume perfect candor in the process. In the spirit of Downs (1957), Festinger (1957), Berelson et al. (1954), Katz and Lazarsfeld (1955), and others, we expect the process to be contingent on the preferences and

---

[3] In this, as in earlier experiments, the value of the public information should not be overstated. The interval boundaries on candidate positions overlap significantly, and hence there is no guarantee that Candidate A lies to the left of Candidate B. In this way the election is more like a primary election within a party rather than a general election contest between parties.

expertise of informants, the range of available informants, and the potential for biased and misleading communication.[4]

HETEROGENEITY AND BIAS WITHIN NETWORKS

In the context of Downs' analysis, the experimental participants should select *well-informed* informants who *share their preferences*. The problem for individual subjects is that the supply of such informants may be limited. Each of the directed graphs in Figure 9.1 illustrates one period (or election) within the experiment. The edges (arrows) point toward the individual from whom information is being requested. The size of the nodes reflects the amount of each individual's investment in private information, and it becomes clear that the more highly informed participants receive more requests for information.

At the same time, Figure 9.1 also shows that participants must often choose between (1) expert informants with preferences that diverge from their own and (2) non-experts with preferences similar to their own. While individuals might prefer to have expert informants who share their preferences, their choices are limited by availability in their local contexts, with important implications for network heterogeneity and the communication of bias. We begin the analysis by examining the first-order effects of our experimental manipulations on the creation of potential for heterogeneity and biased communication that is produced.

CRITERIA FOR SELECTING INFORMANTS

This problem is addressed more systematically in Part A of Table 9.1, where participant information requests are regressed on the amount of information each of the other participants requested, as well as the distance between the preferences within the relevant dyad – the preferences of both the potential recipient of information as well as the potential provider. The response variable equals one if the subject requested information from the dyad's alter in a given period, and equals zero otherwise. The table displays the results for all three social information requests, first pooling these requests, and then for each request individually. Thus, in models 2–4 of the table, each row in the data matrix is a dyad and model 1 pools these observations – hence, each row is at the dyad-request level. This structure means that each individual participant appears multiple times within the data set, and thus we apply a clustering correction on the standard errors of the coefficients (Williams 2000).

---

[4] Do participants understand the relatively more complicated process within which they are participating? While we do not debrief the participants after every session, we pre-tested all the experiments we conducted in this study to make sure that participants understood the procedures. Moreover, at the beginning of every session for every experiment we include a practice period for instructional purposes. Finally, we carefully monitor all the experiments, and it is clear that the participants understood the experimental process and procedures.

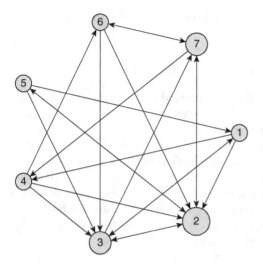

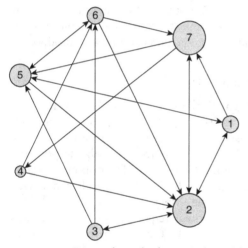

FIGURE 9.1. Directed graphs for typical periods in an experiment. Size of node indexes amount of information purchased. Direction of edge signifies the participant from whom information is being requested.

We do not restrict participants from making multiple information requests from the same participant during the same period. While it is a relatively rare event, Table 9.1 includes a control for whether the subject previously requested information from the potential discussant. Thus, in the second request for information, the indicator variable equals one if the subject's *first* request for information was to this potential discussant. In the third request, the indicator

TABLE 9.1. *Proximate effects of experimental manipulations.*
A. *Creation of dyadic ties: information request by amount of information purchased by the potential informant and absolute distance separating preferences within the potential dyad. (Logit; standard errors corrected for clustering.)*

	1. all choices		2. 1st choice		3. 2nd choice		4. 3rd choice	
	coef.	t-value	coef.	t-value	coef.	t-value	coef.	t-value
Preference distance[a]	−.14	3.56	−.12	2.50	−.17	3.49	−.13	2.34
Information purchased	.39	8.15	.58	8.58	.40	6.23	.24	4.12
Previous information request	−2.20	7.08			−2.20	5.49	−2.37	7.79
Constant	−1.82	14.83	−2.51	14.67	−1.74	11.20	−1.26	6.76
N=	13482 (84 subjects)		4494 (84 subjects)		4494 (84 subjects)		4494 (84 subjects)	
χ^2,df,p =	85, 3, .00		74, 2, .00		50, 3, .00		64, 3, .00	

B. *Predicted probabilities of requesting information by distance separating preferences within dyad and informant information.*

1. ANY CHOICE

	Minimum information	Maximum information	Δ
Minimal distance	.12	.40	.28
Maximal distance	.07	.26	.19
Δ	.05	.14	

2. FIRST CHOICE

	Minimum information	Maximum information	Δ
Minimal distance	.07	.42	.35
Maximal distance	.04	.28	.24
Δ	.03	.14	

3. SECOND CHOICE

	Minimum information	Maximum information	Δ
Minimal distance	.13	.42	.29
Maximal distance	.06	.24	.18
Δ	.07	.18	

4. THIRD CHOICE

	Minimum information	Maximum information	Δ
Minimal distance	.20	.39	.19
Maximal distance	.12	.25	.13
Δ	.08	.14	

C. *Network centrality by information purchased and mean distance of preference from others in network. OLS regression w/ standard errors corrected for clustering.*

	Coefficient	t-value
Mean preference distance from others in network	-.25	1.49
Private information purchased	.73	10.17
Constant	2.33	5.00

N= 749 (84 subjects)
R^2=.29
Root MSE= 1.39

D. *Estimated bias[b] of message by the absolute difference between the preferences of the sender and the receiver. OLS regression w/ standard errors corrected for clustering.*

	Candidate A		Candidate B	
	Coefficient	t-value	Coefficient	t-value
Difference in preferences	.15	3.33	.15	2.93
Constant	.68	4.86	.73	3.90
N=	715 (76 subjects)		715 (76 subjects)	
R^2=	.02		.02	
Root MSE=	1.40		1.51	

[a] Preference differences in Parts A and D of the table are measured as the absolute value of the difference within the dyad.

[b] Bias is estimated as the absolute value of the distance between the message and the messenger's immediately preceding prior judgment regarding the candidates.

A one standard deviation increase in preference divergence .58 produces a reduction in the predicted number of information requests by .145, and an increase across its range (1.5) yields a reduction of .375. In contrast, a one standard deviation increase in the amount of information purchased yields an increase of .88 requests, and an increase across its range (4) yields an increase of 2.92 requests.

variable equals one if the subject's *first or second* request for information was to this potential discussant.

Each model demonstrates statistically discernible effects for the difference in preferences within the dyad, for the amount of information privately purchased by the potential recipient of an information request, and for previous information requests from a provider in the same period. Participants are more likely to request information from other individuals who (1) hold preferences similar to their own and (2) have made personal investments in privately acquired information. The control for repeated requests confirms that they are relatively rare, underlining the consequences of a constrained choice set on the supply of informants.

Based on the estimates in Part A of Table 9.1, Part B shows the corresponding changes in predicted probabilities of information requests across the explanatory variables for respondents, with the dummy variable for previous information requests from a particular individual held constant at 0 or no previous request. The first model generates an effect for the information level of the potential informants that is substantially larger than the effect for preference, but it becomes clear that this first model is an average across the three requests for information that vary systematically across the exogeneous factors. The initial request is highly responsive to the potential informants' information levels, but this importance is increasingly attenuated for the second and third requests. In contrast, the importance of shared preferences on the part of the potential informants stays relatively constant across the three choices, but its effect never exceeds that of the informant's information level.

NETWORK CENTRALITY IN A CONTEXT OF LIMITED CHOICE

The problem is not that the criteria of choice are changing, but rather that the range of choices becomes increasingly limited. The context of the experimental group imposes limits on the ability to implement Downs' advice – participants are unable to locate sufficient numbers of experts with shared preferences. Network formation is thus subject to the constraints imposed by the particular configuration of the surrounding context (Huckfeldt and Sprague 1987). Within this context, perhaps one of the most surprising results of the chapter's analysis is that participants place a higher value on expert information, and hence they confront a heterogeneous stream of information.[5]

This result carries important implications for the structure of the communication network. In particular, it points toward experts as being particularly influential in the communication process, with high levels of network centrality. In Part C of Table 9.1, centrality is defined within a period (or election) as a subject's "indegree" – the number of requests for information received from other participants.[6] Participants with higher levels of indegree are more central to the communication of information within the process – the information they communicate occupies more space within the communication process. When this measure of indegree is regressed on the absolute distance between preferences within dyads and the amount of information that a potential informant has independently acquired, it becomes clear that expertise trumps shared preferences as the most important factor explaining centrality.[7]

---

[5] At the same time, it is important to recognize that the motivation to acquire information from an individual with shared preferences does not necessarily contradict the motivation to acquire information from an expert. One would have more confidence in the capacity of an expert with shared preferences to provide reliable information supporting those preferences.

[6] We report an OLS regression, but the substantive conclusions are unchanged when employing a negative binomial regression.

[7] A one standard deviation increase in preference divergence (.58) produces a reduction in the predicted number of information requests by .145, and an increase across its range (1.5) yields a reduction of .375. In contrast, a one standard deviation increase in the amount of information

IMPLICATIONS FOR BIAS

The fact that participants are more likely to weight expertise over shared preferences in the selection of an informant produces obvious advantages. At the same time, it also has the consequence of exposing recipients to messages from politically divergent sources – messages that are more likely to contain biases introduced by the informant. The participants in our experiment send messages aimed at persuading the recipient, and hence the messages are contingent on the sender's goals. Participants are free to send different messages to different recipients, and messages typically carry a bias that is distinctive to the position of the recipient relative to the sender. Hence, these messages are not unlike those frequently sent in ordinary political communication, where lively conversation is *both* informative *and* strategic.

Part D of Table 9.1 estimates bias in the messages sent by participants, where bias is defined as the distance between the message sent at the first opportunity for social communication during a period and the sender's immediately preceding prior judgment regarding the candidates. This measure of bias is regressed on the absolute distance separating the preferences of the sender and the receiver of the message.[8] The regression shows that bias increases as the distance between the preferences in the dyad increases. The maximum distance between preferences is six units, and hence the maximum predicted effect on a single candidate message is 90 percent of one unit (6 × .15). While these are relatively subtle effects, they are not without consequence, and even minimal levels of bias can be consequential when candidates converge. In short, the participants must take into account the potential for bias as well as the inherent noise that accompanies information taken from a stochastic distribution, and hence it becomes important to address the process through which network effects are realized.

INFORMATION, MEMORY DECAY, AND AUTOREGRESSIVE PROCESSES

Autoregressive models suggest that new information is judged relative to previously obtained information. Thus, new information that deviates from expectations based on past information would yield a diminished effect (Huckfeldt, Johnson, and Sprague 2004). We evaluate such a model in Table 9.2, which considers the subject's final summary judgment regarding a candidate's position as a function of (1) all three social messages, (2) the deviations of these social messages from the subject's judgments immediately prior to receiving the message, and (3) the interaction between the two. The models also include the

---

purchased (1.21) yields an increase of .88 requests, and an increase across its range (4) yields an increase of 2.92 requests.

[8] The number of observations in these models is lower than the previous estimates in Table 9.1 because they exclude the small number of subjects whose requests for information were denied.

TABLE 9.2. *Final judgments by priors and messages, with messages contingent on contemporaneous judgments.*

A. Candidate A	Coefficient	t-value	
Initial (prior) judgment	.16	2.38	
Prior X info. purchased	.10	4.08	N=749 (84 clusters)
Information purchased	−.35	3.75	R^2 = .58
First message deviation	.06	.71	Root MSE = .96
Second message deviation	.20	2.46	
Third message deviation	.50	6.38	
First message	.13	2.75	
Second message	.25	5.01	
Third message	.43	8.81	
First message X deviation	−.02	.92	
Second message X deviation	−.08	4.28	
Third message X deviation	−.13	6.65	
Constant	.18	.63	

B. Candidate B	Coefficient	t-value	
Initial (prior) judgment	.13	2.08	
Prior X info. purchased	.10	4.32	N=749 (84 clusters)
Information purchased	−.43	4.08	R^2 = .59
First message deviation	.12	1.53	Root MSE = .97
Second message deviation	.44	5.42	
Third message deviation	.54	4.93	
First message	.16	3.21	
Second message	.35	7.12	
Third message	.44	7.20	
First message X deviation	−.04	1.60	
Second message X deviation	−.10	4.70	
Third message X deviation	−.12	5.24	
Constant	.28	.81	

Initial (prior) judgment = the subject's initial judgment regarding candidate positions, based solely on the public information and any private information the subject purchased

Information purchased = the number of pieces of information the subject purchased at the beginning of the relevant period

Message deviation = the absolute deviation between the message the subject received from another subject at the current request for information, and the subject's most recent judgment regarding candidate position. (For the first message deviation, the most recent judgment is the prior. For the second and third deviations, the most recent judgments are the updates following the first and second messages, respectively.)

individuals' original prior judgments based on individually purchased private information, the amount of private information purchased, and the interaction between the prior and the amount of private information purchased.

This model provides support for an autoregressive influence model. In general, the ultimate effect of a message is attenuated by the absolute size of

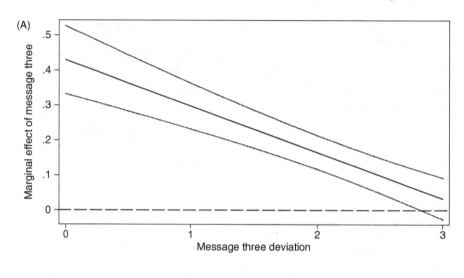

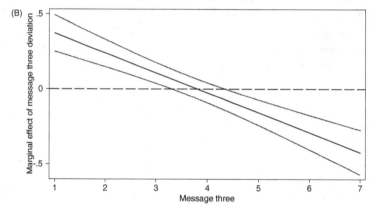

FIGURE 9.2. The autoregressive influence of social information.

A. Marginal effect (with 95% confidence bounds) of the third message on the subject's final judgment by the message's deviation from the subject's immediately prior update.

B. Marginal effect (with 95% confidence bounds) of the third message's deviation from the immediately prior update by the third message.

Data source: Estimates in Table 9.2a.

its deviation from the subject's immediately preceding, contemporaneous judgment regarding the candidates. The first message fails to generate a discernible pattern of effects for candidates, but this is due to a pronounced pattern of decay in the message's effects. More recent messages are consistently more influential because earlier messages tend to be forgotten (Lodge and Taber 2000).

Figure 9.2 graphically displays the autoregressive process for the subjects' final judgments of Candidate A. Part A of the figure demonstrates that the effect of the third message on the subject's final judgment of the candidate diminishes as the message diverges from the subject's previous judgment. When the message is within one unit of the subject's previous judgment, the model predicts that the subject's next judgment will move about 0.3 units in the direction of the message. In other words, if the subject previously believed that the candidate was a 4 and the message suggests that the candidate is a 5, the model predicts that the subject's next judgment will be about 4.3. If the message is two units away from the previous judgment, its effect falls to about .2. Messages that deviate from the previous judgment by three units produce no discernible change on the final judgment. In other words, subjects dismiss such divergent information rather than integrating it into their judgments.

Part B of the figure displays the effect of a socially communicated message on the subject's final updated judgment when the message deviated from the subject's immediately prior update. That is, the figure illustrates the consequences of receiving a message that does not correspond to an individual's contemporaneous opinion. In particular, the figure focuses on the third social message and its deviation from the immediately preceding second update. When the message suggests that the candidate is on the far left (lower values), the effect of the deviation is positive. This positive effect counteracts the effect of the message, which would otherwise pull the subjects' final judgment downward. Conversely, when the message suggests that the candidate is on the right (higher values), the effect of a deviation is negative. Once again, this negative effect offsets the effect of the message, which would otherwise pull the subjects' judgments upward. Thus, the net influence of a message decreases with its deviation from subjects' immediately previous judgment.

In summary, this preliminary analysis shows three things. First, messages that are at variance with the subject's contemporaneous judgments at the time they receive the messages are less likely to be influential in affecting the subject's ultimate judgment. Thus, a subject's summary judgment is *not* based on a fresh look at all of the evidence. Rather, the final judgment depends on the subject's preliminary judgments and the contemporaneous judgment at the moment when a message is received (Lodge and Taber 2000). Second, and just as important, this analysis suggests a dynamic process in which more recent information is generally weighted more heavily than earlier information. Finally, it becomes clear that the experts – those individuals who invest more heavily in the acquisition of information – form prior judgments that are much more likely to endure through this influence process, as well as to register stronger effects on their summary judgments. Hence, we turn our attention to a simple model of the influence process to consider the consequences.

A SIMPLE MODEL OF THE PROCESS

We begin by expressing the updating process for the subjects' judgments as a function of three factors: (1) decay in the most recently updated judgment,

(2) decay in the initial (prior) judgment based on individually purchased private information, and (3) new incoming social information that is communicated by other subjects.

THE EFFECT OF THE PRIOR

The model assumes that the initial (or prior) judgment, formed on the basis of privately purchased information, has an enduring effect that declines at a compound fixed rate between judgments. At the first update, the effect of the prior is wP_0, where w is defined as ($1-d$, or 1 minus the single period rate of decay in the prior) and at the nth update, its effect is thus $w^n P_0$.

THE EFFECT OF UPDATED JUDGMENTS

Updated judgments generate first-order effects that also decline at a fixed rate. At the nth update, the effect of the previous update is αJ_{n-1}, where α is the survival of the previous judgment.

INCOMING INFORMATION

At the same time that the prior and the previously updated judgments are vulnerable to decay, the subject is responding to an ongoing stream of social information communicated by other subjects.

Hence, the current judgment arises as a consequence of the rate of decay in an immediately prior judgment update, the rate of decay in an initial prior judgment, and the effect of contemporaneous social information.

$$\Delta J_t = -dJ_{t-1} + w^t P_0 + eI_t \qquad (9.1)$$

where $\Delta J_t = J_t - J_{t-1}$; d = the rate of decay in the previous judgment, with d expected to lie between zero and 1; P_0 = the prior judgment based on privately purchased information; w^t = the effect of the prior at J_t, with w expected to lie between 0 and 1; I_t = incoming social information received at t; and e = the educative impact of the new social information.

The model is rewritten as:

$$J_t = \alpha J_{t-1} + w^t P_0 + eI_t, \qquad (9.2)$$

where $\alpha = 1-d$ = the memory or survival of the previous judgment.

It is helpful to develop the model through recursion. At the first judgment (J_1) there is no previous judgment to update – only a prior based on private information plus new information, and thus

$$J_1 = w P_0 + eI_1. \qquad (9.3)$$

Subsequent judgments update the immediately previous judgment as well as responding to the prior and new social information. Hence,

$$J_2 = w^2 P_0 + eI_2 + \alpha J_1$$
$$= w^2 P_0 + eI_2 + \alpha w P_0 + \alpha eI_1 \qquad (9.4)$$

$$J_3 = w^3 P_0 + eI_3 + \alpha J_2$$
$$= w^3 P_0 + eI_3 + \alpha w^2 P_0 + \alpha eI_2 + \alpha^2 w P_0 + \alpha^2 eI_1. \qquad (9.5)$$

Pushing the model beyond the reach of our experimental observations yields

$$J_n = (w^n P_0 + \alpha w^{n-1} P_0 + \alpha^2 w^{n-2} P_0 + \ldots + \alpha^{n-1} w P_0)$$
$$+ eI_n + \alpha eI_{n-1} + \ldots + \alpha^{n-1} eI_1. \qquad (9.6)$$

To consider the long-term dynamic logic, we take the equation to its limit. For n sufficiently large, the equilibrium is

$$J_n = (w^n P_0 - \alpha^n w^0 P_0)/(1 - \alpha/w) + eI_n + \alpha eI_{n-1} + \ldots + \alpha^{n-1} eI_1. \qquad (9.7)$$

Assuming that both α and w are bounded by o and 1, the effect of the prior converges on zero and the summary judgments inevitably depend on the continuing stream of incoming information, where the stream of information is weighted to favor the most recent information.

In short, the past is attenuated because this system of behavior forgets past events and past judgments rather than accumulating them – as any stable system must. How fast does the memory of this behavioral system decay? The key lies in the behavior of w^n and α^n. As α increases – as the immediately past updated judgment looms larger in the formulation of the current judgment – the importance of information received earlier maintains its effect longer.

Since the updated judgment is the mechanism whereby the prior is modified by new information, α also provides an index on the temporal durability of effects due to messages from other participants. As w increases, the importance of the prior takes longer to disappear. In this context, it is important to consider the dynamic implications in the short-term as well as the long-term, and hence to obtain estimates for the model parameters.

ESTIMATING THE MODEL

For the purposes of estimation, we multiply both sides of Equation 9.4 by α before subtracting the corresponding sides of the equations from Equation 9.5. Upon rearrangement this yields,

$$J_3 = \alpha J_2 + w^3 P_0 + eI_3 \qquad (9.8)$$

Hence regressing the final updated judgment regarding a candidate's position on the previous judgment, the prior, and the incoming social information, provides statistical estimates for the model parameters – α, w, and e.

Part A of Table 9.3 displays the results of estimating the model in Equation 9.8. For both candidate judgments, the final updated judgment (J_3) is regressed on the immediately preceding updated judgment (J_2), the initial prior judgment (P_0), and the immediately preceding (third) piece of communicated information (I_3). In view of the demonstrated importance of private information consumption, the regressions also include the amount of information purchased as an explanatory variable, as well as its interaction with both the third installment of communicated information and the prior judgment.

First, the table shows that the initial (prior) judgment has no effect in the absence of the interaction with the amount of information purchased. That is, the prior matters only among those participants who invest in private information, and the effect is enhanced by the level of that investment. Second, as would be expected, the table shows a substantial effect due to the immediately preceding update. Third, the model shows a substantial effect due to the final (third) message that appears to be at least modestly attenuated by the amount of private information purchased by the participant.

Part B of Table 9.3 adds an interaction between the third message and its deviation from the subject's immediately preceding (third) updated judgment. This yields no change in the estimates from Part A of the table, and it fails to produce a discernible effect due to message deviation. Hence, we pursue the analysis based on the results in Part A. In view of the results shown in Table 9.2, the lack of an interaction effect due to the deviation between the message and its distance from the subject's immediately previous update warrants explanation. The difference is that the models in Parts A and B of Table 9.3 include updated judgments as regressors, while the models in Table 9.2 only include the prior, the stream of incoming messages, and the interaction with the divergence of these messages from participants' immediately preceding updates. These results thereby support the on-line processing model of Lodge et al. (1995) – the memory of past information is mediated by past judgments. The information is not recalled directly and has no lasting effect, except as it forces updates in judgment.

Part C of Table 9.3 shows the estimated model parameters adjusted for the amount of information purchased by the subject. The results show that the survival of the prior is directly related to the amount of information purchased. Indeed, apart from the interaction of the prior with the amount of information purchased, the prior has no effect. (This result means that we cannot reject the null hypothesis that *w* is 0 for the subjects who purchased no information.) In contrast, however, there is a dramatic effect of information investments on the survival of the prior. If we fail to reject the null that there is no effect among those who did not purchase information, *w* varies from 0 to .64 for the judgment regarding Candidate A.

TABLE 9.3. *Estimating the dynamic model of judgment formation.*
A. *Final updated judgment by initial (prior) judgment, previous update, and final communicated information, with interactions.*

	Candidate A		Candidate B	
	Coefficient	t-value	Coefficient	t-value
Initial (prior) judgment	.004	.09	.04	.97
Immediately previous (third) update	.66	11.81	.63	10.17
Third message	.21	4.88	.21	3.55
Prior X info. purchased	.06	2.82	.07	3.29
Third message X info. purchased	−.03	−2.28	−.04	1.64
Information purchased	−.08	.93	−.16	1.57
Constant	.36	1.62	.53	1.80
N =	749 (84 clusters)		749 (84 clusters)	
R² =	.69		.70	
Root MSE =	.81		.83	

B. *Final updated judgment by initial (prior) judgment, previous update, and final communicated information, with interactions.*

	Candidate A		Candidate B	
	Coefficient	t-value	Coefficient	t-value
Initial (prior) judgment	.007	.14	.04	.95
Immediately previous (third) update	.65	10.23	.63	9.60
Third message	.25	4.19	.21	3.52
Prior X info. purchased	.06	2.74	.07	3.27
Third message X info. purchased	−.03	2.22	−.03	1.54
Information purchased	−.08	.87	−.16	1.63
Third message deviation	.04	.48	.03	.33
Third message deviation X message	−.02	.97	−.002	.09
Constant	.36	1.41	.47	1.95
N_i =	749 (84 clusters)		749 (84 clusters)	
R² =	.70		.70	
Root MSE =	.81		.83	

C. *Model parameters adjusted for individual information purchases, based on the estimates from Part A.*

	Candidate A					Candidate B				
	Amount of information purchased					Amount of information purchased				
	0	1	2	3	4	0	1	2	3	4
W	.16	.40	.51	.58	.64	.35	.49	.57	.64	.69
α	.66	.66	.66	.66	.66	.63	.63	.63	.63	.63
e	.21	.17	.14	.10	.06	.21	.17	.14	.10	.06

The effect of socially communicated information is also dependent on information purchases. Those who did not purchase any private information show an effect that is more than three times larger than the effect among those who purchased four pieces of information on each of the candidates. In short, those who purchase private information do not pay much attention to socially communicated information, and those who do not purchase private information are reliant on socially communicated information obtained from other subjects.

What are the dynamic implications? Part A of Figure 9.3 shows the decay in the prior over time for judgments regarding Candidate A. The figure plots the influence of the prior at the time the prior is given (J_0) through the final judgment (J_3) for individuals purchasing four, two, and zero pieces of information. In general, we see quite rapid decay in the effect of the prior, even among those individuals who purchased the maximum of amount of private information.

In contrast, Part B of the figure shows the decay in the effect of socially communicated messages from the first judgment subsequent to their reception (J_1) through the final judgment (J_3). In this instance the decay occurs relatively more slowly, but, in contrast to the effects of the prior, we see the greater effect of communicated messages on those subjects who purchased less private information. That is, among those who purchased four pieces of private information, their fourth and final judgment relies on approximately 40 percent of the prior, but is virtually independent of the first social message. In contrast, among those who purchased no information, the contribution of the prior has disappeared, and we see a modest effect due to the first social message.

The implications are quite important. While experts play a central role in the process of political communication, we should not view them as wholly independent actors who emit signals but do not receive them. While experts are able to assess incoming signals in the context of their own accumulated knowledge, their judgments based on this knowledge decay with time, and this process of decay is offset by new, socially communicated information. As Katz (1957) informed us more than fifty years ago, politically expert citizens are not immune to the effects of social communication.

Is the process autoregressive? The results show an interplay between recency and primacy in the communication process. Everything else being equal, recent communications matter more than earlier communications, and the decay of earlier communications enhances the relative effect of the most recent communications. At the same time, decay is mediated by expertise. Individuals who invest more heavily in the acquisition of private information demonstrate a more enduring effect due to their priors, at the same time that they rely less heavily on messages obtained from others. As a consequence, they engage in on-line processing (Lodge and Taber 2000), where new information is judged and assessed in the context of pre-existing judgments, and thus they tend to be more intransigent in their opinions.

In contrast, those who do not invest in private information rely less heavily on their prior judgments, and they pay more attention to new messages and new information. Hence, the updating process takes on relatively more importance.

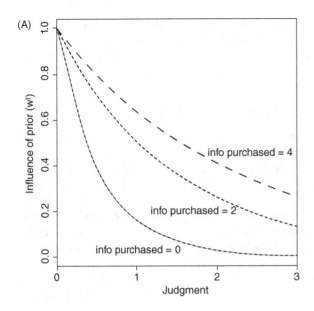

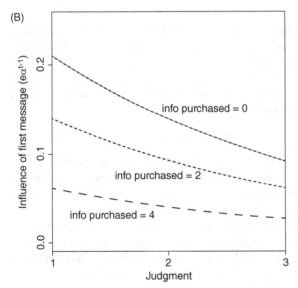

FIGURE 9.3. Implications of the model.
   A. Temporal decay in influence of prior (w^t).
   B. Temporal decay in influence of social messages ($e\alpha^{t-1}$).
Data source: Estimates in Table 9.3a.

The process is still autoregressive – informationally impoverished individuals do not exercise a comprehensive, memory-based processing strategy. It is simply the case that, lacking a strong prior on which to formulate a judgment, they necessarily rely more heavily on contemporaneous information.

HETEROGENEOUS INFORMATION AND THE VOTE

Individuals are thus faced with a heterogeneous stream of incoming information and limits on their ability and willingness to make continuing investments in additional information.[9] Their votes become the culminating events in a dynamic process where people sift and weigh the information they obtain by their own efforts, as well as the information they receive from others. In this context, we consider the participant's vote choice as a function of the entire process, in the context of their priors, their updates, and the final information purchase. How do individuals aggregate this heterogeneous stream of information in order to arrive at a binary vote decision?

We define a vote propensity measure that is defined in terms of the logit (L), or the log of the odds ratio, and the probability of voting for Candidate B is defined as:

$$P = 1 / \left(1 + e^{(-L)}\right), \tag{9.9}$$

The propensity measure is defined as a linear function of the subjects' accumulated experience – privately purchased information, socially communicated information, and their own judgments and relative assessments of the candidates. The assessments constitute a combined response to both candidates, based on the perceived distance between each of the candidates and the position of the particular subject.

A_t = the relative assessments of the candidates at time t

$$= |J_{at} - \text{ideal}| - |J_{bt} - \text{ideal}| \tag{9.10}$$

Where J_{at} is the individual's judgment regarding the position of Candidate A at time t, J_{bt} is the judgment regarding Candidate B at time t, and "ideal" is the individual's ideal – their own position on the seven-point scale. The range of the resulting measure is from –6, for the most positive relative assessment of Candidate A, to 6 for the most positive relative assessment of Candidate B.

One might thus conceive the propensity as a consequence of all the privately purchased and socially communicated information an individual has obtained, as well as each of their four preliminary judgments regarding each candidate. Alternatively, the same logic that produced Equation 9.8 also generates:

[9] Analyses not shown here suggest that participants who obtained more heterogeneous information, as well as participants with more heterogeneous priors and updated judgments, are no more likely to purchase information at the final opportunity, immediately prior to the vote. In short, investing in additional information does not seem to be a commonly adopted solution to noisy information streams.

$$L = f(A_3, A_0, eI_4, dD_4) \qquad (9.11)$$

where:

A_0 = the individuals' initial or prior assessments of the two candidates, based on their initial judgments of the candidates' position relative to their own positions

A_3 = the individuals' final updated assessments of the two candidates, based on their final judgments of the candidates' positions relative to their ideals

D_4 = 1 for subjects who purchased information at the last opportunity; 0 otherwise

I_4 (for individuals who did not purchase information at final opportunity) = 0

I_4 (for individuals who purchased information at final opportunity) = $|I_{a4} - \text{ideal}| - |I_{b4} - \text{ideal}|$

I_{a4} = information regarding the position of Candidate A at the final opportunity (t=4)

I_{b4} = information regarding the position of Candidate B at the final opportunity (t=4)

ideal= the participant's fixed ideal position

While the non-linearity of the logit model precludes the direct estimation of the decay rates (w and α), we can still evaluate the relative importance of the priors through time and across levels of investment in private information.

The model is estimated in Table 9.4, where the prior assessment, the final assessment, and the final information purchase are also included in interaction variables with the amount of information purchased by the subject at the first opportunity. The estimates show that both the prior assessment and the final assessment are contingent on the initial acquisition of information. The final judgment has an independent effect that is further enhanced by the initial information purchase. The prior has an effect that is wholly contingent on the initial information purchase, and indeed the prior has no effect among those participants who did not purchase information. Finally, the final information purchase has no effect, either independently or contingently.

The magnitudes of the effects estimated in Table 9.4 on the probability of voting for Candidate B are shown in Table 9.5, where each part of the table corresponds to a different level of investment in privately purchased information at the outset of an experimental round. And it comes as no surprise that, in all three parts of the table, we see a much more pronounced effect of the final candidate assessments in comparison to the prior assessments. If the final assessment is unambiguous – if the subject's judgments regarding the candidates lead to *a clear and certain preference* – the prior appears to be largely irrelevant.

In contrast, we see a pronounced effect of the prior when either of two circumstances are present: (1) when the subject's final candidate assessment

TABLE 9.4. *Candidate vote by prior assessment, final assessment, and information purchased at the last opportunity, contingent on amount of initial information purchase. Standard errors are corrected for clustered observations on subjects.*

	Coefficient	t-value
Prior assessment (A_0)	−.12	−1.18
Final assessment (A_3)	.35	2.62
Final formation purchase (I_4)	.29	0.63
Prior assessment X amount of initial information purchase	.13	2.13
Final assessment X initial information purchase	.21	3.15
Final information X amount of initial information purchase	.07	0.42
Amount of initial information purchase	.12	1.50
Last information purchase (D_4)	−.03	−0.12
Constant	−.19	−1.17

N = 749 (84 subjects)
χ^2, df, p = 112, 8, .00

prior to voting is ambiguous, thereby creating a *higher level of uncertainty* (Tversky and Kahneman 1974), and (2) when the subject invested more resources in the purchase of information at the beginning of the round. If either of these conditions is absent, the importance of the prior judgments is greatly reduced. In this context, it is important to emphasize that, on average, the candidates tend to lie close together on the seven-point scale. Nearly 80 percent of the candidate pairs lie within 3 points of each other on the scale, and the mean distance is 2.4. Hence, a great deal of the activity involves close calls, where both actual and perceived best choices are ambiguous and uncertain. This means, in turn, that the priors are highly relevant in most circumstances, but only when subjects have invested heavily in privately acquired information. In ambiguous decision-making settings, the highly informed experts make up their minds early, and they are highly unlikely to change their minds (Lodge and Taber 2000).

The survival of the prior judgment is shown in Figure 9.4 as a function of the certainty of the final judgment and individual information purchases. The figure clearly demonstrates the dramatic and contingent effects of both final judgment certainty as well as expertise on the survival of the prior's influence.[10] This analysis provides a formidable test of the autoregressive argument. One might expect that earlier judgments would be subsumed in subsequent judgments. This analysis reveals, however, that past judgments take on lives of their own.

[10] The certainty of the final judgment is defined as the absolute value of the candidate propensity reflected in the final judgment, and hence it varies from 0 to 6.

TABLE 9.5. *Predicted probabilities of voting for Candidate B by candidate propensities of prior and final judgments.*
A. *Participants who purchased four pieces of information.*

Candidate propensity of final judgment	Candidate propensity of prior judgment							
	−6	−4	−2	0	2	4	6	Δ
−6	0	0	0	0	0	.01	.02	.02
−4	0	0	0	.01	.02	.06	.16	.16
−2	0	.01	.03	.08	.21	.43	.68	.68
0	.04	.11	.26	.50	.74	.89	.96	.92
2	.32	.57	.79	.92	.97	.99	1	.67
4	.84	.94	.97	.99	1	1	1	.16
6	.98	.99	1	1	1	1	1	.02
Δ	.98	.99	1	1	1	.99	.98	

B. *Participants who purchased two pieces of information.*

Candidate propensity of final judgment	Candidate propensity of prior judgment							
	−6	−4	−2	0	2	4	6	Δ
−6	0	0	.01	.01	.02	.03	.04	.04
−4	.01	.02	.03	.04	.07	.12	.18	.17
−2	.04	.07	.11	.18	.27	.38	.50	.46
0	.17	.26	.37	.50	.63	.74	.83	.66
2	.50	.62	.73	.82	.89	.93	.96	.46
4	.82	.88	.93	.96	.97	.98	.99	.17
6	.96	.97	.98	.99	.99	1	1	.04
Δ	.96	.97	.97	.98	.97	.97	.96	

C. *Participants who purchased no information.*

Candidate propensity of final judgment	Candidate propensity of prior judgment							
	−6	−4	−2	0	2	4	6	Δ
−6	.11	.11	.11	.11	.11	.11	.11	0
−4	.20	.20	.20	.20	.20	.20	.20	0
−2	.33	.33	.33	.33	.33	.33	.33	0
0	.50	.50	.50	.50	.50	.50	.50	0
2	.67	.67	.67	.67	.67	.67	.67	0
4	.80	.80	.80	.80	.80	.80	.80	0
6	.89	.89	.89	.89	.89	.89	.89	0
Δ	.78	.78	.78	.78	.78	.78	.78	

Data source: Estimates in Table 9.4.

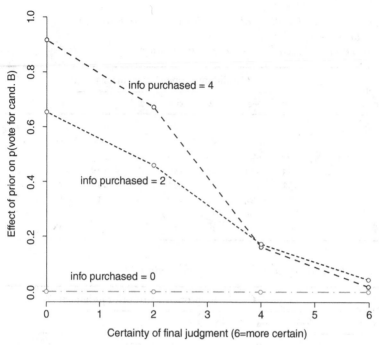

FIGURE 9.4. The effect of prior judgment on the probability of voting for Candidate B as a function of the certainty of the final judgment.
Data source: Estimates in Table 9.5. Certainty is measured as the absolute distance between the subject's final pre-vote assessments of the two candidates.

Particularly in ambiguous, uncertain decision-making environments, the memory of past judgments affects contemporaneous behavior among the high-volume consumers of information, even when contemporaneous judgments are taken into account.

IMPLICATIONS AND CONCLUSIONS

Political information is both noisy and biased, as a direct and inevitable consequence of its subject matter. For many people in many circumstances, political issues are complex and ambiguous, with frequently high levels of uncertainty. At the same time, many other individuals are deeply invested in particular opinions and attitudes and hence care very deeply about political issues and outcomes. Communication regarding politics thus reflects both the complexity of the subject matter and the existence of strongly held opinions. Moreover, the attentive are being continually bombarded by heterogeneous streams of information that are both biased and difficult to validate.

In this context, citizen experts play an important role, even if most experts are self-appointed. In the context of citizen politics, the experts are those activists who care enough about politics to pay the costs of becoming informed. For many, the costs are not so terribly high for the simple reason that they thrive on the acquisition and analysis of political information. Whether the favored information source is the *New York Times*, *The Daily Show*, Fox News, or Rush Limbaugh, the expert is often ready and willing to pay the costs of becoming informed. Or, alternatively, the experts encounter no costs because they enjoy the process of becoming informed. Who are these people who realize no costs? They are likely to be the activists who thrive on, and are motivated by, their fascination with the world of politics.

The citizen experts are important for several reasons. They fill the social airwaves with political content. They package the information they transmit within inevitable patterns of bias that reflect their own interests and concerns. They provide an information source for those political non-junkies who would just as soon spend their time in the pursuit of other interests and avocations. Most importantly, they inject political content into the everyday patterns of communication and interdependence that exist among citizens in democratic societies.

In some ways, political experts display high levels of political self-reliance. Through their private investments in political information, they develop their own political priors regarding a vast array of issues and problems. At the same time, this analysis also suggests that the independence and self-reliance of experts can be overstated. Knowledge and information are indeed fleeting, if only due to the inevitable processes of decay that undermine the certainty of almost any judgment. Hence, political junkies sustain their positions as experts, not by the breadth of their knowledge regarding things political, but rather by their continuing pursuit of political information. Their energy in the pursuit of politics gives rise to the continual formulation of new prior judgments regarding a great variety of issues and problems.

Moreover, this chapter's analysis suggests that even experts are affected by patterns of communication with others, and sometimes these others may be less politically expert. Indeed, a defining ingredient of the expert is a willingness to engage in political communication with others, and our results show that this communication is not without consequence. Hence, the influence of political communication may sneak in through the back door, integrating the expert within patterns of communication that rebound as a source of influence on the prime mover.

Finally, the analysis suggests that the process of becoming informed is autoregressive – individuals encounter and digest new information in the context of old information. This autoregressive process is best understood as an on-line process among the politically expert because these are the individuals with well-developed attitudes, opinions, and beliefs. As we have seen, strongly held opinions survive the process of on-line updating, and hence the experts tend to be only modestly affected by new information. In contrast, the judgments formed by the less expert are not anchored in strongly held priors, and hence they are much more susceptible to messages received from others.

A question that naturally arises is whether the social communication process we have specified resembles a Bayesian updating process – that is, are the subjects in our experiment employing Bayesian reasoning when they formulate prior judgments based on private investments in information and then update those judgments based on information that is socially communicated? If the process is Bayesian, the updated judgment should represent both the prior and the newly acquired information, where both are weighted inversely by their respective variances (Bullock 2009; Bartels 2002; Gerber and Green 1999). Such an account runs at least partially parallel to the social communication process analyzed here. Individuals form final judgments based on priors weighted by the amount of unbiased information they use in formulating the prior. This weight is an entirely reasonable (inverse) function of the variance around the prior, where a higher level of information consumption thus indexes a reduced level of variance. Moreover, the analysis suggests that participants are cautious regarding the value of new information. They seek to minimize misleading bias by locating informants whose interests coincide with their own, and they are skeptical regarding new information, particularly information taken from non-experts whose judgments they do not trust.

The comparison to a Bayesian process thus provides an interesting frame of reference for evaluating the implications of social influence in politics. While there is certainly no evidence to suggest that the participants in our experiment are self-consciously invoking Bayes' theorem, they appear to be invoking standards of judgment that approximate a Bayesian process. Alternatively, this social communication process might also be understood in terms of motivated reasoning. After investing more heavily in the formulation of their own prior judgments, the experts among our participants are personally committed to these judgments and less likely to be swayed by information to the contrary (Kunda 1999; Lodge and Taber 2000). Thus, in several different ways, a social influence process might ironically result that, quite apart from any intent on the part of the participants, parallels Bayesian updating.

The implication is that, in terms of May's (1976) observation with which we began this chapter, we are indeed observing patterns of behavior marked by pronounced levels of non-linear interdependence. Not only does current behavior depend on past behavior, but it also depends on the behavior of others within the context where the individual is located. Some of these individuals – those with strong commitments to their own prior beliefs – are relatively less susceptible. For those without strongly held priors, their behavior is highly dependent on the behavior of others, and the implications for political dynamics are quite profound (Huckfeldt 1990).

This analysis is extended in Chapter 10, with a focus on higher-order dynamic implications. Communication networks generate a sequential dynamic process that is inherently endogenous with important higher-order consequences. Mort talks to Harvey; Harvey talks to Ted; Ted talks to Doris; Doris talks to Harvey; and Harvey talks to Mort. The system is inherently dynamic, and Mort's influence stops with neither Harvey nor Ted, but percolates through the system of relationships, ultimately coming back to register a potential effect on its originator. We address these issues in the context of memory decay and the role of well-informed, durable priors in opinion leadership.

CHAPTER 9 APPENDIX

INSTRUCTIONS TO PARTICIPANTS

The following instructions were read to all subjects before the experiment began. These instructions reference screens that can be viewed at johnbarryryan.com.

Thank you for participating in today's experiment. I will be reading from a script to ensure that every session of this experiment receives the same instruction. Feel free to ask questions if you require clarification. This instruction explains the nature of today's experiment as well as how to navigate the computer interface you will be working with. We ask that you please refrain from talking or looking at the monitors of other participants during the experiment. If you have a question or problem please raise your hand and one of us will come to you.

Please turn to your informational handout while I read from it.

Instructions for the experiment

This experiment is about information and voting, and it takes place over approximately ten rounds.

During each round, you will consider two candidates.

Your goal is to elect the candidate at each round whose position is closest to your own position.

Each participant in the group receives 100 ECUs at the beginning of each round. Participants **earn** *an additional 50 ECUs if the candidate whose position is closest to their own position wins the election for that round. And they lose 50 ECUs if the candidate closest to their position loses the election for that round. If there is a tie, nobody earns nor loses ECUs. Participants also* **spend** *ECUs by purchasing information during each round.*

Each ECU is worth 1 cent. So, over ten rounds you will receive a total of 10 dollars as your endowment.

Your total earnings will grow when the candidate closest to you wins, and decrease when the candidate closest to you loses. You will also have the opportunity to spend your ECUs on additional information about the candidates.

Your total payout will be: $5 for being willing to participate, plus your earnings.

Positions of candidates and participants

Your position and the candidates' positions are represented on a scale that varies from 1 to 7. You will be assigned a precise position on the scale, and hence you will know your own position exactly, as well as the positions of the other participants.

The candidate's position will be more difficult to determine. Candidate A's position lies somewhere between 1 and 6. Candidate B's position lies somewhere between 2 and 7.

Your position is fixed throughout this session. The candidates' true positions change between rounds. This means that the candidate closest to your position at one round may not be closest to your position at the next round.

Information

You will have two different types of information to use in estimating the candidates' positions:

1. *Information about the candidates that you purchase with ECUs. You can purchase information regarding the candidates. The problem is that, while this information is accurate on average, any single piece of information is likely to diverge from the candidate's true position.*
2. *Information about the candidates obtained from others. You will also have the opportunity to obtain information from other members who are participating with you. In making this request, you will know each participant's exact position, as well as the amount of information each participant has purchased. All information obtained from others is free, but the information that the participant provides may or may not reflect that participant's true beliefs regarding the candidate's position.*

Now, please turn to your computer screens. We have prepared several demonstration screens to help you get familiar with the actual screens you will see during the experiment.

(SCREEN ONE) This is the first screen you will see in each period. The top of each screen displays the period and the time remaining for this screen. We suggest that you make your decisions for a screen within the time limit, but you will not be forced to make decisions in that time.

In the upper left hand corner, you will see your participant number and your position. This information will be in the upper left hand corner on every screen.

On this screen, you will be allowed to purchase private information about the candidates. Information costs a certain amount of money. You may purchase up to four pieces of information, so long as you spend less than with 50 ECUs. You may also purchase no private information. For this practice round, please *purchase at least one piece of private information. Please purchase some information and click "OK."*

(SCREEN TWO) This screen displays the private pieces of information that you bought. On average, private information accurately represents the candidates' true position, but any single piece of information could be inaccurate.

Each piece of information is a number randomly drawn from an interval centered on the candidate's true position and extending 3 positions above and below that true position. So, while the candidate's proposals are bound between 1 and 7, the information you receive could fall outside of those bounds.

Based on the information you see, you are asked to estimate the candidate's positions. Enter estimates for the two candidates and click OK.

(SCREEN THREE) You are also able to request information from other participants. You are accurately told the other participants' number and position as well as the amount of private information the other participant received on the previous screen. There is no cost for requesting this social information. Please enter the participant number from the player you wish to request social information from and click OK.

(SCREEN FOUR) On this screen, you provide social information to participants that requested social information from you. You are accurately told the other participants' number and position, as well as the amount of private information the participant has purchased. You do not need to provide information to the other participants, nor do you need to provide identical information to each of the participants who asked information from you. You are reminded of the positions that you thought the candidates held after receiving the private information. Enter the information about the candidates that you want to provide to the other participants and then click OK. If no one requested information from you, simply click OK.

(SCREEN FIVE) On this screen, you receive information from the participant you requested information from. You are accurately told the other participants' number and party as well as the amount of private information the other participant received on the first screen. You are also given the participant's stated estimate of the candidates' position.

Once again, you are asked to estimate the candidate's benefit. You are reminded of your previous estimate. Enter estimates for the two candidates and click OK.

(SCREENS SIX/SEVEN/EIGHT/NINE/TEN/ELEVEN) You will request and provide information two more times from and to other participants. Each time you request information, you will be reminded of the participants you have previously requested information from. Enter the next candidate that you would like to request information from and click OK.

(SCREEN TWELVE) On this screen, you will have the opportunity to purchase a final piece of private information for 10 ECUs. Choose whether you would like to purchase an additional piece of information and click OK.

(*SCREEN THIRTEEN*) *Once again, you are reminded of your previous estimate. If you purchased another piece of private information, it will show up on this screen. Now, it is time to vote. You should vote for the candidate that you think will be closer to your issue position. Your final cash payoff is calculated by adding what is left of your initial endowment to the 50 ECU bonus you receive from the candidate closer to your issue position winning or subtracting the 50 ECU penalty you receive from the other candidate winning. For example, if you had 80 ECUs left from your initial endowment after purchasing private information, and your ideal candidate won, you would end the round with 130 ECUs (80 plus 50). If the other, less ideal, candidate won, you would end the round with 30 ECUs (80 minus 50).*

Vote for one of the two candidates and click OK.

(*SCREEN FOURTEEN*) *This is the final screen. The two candidates' positions are revealed as is the outcome of the election. You will also learn the number of ECUs you earned in this period as well as the number of ECUs you have earned up to this point in the experiment.*

The experiment will consist of 10 periods like this one. At the end of these 10 periods, you will be asked a couple of questions about the experiment, asked to provide some demographic information, and a couple of questions about your general political leanings. All of your responses are anonymous.

This concludes the demonstration screens. We are now ready to begin the actual experiment. We ask that you follow the rules of the experiment. Anyone who violates the rules may be asked to leave the experiment with only the $5 show up fee. Are there any questions before we start?

The complex dynamics of political communication

Robert Huckfeldt, Matthew T. Pietryka, and Jack Reilly

> Each ant lives in its own little world, responding to the other ants in its immediate environment and responding to signals of which it does not know the origin. Why the system works as it does, and as effectively as it does, is a dynamic problem of social and genetic evolution.
>
> Thomas Schelling (1978: 21)

Particularly in the context of complex political processes involving hundreds or thousands or millions of citizens, the whole is typically an unintentional byproduct viewed from the vantage point of the participant. Just as the formation of political beliefs and opinions is not solely due to a cognitive process occurring between the ears of isolated individuals, so too the implications of political communication among citizens is not solely due to an isolated process occurring within self-contained dyads. Not only do the beliefs of individuals depend on what happens within dyads, but the effects of single dyads are contingent on the other dyads within which individuals are simultaneously located (Huckfeldt, Johnson, and Sprague 2004). Moreover, these network effects are not simply cumulative across an individual's range of contacts. To the contrary, the effects are sequential, dynamic, and interdependent. While voters certainly do not resemble Schelling's ants, public opinion in the aggregate is created through complex processes of interaction and communication, located in both space and time, which are at least as complex as those producing the anthill.

This chapter takes a modest step toward understanding an important micro–macro problem in democratic politics (Eulau 1998). In particular, our concern is whether individual levels of political expertise serve to inform the aggregate through the patterns of communication existing among interdependent individuals. We address this problem by extending the analysis of the small group experiments in Chapter 9 to address the consequences of dynamic interdependence for aggregate rather than individual outcomes.

EXPERT CITIZENS AND HIGHER-ORDER
COMMUNICATION EFFECTS

Complex patterns of communication and inter-connectedness create analytic opportunities as well as methodological challenges. Opportunities arise to move seamlessly back and forth between aggregates and individuals, guided by the observed patterns of connections between and among the individual members of aggregate populations. At the same time, this potential carries with it a variety of observational challenges. These challenges include endogeneity problems that are endemic to any effort aimed at studying individuals within their ongoing patterns of communication and social interaction – problems that plague any effort aimed at establishing causality in post hoc observational studies of social and political influence. Without experimental control over the flow of communication, it becomes difficult to make assertions that are not hotly contested regarding the effects of expertise on either the flow of communication or its influence, and hence observational studies confront substantial problems with respect to their internal validity.

While post hoc observational studies make it difficult to address endogeneity problems, they also pose problems for studying the higher-order consequences of individual expertise. While inroads have been made in addressing the implications of expertise for political influence and the formation of relationships at the level of dyads, less has been accomplished in addressing the diffusion of expertise through larger populations (but see Nickerson 2008). What are the implications for you if your life partner regularly discusses politics with a knowledgeable person at his or her work place? What are the implications for your life partner that arise due to the coworkers with whom *you* discuss politics?

Moreover, while the social communication of political information carries the potential to create efficiency gains, it also creates the potential for politics and persuasion to be played out in countless social exchanges, with consequences reaching far beyond the immediacy of a dyad (Christakas and Fowler 2009). As we have argued, the social transmission of political information is not an antiseptic exercise in civic betterment. Rather, it is a process characterized by informational asymmetries among participants, as well as frequently passionate advocacy on the part of those who are politically engaged. Thus, it creates the potential for opinion leadership and the social mobilization of bias within the communication process – a process that extends far beyond dyads to generate policy moods (Stimson 1999) and other aggregate consequences.

As a consequence, some individuals are more influential than others, and our goal in this chapter is to assess the higher-order implications of their influence. In particular, we are interested in the extent to which influence reaches beyond dyads. How does political influence extend beyond the immediate range of contacts to penetrate the larger population? Does this penetration serve to amplify the influence of the activists and experts? Here again we confront complex endogeneity problems that are not easily resolved in the absence of an experimental design (Erbring, Goldenberg, and Miller 1980), and hence we extend the analysis of the experiment and experimental results taken from Chapter 9.

A DEGROOT MODEL OF SOCIAL INFLUENCE

The analysis of this chapter employs a DeGroot model (DeGroot 1974; Jackson 2008) to focus on the higher-order consequences of complex communication processes. While we expect the process to be contingent on the preferences and expertise of informants and message recipients, we are less concerned with the direct effects that occur within dyads, and more concerned with the socially mediated effects that arise due to the informants of informants. In the previous chapter we focused on the individual updating process within rounds. In this chapter we employ those results, but our concern turns to the higher-order, longer-term dynamic implications.

The DeGroot model draws on basic theorems regarding Markov chains, where individuals formulate prior beliefs and then update these beliefs on the basis of information taken from other individuals. The updating process is not random, but rather occurs through networks of communication within a larger population. The basic model is

$$p_{t+1} = Tp_t \qquad (10.1)$$

where:

p_t = is a N×1 column vector, where each of the entries is an individual's belief regarding a particular candidate and p_o is a vector of individual priors. For example, each entry might be the nth individual's belief regarding the position of Candidate A.

T = a row stochastic matrix, such that T_{ij} is the persuasive weight of the jth individual's belief regarding the candidate at any time period (t) on the ith individual's belief at the subsequent period (t+1). Each row sums to unity, where the main diagonal is the weight that the ith individual places on her own prior belief (at t) in the formulation of her current updated belief (at t+1).

We are especially interested in the T matrix, as well as its long-term dynamic consequences. The focus of this analysis is not on the formation of initial beliefs, but rather on the relative weights that individuals place on their own prior beliefs versus the beliefs of others. In particular, we are concerned with the ways in which the evolution of beliefs in the aggregate depends on the underlying distribution of expertise within the aggregate. And we can readily obtain an estimate of T based on our experimental data from Chapter 9.

TABLE 10.1. *Subject's final judgment regarding Candidate A at each round by their initial (prior) judgment as well as the information conveyed by each of their informants. (Least squares models absent intercepts. Standard errors are adjusted for clustering on subjects.)*

A. *All subjects, with no weights for information purchases.*

	Coefficient	t-value
Prior judgment	.51	12.61
First message	.17	9.46
Second message	.14	5.36
Third message	.17	5.80
N =		749 (84 subjects)
R^2=		.92
Root MSE=		1.06

B. *Subjects who purchased more than 1 piece of information on candidates.*

	Coefficient	t-value
Prior judgment	.67	15.12
First message	.10	4.90
Second message	.10	3.85
Third message	.14	5.05
N =		454 (74 subjects)
R^2=		.95
Root MSE=		.86

C. *Subjects who purchased less than 2 pieces of information on candidates.*

	Coefficient	t-value
Prior judgment	.35	5.95
First message	.23	6.39
Second message	.16	3.85
Third message	.21	3.46
N =		295 (59 subjects)
R^2=		.89
Root MSE=		1.23

In Table 10.1 we address the subjects' final judgments regarding the position of Candidate A at each round.[1] In each part of the table, these judgments are

---

[1] The results for Candidate B are highly comparable, and the empirical results in Table 10.1 can be compared to those of Table 9.2. We suppress the constant in order to translate the combined effects approximately into a unit interval.

regressed on the subject's prior judgment and each of the three messages that the individual obtained from other subjects. Part A of the table shows the pattern of simple direct effects for all subjects, independently of individual information levels. The coefficients suggest that the effect of the prior is roughly equal to the cumulative effect of the three communicated messages, with comparably sized message effects. In parts B and C of Table 10.1, the model is re-estimated for high- and low-information consumers respectively. We see that the effect of the prior judgment is nearly twice as large among the more informed subjects, with an average message effect that is almost twice as large among the less informed subjects. We explore the aggregate, dynamical implications of these results in the remainder of this paper.

ESTIMATES FOR THE MODEL

The first step is to arrive at estimates for the rows of T – the relative weights that are attached to an individual's own immediately previous judgment, as well as the judgments of others, in arriving at that individual's contemporaneous judgment. The empirical results in Part A of Table 10.1 suggest that, for the subjects as a combined group, approximately 50 percent of current judgments are based on the immediately prior judgments, with the remainder depending approximately equally on the three messages obtained from other participants in the experiment. Hence, the non-zero elements of each row in the T matrix should consist of .5 on the diagonal, with three of the remaining six entries set to .167. (The final message effect is set to .166 in order that the rows sum to 1.)

This raises the obvious question, which three entries? We pursue the objective of considering the long-term implications of the communication choices selected by the participants in two randomly chosen sessions – round 6 of session 5 and round 3 of session 8.[2] These sessions are shown in the directed network graphs of Figure 10.1, where each node is numbered according to the individual's preference, and where the size of the node is indexed on the amount of information purchased by the individual.

These network graphs tell a similar story to the empirical results of Table 9.1. Larger nodes (better-informed participants) attract more requests for information, and higher levels of communication generally occur among individuals with similar preferences. A close inspection of the graphs produces some surprises, and many of these seeming aberrations can be explained on the basis of expertise and preference proximity as competing criteria. This reflects a reality where the choice of informants is complex, and the process is inherently

---

[2] Each of 12 sessions involved seven subjects and the number of rounds (each of which constituted a separate election) varied from 7 to 10.

stochastic.[3] For the purposes of illustration, the T matrix implied by Part A of Table 10.1 and Part A of Figure 10.1 is shown below.

(A)

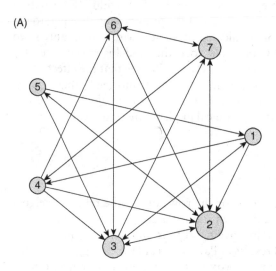

(B)

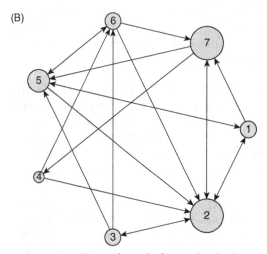

FIGURE 10.1. Directed graphs for randomly chosen rounds. Size of node indexes amount of information purchased. Direction of edge signifies the participant from whom information is being requested.
   A. Session 5, Round 6
   B. Session 8, Round 3

---

[3] The stochastic component of participant choices is well illustrated in these two sessions of the experiment. If we regress information purchases on information costs for all the subjects in each round of every session, the R^2 is .23. In contrast, the R^2 for the session in Figure 10.1A is .05 and

$$T = \begin{matrix}
.500 & .167 & .167 & .166 & .000 & .000 & .000 \\
.000 & .500 & .167 & .000 & .167 & .000 & .166 \\
.167 & .167 & .500 & .000 & .000 & .000 & .166 \\
.000 & .167 & .167 & .500 & .000 & .166 & .000 \\
.167 & .167 & .166 & .000 & .500 & .000 & .000 \\
.000 & .167 & .167 & .000 & .000 & .500 & .166 \\
.000 & .167 & .000 & .167 & .000 & .166 & .500
\end{matrix} \qquad (10.2)$$

Each row is a vector of weights corresponding to the network's contemporaneous, single-period effect on a particular individual's judgment update. Based on the results of Table 10.1A, we set each participant's current judgment as the weighted sum of the immediately prior judgments, with a 50 percent weight on the immediately prior judgment, and the remaining 50 percent partitioned equally among the three informants. Hence, each individual in this specification is influenced directly by her own prior judgment, as well as the judgment of three other participants. Each column corresponds to the contemporaneous, single-period effect of a particular individual's judgment on each of the other individuals' judgments. For example, the fifth column characterizes the very limited short-term effect of the individual who holds preference 5 in Part A of Figure 10.1. Only the individual with preference 2 requests information from the person who holds preference 5.

These short-term direct effects are not, however, simply additive across time. Instead, the information provided by preference holder 5 to preference holder 2 produces indirect effects on all 6 individuals (including preference holder 5) who request information from preference holder 2 at the subsequent time period. Hence, the short-term contemporaneous effects ignore much of the dynamic interdependence underlying communication and persuasion. In this experiment, we do not require individuals to maintain the same contacts across all the experimental sessions, and thus we do not empirically trace effects across the entire session. Rather, our intent is to consider the long-term implications of the short-term contacts that are established by the participants in the experiment, in an effort to consider both the direct and indirect effects of experts and information in political communication.

LONG-TERM DYNAMICS OF POLITICAL COMMUNICATION

The process described in Equation 10.1 is recursive, and hence

the R^2 for the session in Figure 10.1B is .20. In short, while the information cost incentives we have established are clearly related to information purchases, the strategic choices of the participants include a significant idiosyncratic component.

$$p_1 = Tp_0$$
$$p_2 = Tp_1 = T^2 p_0$$

$$.$$
$$.$$ (10.3)
$$.$$

$$p_t = T^t p_0$$

This is a particularly helpful formulation because it suggests that each entry in T^t provides the long-term effect of the jth individual in moving the ith individual from p_0 to p_t. If at any value of t, some column of T includes all non-zero elements, it suggests that every individual in the entire population is affected, either directly or indirectly, by every other individual in the entire population, and thus the process leads to convergent beliefs. We are thus assured that the T matrix for round 6 of session 5 leads to convergent beliefs because, in the first order matrix, the column for preference holder 5 contains all non-zero elements, and T raised to successively higher powers converges on the following set of identical row vectors.

$$
T^* =
\begin{matrix}
.096 & .250 & .205 & .093 & .084 & .091 & .181 \\
.096 & .250 & .205 & .093 & .084 & .091 & .181 \\
.096 & .250 & .205 & .093 & .084 & .091 & .181 \\
.096 & .250 & .205 & .093 & .084 & .091 & .181 \\
.096 & .250 & .205 & .093 & .084 & .091 & .181 \\
.096 & .250 & .205 & .093 & .084 & .091 & .181 \\
.096 & .250 & .205 & .093 & .084 & .091 & .181 \\
\end{matrix}
\qquad (10.4)
$$

Hence we can identify an equilibrium vector for participants' judgments, which is simply the judgmental priors of the participants weighted by T^*.

$$p^* = T^* p_0 \qquad (10.5)$$

Assume for the moment that p_0 provides the participants' initial estimates regarding the position of Candidate B, specified as $(2,2,2,3,4,4,4)$. This leads to an equilibrium vector of $(2.8, 2.8, 2.8, 2.8, 2.8, 2.8, 2.8)$. If we reversed the order of priors in p_0, p^* would become an equilibrium vector $(3.2, 3.2, 3.2, 3.2, 3.2, 3.2, 3.2)$. In short, these alternative outcomes reflect the greater influence of those individuals with preferences 1 through 3 relative to preferences 5 through 7.

A row of T^* becomes the unit eigenvector for T,[4] and it provides a relative measure of each participant's influence, capturing both their direct and indirect

---

[4] A row vector in T^* provides the unit eigenvector of T – the row vector that, when multiplied times T, returns the same row vector, or $tT=t$.

TABLE 10.2. *Unit eigenvectors for experimental periods. Expert effects in bold italics.*

	Participant with preference:							
	1	2	3	4	5	6	7	Σ expert
A. Baseline condition.								
Group 5, Period 6:	(.096	*.250*	*.205*	.093	.084	.091	*.181*)	.64
Group 8, Period 3:	(.141	*.250*	.084	.057	*.173*	.123	*.171*)	.59
B. With information weights.								
Group 5, Period 6:	(.059	*.305*	*.249*	.057	.052	.056	*.222*)	.78
Group 8, Period 3:	(.090	*.312*	.053	.036	*.217*	.078	*.214*)	.74

effects within the network. By comparison to Figure 10.1A, we see that the individuals who purchased the most information become the opinion leaders in the process. Indeed, the participants in columns 2, 3, and 7 combine for 64 percent of the total network influence.

The network in Part B of Figure 10.1 produces a similar outcome. Part A of Table 10.2 shows the unit eigenvectors for both networks. In each instance, the individuals who purchased the most information demonstrate the strongest relative effects. Indeed, as shown in part A of Table 10.2, the three highest consumers of information in the two randomly selected experimental rounds account for 64 and 59 percent of opinion leadership, respectively.

These networks are inherently stochastic. Individuals need not purchase information, and even individuals who can obtain it for free do not necessarily obtain the full amount that is available. The relationship between information costs and preference is the same in both experimental periods, yet we see variation between the rounds in information purchases. No one in Part A obtained four pieces of private information, but two individuals in Part B purchased the maximum. In short, information costs and preference proximity generate important effects on network structure, but these effects are certainly not deterministic, and we see pronounced differences in networks between the two experimental periods.

Finally, it is important to recognize that the empirical model of opinion leadership in Part A of Table 10.1 is wholly due to the specification of network selection. That is, we are assuming network effects that are wholly mediated by an individual's choice of discussion partners, without any effects due to the inherent effects of information abundance and scarcity on the processing of either private information or socially communicated information. We turn to the consequences of information and expertise for the behavior of individuals, both with respect to the confidence they place in their own priors, as well as the extent to which they update their priors based on socially communicated information.

INFORMATION, EXPERTISE, AND OPINION LEADERSHIP

As Parts B and C of Table 10.1 suggest, information has important effects on the extent to which individuals depend on their own priors versus the extent to which they depend on messages received from other individuals. That is, individuals who purchase more information reveal more confidence in their own prior judgments, as well as relatively less confidence in the judgments of others. This moves us beyond a strictly sociological view of the problem based on the structure of the relationships among participants, introducing a psychological perspective regarding the cognitive processing of new information, as well as a decision-making process whereby individuals update their own preconceived judgments in a highly uncertain environment with information provided by others.

Unfortunately, major advances in the cognitive processing of information are rarely considered among network scientists, and major advances in network science appear to be unknown among students of cognition. It is as if network scientists ignore the nodes, and cognitive scientists ignore the edges![5] The reality is that, as Parts B and C of Table 10.1 show, it is not simply the existence of the communication pathways among actors that is important. Indeed, the relative efficacy of those pathways depends on the commitment of individual actors to their own pre-existent beliefs, as well as their relative openness to communication on the part of the individuals (nodes) populating the pathways. These results reinforce the work of Lodge and Taber (2000) – those who know the most are the least willing to be moved by new information.

We build on these results by constructing T matrices that take account of these contingent effects for both network graphs in Figure 10.1. The matrix for Figure 10.1A is shown here:

$$T = \begin{bmatrix} .350 & .217 & .217 & .216 & .000 & .000 & .000 \\ .000 & .670 & .110 & .000 & .110 & .000 & .110 \\ .110 & .110 & .670 & .000 & .000 & .000 & .110 \\ .000 & .217 & .217 & .350 & .000 & .216 & .000 \\ .217 & .217 & .216 & .000 & .350 & .000 & .000 \\ .000 & .217 & .217 & .000 & .000 & .350 & .216 \\ .000 & .110 & .000 & .110 & .000 & .110 & .670 \end{bmatrix} \quad (10.6)$$

Reflecting the results of Parts B and C of Table 10.1, the better-informed rely more heavily on their priors and less heavily on social communication than the lesser-informed. This produces, in turn, the unit eigenvector in Part B of Table 10.2, which displays an enhanced level of influence for the informed relative to the uninformed.

---

[5] For particularly notable exceptions see Levitan and Visser (2009) and Lazer et al. (2010).

In summary, opinion leadership is both a sociological as well as a psychological phenomenon. Not only is the influence of opinion leaders related to their centrality within communication networks and the frequency with which they engage in political communication, but it is also due to the resilience and durability of their judgments. Experts are resistant to persuasion and committed to their own prior judgments, thereby providing a persuasive advantage in the collective deliberations of democratic discussion.

THE DECISIVE EFFECTS OF SLOWLY DECAYING PRIORS

Finally, limits on cognition encourage us to take the mechanics of memory seriously in the analysis of political communication. Working memory is dramatically limited in its capacity, and objects in working memory can be lost after they are passed to long-term memory. Hence, memory decay plays a role in the duration of even the strongest beliefs and judgments.

Analyses of these same experimental results support even short-term effects on memory decay (see Chapter 9) – that is, participants in the experiment update their prior judgments three times during a round, and during that short period of time we see a rate of decay in the priors that is especially precipitous among the least informed. At the same time, even the priors of the most informed show the short-term consequences of memory decay.

Our goal is to consider the implications that arise due to differential rates of decay among experts and non-experts, and we modify the general model accordingly (see Friedkin and Johnsen 1990; Jackson 2008). Suppose that an individual's prior judgment competes directly with the updating process, but that the importance of the prior declines in time as a consequence of memory decay. We incorporate this idea into a revised model,

$$p_{t+1} = D^{t+1}p_0 + (I - D^{t+1})Tp_t \qquad (10.7)$$

where the T matrix is taken from (10.6); D is a diagonal matrix with the rates (defined on a 0,1 interval) at which individuals' prior judgments survive in a single period of time; I is the identity matrix; and I-D is a diagonal matrix reflecting the complement of D – the rates at which individuals base their judgments on the messages received from informants *as well as* their own immediately previous judgments.

Hence, the importance of an individual's prior declines both in time and across individuals. For the purposes of illustration, we set the rate of decay to .2 for individuals who purchased 2 or more pieces of information, and to .6 for individuals who purchased 0 or 1 piece of information. (These rates of decay are compatible with the earlier analyses in Chapter 9 showing rates of decay structured by private investments in information.)

First, the impact of memory decay declines over time in this formulation – that is, D^{t+k} converges to zero as k increases, but it converges more rapidly among the least informed. Second, and in a similar fashion, $I-D^{t+k}$ converges on I (the identity matrix), as k increases. And hence, in the long run, the effect of memory decay disappears and we are left with the process described in the basic model (see Equation 10.1). The end result is the same unit eigenvector that is displayed in Table 10.2B for Group 5, Session 6. The difference is that the system takes much longer to converge on the same equilibrium vector of shared judgments, and *during that slow path to equilibrium, the judgments of the opinion leaders are more influential.*

The question that arises is whether the long term makes much difference in the deliberations of democratic societies, and the answer is a resounding "sometimes"! Many issues play out on a short timescale, and in these instances opinion leaders are likely to be particularly influential because their priors decay so slowly. Other issues are of longer duration, and we should expect an inevitable convergence toward a long-term equilibrium which serves to diminish the role of enduring priors even among opinion leaders. Indeed, some issues are initially controversial, but eventually become settled matters after long periods of public discussion. Universal suffrage is one example, and the existence of global warming is likely to be another. This does not mean that everyone ends up holding the same opinion, but in these cases divergence from the conventional view become notable because they are so rare and idiosyncratic.

INCORPORATING THE MODEL OF MEMORY DECAY

While memory constraints certainly operate on prior judgments, they also operate on the updates to these priors, as well as the messages that are communicated by others. Memory decay can be portrayed at the individual level by expressing the updating process for the subjects' judgments as a function of three factors: (1) decay in the most recently updated judgment, (2) decay in the initial (prior) judgment based on individually purchased private information, and (3) incoming information communicated by other subjects. For the reader's convenience, we briefly recapitulate the model developed in Chapter 9.

THE EFFECT OF THE PRIOR

The model assumes that the initial (or prior) judgment, formed on the basis of privately purchased information, has an enduring effect that declines at a compound fixed rate between judgments. At the first update, the effect of the prior is wP_o, where w is defined as (1–rate of decay) and at the nth update its effect is thus w^nP_o.

THE EFFECT OF UPDATED JUDGMENTS

Updated judgments generate first-order effects that also decline at a fixed rate. At the nth update, the effect of the previous update is αJ_{n-1}, where α is the survival of the previous judgment.

INCOMING INFORMATION

At the same time that the prior and the previously updated judgments are subject to decay, the subject is responding to an ongoing stream of social information communicated by other subjects. This incoming information is incorporated within the update, and thus its effect decays as the updated judgment decays.

Hence, the current judgment arises due to the persistence of the immediately preceding judgment update, the rate of decay in an initial prior judgment, and the effect of contemporaneous social information.

$$J_t = \alpha J_{t-1} + w^t P_o + eI_t \text{, or} \qquad (10.8)$$

where α = the memory or survival of the previous judgment ($0 < \alpha < 1$); P_o = the initial or prior judgment based on privately purchased information; w^t = the effect of the prior at t ($0 < w < 1$); I_t = socially supplied information received at t; and e = the educative impact of the new social information.

By employing recursion to push the model beyond the reach of our experimental data, we take the equation to its limiting behavior. For n sufficiently large,

$$J_n = (w^n P_o - \alpha^n w^o P_o)/(1 - \alpha/w) + eI_n + \alpha eI_{n-1} + \ldots + \alpha^{n-1} eI_1.$$
$$(10.9)$$

Assuming that both α and w are bounded by 0 and 1, the effect of the prior converges on zero and the summary judgments inevitably depend on the continuing stream of incoming information, where the stream of information is weighted to favor the most recent information.

The crucial issue is how rapidly the memory of this behavioral system decays. The key lies in the behavior of w^n and α^n. As α increases – as the immediately past updated judgment looms larger in the formulation of the current judgment – the importance of information received earlier maintains its effect longer. Since the updated judgment is the mechanism whereby the prior is modified by new information, *α* also provides an index of the temporal durability of effects due to messages from other participants. As *w* increases, the importance of the prior takes longer to disappear. In this context, it is important to consider the dynamic implications in the short-term as well as the long-term, and hence to obtain estimates for the model parameters.

OBTAINING ESTIMATES FOR THE DEGROOT MODEL

The three model parameters are re-estimated for low- and high-information subjects relative to both candidates in Table 10.3, based on the procedures outlined in Chapter 9. Part A of Table 10.3 displays the results of estimating the model in Equation 10.8 for high-information subjects, defined as subjects who purchased more than 1 piece of information. Part B shows the results for low-information

TABLE 10.3. *Final judgment regarding candidate positions by initial prior judgment, immediately previous judgment, and previous (third) message received from other participants, for high-information and low-information subjects.*
A. *High-information subjects who purchased more than 1 piece of information.*

	Candidate A		Candidate B	
	Coefficient	T-value	Coefficient	T-value
Prior	.19	2.85	.28	4.07
Previous judgment	.65	8.88	.60	7.27
Previous message	.12	5.32	.10	5.09
Constant	.12	1.22	.12	1.05
N=	454		454	
Subjects=	74		74	
R2=	.79		.83	
Root MSE=	.67		.62	
		parameters		
	w=.57		w=.65	
	α=.65		α=.60	
	e=.12		e=.10	

B. *Low-information subjects who purchased less than 2 pieces of information.*

	Candidate A		Candidate B	
	Coefficient	T-value	Coefficient	T-value
Prior	.02	.59	.06	4.07
Previous judgment	.67	9.01	.64	7.27
Previous message	.18	4.15	.20	5.09
Constant	.33	1.98	.41	1.66
N=	295		295	
Subjects=	59		59	
R2=	.55		.53	
Root MSE=	.99		1.07	
		Parameters		
	w=.27		w=.39	
	α=.67		α=.64	
	e=.18		e=.20	

subjects who purchased less than 2 pieces of information. In each case, the final updated judgment (J_3) is regressed on the immediately preceding updated judgment (J_2), the initial prior judgment (P_0), and the immediately preceding (third) piece of communicated information (I_3).

The estimated model parameters are consistent with the Chapter 9 results, showing that the effect of the initial (prior) judgment is dramatically dependent on the amount of information purchased by a subject – the effect of the prior persists only among those participants who invest in private information. The table also shows a substantial effect due to the immediately preceding update that is comparable among high- and low-information individuals. Finally, we see a substantial effect due to the contemporaneous message that is attenuated by the amount of private information purchased by the participant.

Returning to the modified DeGroot model in Equation 10.7, not only can we specify the rates of memory decay in the priors, but we can also take account of memory decay with respect to the social communication process that is captured in the T matrix. First, the effect of the immediately preceding judgment is α, and the effect of the incoming information is e. All the model parameters are represented in the T matrix as summing to unity across the rows. This involves adjusting the parameter magnitudes so that their effects relative to one another are maintained. Hence, at each social iteration, the normed effects for α and e are set at $\alpha/(\alpha+e)$ and $e/(\alpha+e)$.

As the model in Equation 10.9 suggests, earlier messages are subject to decay. The most recent message effect is "*e*," and earlier messages are discounted by raising α^{n-1} to successively higher powers. This occurs automatically, as the updated judgments which incorporate the new information are adjusted by α at each iteration.

The model assumes that each individual has three informants, and that each individual cycles through the informants in the order in which they were initially chosen, receiving and responding to each message in the order in which it is received. Hence, the first informant sends messages at t = 1, 4, 7, etc. The second informant sends messages at t = 2, 5, 8, etc. And the third informant sends messages at t = 3, 6, 9, etc. Correspondingly, we construct three T matrices, corresponding to the subjects' first, second, and third choices of informants.

Hence the T_1 matrix becomes:

			Informant Preference					
		1	2	3	4	5	6	7
	1	.79	.00	.21	.00	.00	.00	.00
	2	.00	.84	.00	.00	.00	.00	.16
Requestor	3	.00	.16	.84	.00	.00	.00	.00
Preference	4	.00	.00	.21	.79	.00	.00	.00
	5	.00	.00	.21	.00	.79	.00	.00
	6	.00	.21	.00	.00	.00	.79	.00
	7	.00	.00	.00	.00	.00	.16	.84

$$(10.10)$$

The T_2 matrix becomes:

		Informant Preference						
		1	2	3	4	5	6	7
	1	.79	.00	.00	.21	.00	.00	.00
	2	.00	.84	.16	.00	.00	.00	.00
Requestor Preference	3	.00	.00	.84	.00	.00	.00	.16
	4	.00	.21	.00	.79	.00	.00	.00
	5	.00	.21	.00	.00	.79	.00	.00
	6	.00	.00	.00	.00	.00	.79	.21
	7	.00	.16	.00	.00	.00	.00	.84

$$(10.11)$$

And the T_3 matrix becomes:

		Informant Preference						
		1	2	3	4	5	6	7
	1	.79	.21	.00	.00	.00	.00	.00
	2	.00	.84	.00	.00	.16	.00	.00
Requestor Preference	3	.16	.00	.84	.00	.00	.00	.00
	4	.00	.00	.00	.79	.00	.21	.00
	5	.21	.00	.00	.00	.79	.00	.00
	6	.00	.00	.21	.00	.00	.79	.00
	7	.00	.00	.00	.16	.00	.00	.84

$$(10.12)$$

where the rows and columns for well-informed subjects are shown in bold parentheses.

In a similar fashion, we can estimate the weights that subjects place on their own priors (w), and on this basis construct the D matrix in Equation 10.7. As we will see, this dramatic difference carries important consequences for the social dynamic, and it produces the following D matrix.

$$
D = \begin{matrix}
.27 & .00 & .00 & .00 & .00 & .00 & .00 \\
.00 & .57 & .00 & .00 & .00 & .00 & .00 \\
.00 & .00 & .57 & .00 & .00 & .00 & .00 \\
.00 & .00 & .00 & .27 & .00 & .00 & .00 \\
.00 & .00 & .00 & .00 & .27 & .00 & .00 \\
.00 & .00 & .00 & .00 & .00 & .27 & .00 \\
.00 & .00 & .00 & .00 & .00 & .00 & .57
\end{matrix}
\qquad (10.13)
$$

Based on these D and T matrices, as well as Equation 10.7, we can iteratively estimate convergence paths for the individual requestors. Figure 10.2a displays

(A)

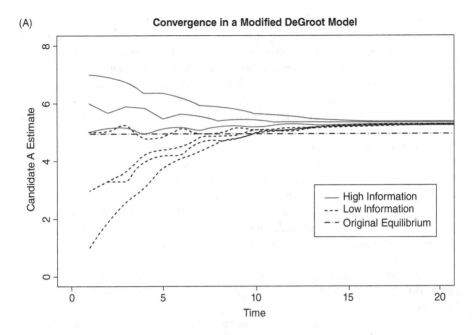

(B)

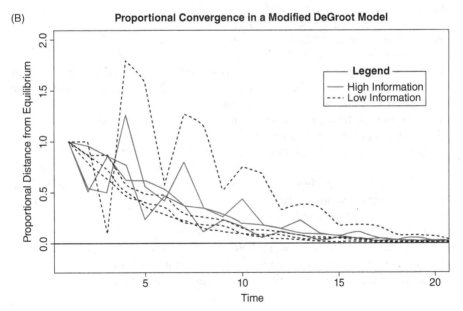

FIGURE 10.2. Convergence to equilibrium.
   A. Estimated convergence to equilibrium among subjects by expertise.
   B. Estimated proportional convergence to equilibrium among subjects by expertise.

the modified DeGroot estimates of the requestors' judgments regarding candidate positions across time. Highly informed individuals (2, 3, and 7) are shown with solid lines, whereas low-information individuals are shown with dashed lines. A few things are particularly notable about this graph. The highly informed individuals, most of whom begin estimating Candidate A's position at the high end of the scale, are more influential to the creation of the final equilibrium than low-information individuals. The three high-information subjects estimated Candidate A's position as a 6 on average, while the low-information subjects averaged a 3. However, the final equilibrium value estimated by our modified DeGroot model (5.30) is far closer to the estimates of the high-information, rather than the low-information, voters.

The influence of the experts arises as a consequence of two factors. First, high-information voters have a ***much stronger attachment to their priors*** than low-information voters. Second, high-information voters are ***asked to provide information more often*** than low-information voters, so their viewpoints are more influential throughout the network. As can be seen in Figure 10.2a, high-information voters also tend to be slower to converge to equilibrium – especially early on – as their attachment to their prior makes them much more resistant to change.

Figure 10.2b displays the convergence toward equilibrium as a proportion of the distance between the subject's initial prior judgment and the final equilibrium. By definition, every subject starts at "1," and subsequent values greater than 1 indicate that the subject has diverged (moved farther away) from the eventual equilibrium.[6] As before, solid gray lines indicate high-information individuals, whereas dashed black lines indicate low-information individuals. Equilibrium is represented by a solid horizontal line at zero. Hence, the criterion variable standardizes a subject's distance from equilibrium at any point in time relative to the initial distance from equilibrium at the beginning of the process. This serves to enhance the observed magnitude of change among those individuals who begin the process near to the ultimate equilibrium.

In this graph we see that most individuals behave roughly as expected: three low-information individuals, relatively unattached to their priors, converge to equilibrium more rapidly on average than the high-information subjects. The high-information subjects also converge to equilibrium, but the slow decay in their priors delays the convergence.

The seeming exception is the low-information individual whose behavior is characterized by a few wild swings before she or he also begins to converge. This path to equilibrium is explained by the particular patterns of interaction within the communication process – the subject requested information from particular

---

[6] In theory, values under zero indicate that the subject, after having prematurely converged rapidly upon equilibrium, has overshot and diverged away from equilibrium to the other side. However, there are no cases of this in our currently selected round.

individuals who provided initially divergent signals, pushing the subject farther away from the ultimate equilibrium. (While the swings are not as pronounced, substantial shifts can also be seen in two of the high-information subjects.) While this initial advice was eventually attenuated, the impact of that information persisted due to the subject's reliance on his or her own immediately prior judgments.

Hence, Figure 10.2 serves to illustrate the noisy nature of the communication process. While strong pressures toward equilibrium tend to filter and dampen aberrant messages, particular time paths are highly dependent on particular communication patterns and events, as well as the order in which information is received, leading to highly diverse and variable dynamics across individuals and groups.

IMPLICATIONS AND CONCLUSIONS

Several features of this chapter's argument are particularly important. Perhaps most crucially, the model supports a compelling dynamic analysis regarding the role played by opinion leaders. The role of opinion leaders – the experts in this analysis – is enhanced by two immediate factors. First, they rely more heavily on their own priors and immediately past judgments in responding to socially communicated information, and they are secondarily affected by socially communicated information.

The dynamic implications are quite important. Opinion leaders have sticky priors and past judgments – their prior beliefs persist even under the onslaught of new socially communicated information. This means that opinion leaders are much less likely to dramatically modify their own opinions due to changing opinion distributions in the aggregate. Their staying power, in turn, serves as an anchor on changes in public opinion. Rather than moving toward new opinions, they tend to pull the movement of public opinion back toward their own beliefs.

The persistence of expert priors carries several important implications. Most particularly, the role of experts does not depend on their own loquacious arguments and compelling analyses of public affairs. *Their influence is as much due to their unwillingness to move as it is their ability to encourage movement among others.*

This result helps to make sense of the otherwise puzzling cross-sectional analyses of opinion leadership. These results tend to show weak or non-existent expertise effects on the levels of persuasiveness within dyads. Thus, in Chapter 3, we addressed survey respondents who were very likely to recognize expertise among their discussion partners, but were not necessarily more responsive to the arguments of these experts in comparison to the arguments of their less expert associates. By moving to a dynamic experimental analysis, we are able to address the effect of new socially communicated information within the context of a dynamic process where the participants hold priors, based on varying levels of information and commitment, and are willing to update their opinions accordingly. Such an analysis depends on a highly dynamic treatment of opinion leadership and the influence of opinion leaders.

Finally, the DeGroot model produces a single equilibrium that serves as an attractor for all of the participants. Lacking new information from the surrounding environment, the analysis suggests that a dynamic process occurs in which consensus is reached and that opinions converge toward a particular level. This is both encouraging and discouraging. On the one hand, it conforms to what we have come to see as the news cycle, where (1) new information is communicated through print and electronic media, (2) public responses are initially at disequilibrium, (3) opinions in the population crystallize and stabilize toward a new consensus (see McPhee 1963).

At the same time, this feature of the model poses an inherent limitation – not only is a population equilibrium reached, but this equilibrium consists of a single belief. That is, the model predicts that all groups tied together by direct and indirect ties will inevitably converge toward a consensual equilibrium of shared opinions. At the same time, the empirical record demonstrates the survival of heterogeneous opinions within self-contained populations. Not only do the friends of your friends hold views with which you disagree, but you probably have at least a few friends with whom you are not in perfect harmony. In short, portraying the dynamic that yields a stable, heterogeneous equilibrium is an ongoing challenge in the study of communication networks that reveals the need for non-linear models (Huckfeldt, Johnson, and Sprague 2004) and points toward the inherent complexity of non-linear interdependence (see May's 1976 observation at the beginning of Chapter 9).

Once again, we see the role played by the division of labor in the communication of political information (Berelson et al. 1954). This chapter suggests that the influence of opinion leaders lies in their own unwillingness to change their beliefs. The experts and activists in our midst, correctly or incorrectly, carry with them the courage of their own convictions. The resulting patterns of communication sometimes produce an electorate that makes surprisingly expert choices – at least relative to the low mean levels of political awareness among individuals within the electorate (Converse 1964; Zaller 1992; Delli Carpini and Keeter 1996; Page and Shapiro 1992; Erikson, MacKuen, and Stimson 2002). Alternatively, we have no guarantees that the experts and the activists are always right. Indeed, the experts and activists reading these words would have a difficult time arriving at their own consensus!

When people share their opinions, they are not only learning from one another, but are also persuading one another. The accumulated record, based on surveys and experiments, suggests that the process tends to be driven by activists and experts. That is, the process is skewed in favor of politically engaged participants with more information – the same individuals identified by Lodge and Taber (2000) as being most opinionated and most likely to demonstrate motivated reasoning. Moreover, because the experts are often activists within their own closely held networks of communication – that is, they are not dispassionately neutral – they have the potential to mislead as well as to inform. The information they communicate is typically biased, reflecting the interests of the informant, and thus we cannot assume that all crowds are "wise" crowds (Surowiecki 2005). Even when it comes to "facts" as opposed to "interpretation," not only information diffuses through communication networks, but misinformation as well.

In short, political communication among citizens is not simply an exercise in civic enlightenment – it is instead an inherently political process that plays a central role in democratic politics. Hence, the process carries no guarantees of producing wise or enlightened outcomes. Rather, such a result depends on the continued effort and vigilance of those engaged experts and activists who value democratic outcomes.

Experts, activists, and democratic prospects

T. K. Ahn, Robert Huckfeldt, and John Barry Ryan

> There may be many group members who are not really aware of the goals of their own group. And there may be many who, even if they were aware of these goals, would not be sufficiently interested in current events to tie the two together consciously. They acquiesce to the political temper of their group under the steady personal influence of their more politically active fellow citizens.
>
> Lazarsfeld, Berelson, and Gaudet (1968: 149)

Are electorates self-educating? Does an electorate full of interdependent, interacting citizens make collective decisions and choices that are in some sense better than the decisions that would be made if they all acted individually? Are the experts and activists who act as opinion leaders responsible for the improvement? These are the fundamental questions lying behind our effort.

The most optimistic assessment regarding self-educating electorates points toward the superior civic qualities of aggregates relative to individuals. A distinguished stream of research on political knowledge and civic capacity shows that individual levels of knowledge and awareness regarding political affairs typically are disappointing (Converse 1964; Kuklinski et al. 2000; Sniderman et al. 1991). Individual responses to a wide variety of survey questions and knowledge batteries reveal a deep and troubling chasm of "don't knows," "refuse to answers," inconsistent responses, and mistaken perceptions. Just as troubling, interest and attentiveness are quite low as well, and except in the most media-saturated elections, turnout levels in American elections fall well below 50 percent.

At the same time, the electorate as a whole performs in ways that are typically predictable, explicable, and seemingly based on comprehensible responses to political circumstance (Page and Shapiro 1992; Erikson, MacKuen, and Stimson 2002). When unemployment increases, when scandals rock government, or when international crises strike, opinion polls show that citizens in the aggregate turn their attention to the problem at hand, embracing measures, candidates, and political leaders who appear to address the problem. This occurs even though the disappointing picture of individual political competence does not change, with most individuals still unable to provide cogent, meaningful responses to many of the challenges and problems that wait to be addressed by the political system.

The question thus arises, if so many individuals are so inept, how and why does democratic governance work as well as it does when viewed in terms of its aggregate performance? One explanation has been that poorly informed citizens depend on the judgment of the politically knowledgeable individuals in their midst through a process of civic engagement and discussion. Indeed, even critical assessments of citizenship capacity have recognized that a substantial proportion of the population is well-informed (Converse 1964). Hence, these knowledgeable individuals may be well-equipped to play an important role as opinion leaders who educate and inform their fellow citizens. The net result is that, through a process of civic engagement and discussion, the poorly informed act as though they are fully informed based on the expert guidance of others.

This last point, however, is where our own account pivots from such an explanation. We fully endorse the crucial roles of interdependent citizens and opinion leadership in democratic politics, and we do not dispute that the electorate is self-educating. At the same time, our own view does not overlook the intrinsically political motivation of opinion leaders; the inherently political aspects of the self-educating electorate; and a result in which the poorly informed do not necessarily act as if they were, in fact, fully informed. That is, we entertain the potential for citizens to be led astray by politically motivated opinion leaders providing guidance that does not coincide with these recipients' self-identified interests and political evaluations.

THE ROLE OF OPINION LEADERS

The most effective opinion leaders are seldom motivated by a commitment to civic education, but rather by their own political viewpoints, loyalties, and orientations. These highly motivated individuals are unlikely to be politically neutral. Moreover, they are unlikely to change their political stripes through a process of discussion and communication with other citizens (Lodge and Taber, 2013), and hence they lie at the heart of an inherently political process of communication among citizens.

Levels of citizen sophistication are typically measured in terms of an individual's ability to recall isolated political facts from long-term memory, but this may bear little relationship to citizenship capacity (Lodge, McGraw, and Stroh 1989). To the contrary, the capacity to participate effectively often depends on the development of long-term orientations, attitudes, and loyalties that allow citizens to act expertly – to make informed judgments based on their own self-identified interests and political evaluations.

Moreover, these are some of the same abilities that also give rise to opinion leadership. Those who serve as opinion leaders need not necessarily be seen as either (1) the policy wonks who devote their lives to intricate understandings of politics and policy or (2) the zealots who spend their time on organizing committees and neighborhood canvasses. Rather, they are defined by a mixture of activism and expertise that motivates them to pay attention as well as leads them to arrive at these basic subjective understandings of their own interests, beliefs, and concerns. Their levels of expertise and activism are thus defined modestly and locally, within the contours of their day-to-day interactions with others.

As we have seen, these opinion leaders do not serve as the reference librarians of democratic politics – individuals who are on call to respond to information requests based on their own politically neutral expertise. To the contrary, opinion leaders tend to be *both* experts *and* activists. They are *motivated* to become knowledgeable either because information about politics is relevant to their own interests, passions, and commitment, or because they value information as an end in itself (Fiorina 1990). In either event, opinion leaders are much more likely than the general public to possess strong, well-informed, and consistent views regarding ongoing political issues and debates. They are also the individuals who are *least* likely to be swayed by the informal discussions and debates in which they play such a central role. Indeed, the stability and durability of their political commitments are central to the influence they exercise within the political communication process, and this can be seen in both the network surveys and the experiments.

Hence, we do not view political discussion and communication among citizens as a politically neutral exercise in civic betterment. The goal of opinion leaders is *not* to make people better citizens – to make the world safe *from* democracy. Rather, the political communication process is better seen as an extension of the democratic political process – a process in which the primary actors have self-defined interests and goals they realize through their communication with others.

Such a view may seem hopelessly naïve. In a world where individual votes are pivotal with a probability that converges on zero, why should anyone bother trying to convince another individual how to vote? While a single individual can magnify their own influence on the outcome of an election by persuading other individuals how to vote (Fowler 2005), even the combined effect of the most diligent and committed opinion leaders is insufficient to explain their activity in terms of an instrumental cost-benefit analysis. Why do opinion leaders bother?

The answer is that they communicate with others for the same reason that they stay informed – because they are motivated to do so (Lodge and Taber 2013). What is the source of that motivation? They may thrive on talking (and arguing) about politics as much as they thrive on staying informed. Moreover, having already paid the costs of becoming informed, they have reduced the costs of playing an influential role in the larger democratic conversation. Alternatively, they may be emotionally invested in political outcomes, and such an emotional commitment is likely to generate a great many moth-and-flame moments – that is, the opinion leader's response to politics is likely to be preconscious (Fazio 1995; Huckfeldt et al. 1999). When politically motivated opinion leaders confront viewpoints with which they disagree, they may have a difficult time ignoring the stimulus to voice their own opinions. Hence, engagement and involvement are virtually automatic and inevitable.

THE PERCEPTION OF EXPERTISE

An encouraging empirical footprint regarding the nature of opinion leadership comes from snowball surveys of social networks – the perhaps surprising evidence that citizens generally recognize political expertise when they encounter it! That is, people make judgments regarding the expertise of their informants anchored in the actual political expertise and engagement of these individuals. Not only do they tend to judge the level of expertise among their opinion leaders quite reasonably based on actual underlying characteristics, but they also report more frequent conversations with those whom they view to be expert.

At the same time, opinion leadership is not simply a function of expertise. First, the self-reported political interest and engagement of the informant is at least as important as objectively defined knowledge in affecting the recipient's judgment regarding informant expertise. In other words, opinion leaders tend to be activists as well as experts.

In contrast to the roles in opinion leadership played by expertise and activism, shared preferences play a less pronounced role – that is, agreement is not a precondition for political communication, and its role is less consequential. When faced with a choice between expert informants with whom they disagree and less expert informants with whom they agree, both survey evidence and experimental evidence demonstrate that the potential recipients tend to communicate with the disagreeable experts – a situation in which the incentive for informants to mislead is particularly clear.

Abundant evidence supports the existence of important gender biases in opinion leadership. Even after taking account of interest and knowledge, both men and women tend to discount the expertise of women. Not only does this serve to reinforce the gender biases in the perception of political expertise, but it also points toward a larger political dialogue that is insufficiently informed by the participation of women.

Finally, it is particularly important to remember that the communication of a political message is not only a function of the potential recipient looking for an informant, but also of the motivated messenger looking for an opportunity to make an argument. Hence, in the real world, it is not enough to be an expert. The most influential opinion leaders are also highly motivated activists – so highly motivated that their automatic response to politics often involves them in communication processes that more judicious and conflict-averse citizens might avoid.

INTERDEPENDENCE AND THE MICRO–MACRO DIVIDE

Just as engagement and communication do not depend solely on the attributes of individuals, neither do they depend solely on isolated communication dyads. Individuals are located within dyads, and dyads are located within larger networks of communication and interaction. This gives rise to the socially imbedded nature of political communication and activation, as well as to complex patterns of communication and interdependence. These complexities exist in both space and time, and the dynamic sequences of communication and response play a central role in both individual and aggregate outcomes.

Just as aggregate political outcomes are contingent on the beliefs and viewpoints of individuals, the behavior of individuals is also contingent on the aggregate distributions of preferences in the surrounding social context. Indeed, both survey and experimental analyses show that individuals affect aggregates just as aggregates affect individuals. First, the supply of political informants is constrained by aggregate characteristics in a variety of ways. If expertise and preference are correlated at the individual level, it may be quite difficult for many individuals to locate expert informants who hold their own political orientations. Moreover, if left-leaning informants are more politically expert than the right-leaning informants, the political course of the aggregate is likely to take a port tack.

Similarly, the influence of individual experts is contingent on the aggregate availability of experts in local populations. As the experimental analyses show, when experts are relatively scarce, the lone expert is more likely to be central within locally defined communication networks. Moreover, and as the experimental analyses also demonstrate, the location of individuals within aggregates that vary in terms of preferences and expertise levels carries important consequences for the transmission of political bias. In short, interdependent networks of political communication create a seamless set of endogenous transitions between aggregates and individuals.

CONFLICT, CONTROVERSY, AND OPINION LEADERSHIP

Moreover, opinion leadership does not depend only on the capacity of the informant and the susceptibility of the communication recipient – it also depends on the contextual distributions of aggregate opinion. In particular, opinion leaders are most influential when aggregate opinion is most controversial. As we have seen, aggregate distributions of opinion are reflected within communication networks. Hence, issues that are controversial within the larger population are also influential within communication networks. Perhaps surprisingly, the opinions of others become most clear when issues are controversial – at the moment when the opportunity for opinion leadership is at its height.

None of this means that people enjoy political disagreement and controversy. Indeed, while aggregate levels of controversy are reflected in the level of controversy within communication networks, people are less likely to report political discussion regarding controversial subjects. How can we thus explain opinion leadership regarding controversial issues?

At the same time that political disagreement impedes discussion, political discussion enhances the likelihood of disagreement. Hence, we see a dynamic in which people who talk about politics more frequently with their associates are also more likely to experience disagreement. While this disagreement serves as negative feedback on the frequency of political discussion, it does not necessarily serve to eliminate discussion. Indeed, the motivation of opinion leaders lies at the core of their willingness to tolerate disagreement even if they do not enjoy it. In this sense it is entirely possible to think of the opinion leaders as being self-selected. Their interest and attentiveness to politics makes their involvement unavoidable, even when it simulates controversy within their own circles of associates.

As McPhee (1963) observed fifty years ago, disagreement and the experience of political diversity hold the key to the creation of public opinion. Opinion leaders play important roles in the democratic process because they introduce new information and new ideas, and this often involves encountering diverse views.

NOISE, BIAS, AND DYNAMIC INTERDEPENDENCE

The process of becoming informed generates intrinsic rewards among politically motivated individuals, and thus the acquisition of information becomes a self-reinforcing behavior. Among others, the costs of information might very well overpower any benefit an individual could realistically expect to obtain. As a consequence, when left to their own devices, some individuals become politically expert while others remain politically naïve. Complications arise because participation in the communication process is politically motivated, and thus socially communicated information typically is biased at its source, adding to the complexity of citizen decision-making. Quite apart from these partisan biases, many of the underlying issues are imbedded in uncertainty, and even fully engaged individuals with shared political orientations might arrive at divergent political judgments. Thus, individuals send and receive information that is not only noisy, but also biased.

The central role of experts is enhanced in communication processes characterized by noisy, biased information – processes in which people with variable levels of expertise and strength of preference select informants, as well as being influenced by them. The experimental evidence shows that participants in the communication process formulate judgments that decay in time, but the decay occurs more slowly among the better informed. Hence, the influence of experts is not simply due to their powers of persuasion, but, more importantly, is also due to the durability of their own privately formulated opinions. In short, it is not simply the persuasive power of expert opinion that makes it influential. Rather, influence also arises due to the stickiness of expert opinion – expert opinion that is more committed, less malleable, and thus tends to survive and dominate the democratic conversation.

The role of expertise in the communication process is further heightened by two additional factors. First, as both survey and experimental analyses show, potential message recipients often are exposed to a heterogeneous and hence potentially influential stream of information *because* recipients place a higher value on expert opinion. In a perfect world, everyone would seek out expert informants with compatible preferences (Downs 1957), but the constraints of supply within the locally defined contexts often mean that agreeable experts may not be locally available.

Second, not only do individuals frequently gravitate toward informants who are expert, but many informants do not wait to be asked for their opinions and viewpoints. Their higher levels of motivation mean that they are likely to engage in political communication quite spontaneously, regardless of the level of agreement within a dyad.

BIASED MESSENGERS AND CORRECT VOTES

Our experiments specify a tradeoff between expertise and shared preferences in the selection of political discussion partners. This is a useful abstraction, as most reasonable people choose their associates because they enjoy their company, or because they have no choice, and not due to a strategic calculation regarding expected political benefits! At the same time, individuals can differentially attend to messages communicated through social exchange based on the political engagement, expertise, and shared interests of the messenger, and they can avoid political conversations with purveyors of particularly objectionable political views.

Indeed, our experimental subjects control the flow of information, not only through their choice of discussion partners, but also by accepting and rejecting the messages those discussion partners send. The experimental participants place a premium on expertise in the choice of advisor, and they are even willing to pay a cost to seek advice from experts. At the same time, experts with divergent preferences fail to persuade when their messages differ wildly from the recipient's own judgment. Participants rightly view these messages as attempts to promote the messenger's favored candidate rather than as sincere efforts to provide candid information.

While experimental participants reject messages that are wildly biased, they are more vulnerable to more modestly biased messages. These more slightly biased messages are more likely to matter when (1) the recipients are uncertain or (2) when they receive multiple biased messages. Thus, some uninformed individuals learn which candidate they should support based on the objective criterion of a higher payoff, while others are persuaded to vote for a candidate offering them a lesser payoff, and the two cancel each other out. Partially as a consequence, the experiments fail to show an increase in the aggregate level of "correct" voting as a consequence of social communication.

At the same time, it would be a mistake to conclude that discussion in the real world necessarily leads to worse decisions, just as it would be wrong to conclude that socially interdependent voters are necessarily more likely to reach enlightened decisions. The communication process is inherently political and often defies objectively based judgments regarding "correctness." Indeed, the correctness of ultimate decisions is dependent not only on the distribution of expertise and bias of the individuals within a network, but also on the perspectives of both participants and observers.

ACTIVISM AND EXPERTISE IN A POLITICAL PROCESS

Communication among citizens is an integral part of the larger process of democratic politics, and hence we cannot expect opinion leaders to provide information that is balanced, objective, and value free. Indeed, socially communicated information is likely to include high levels of both noise and bias. In this context, can we still say that electorates are self-educating?

The answer to this question depends on whether we view political communication among citizens as a civic exercise or as a political process. Students of citizens and politics often act as though persuasion and politics end at the citizenship shoreline – that is, the professional politicians do the politics, and amateur citizens attempt to be the arbiters who figure it all out. Our own view is that this can be a misleading vantage point from which to assess politics and representation. To the contrary, we see political communication among citizens as an *extension* of the political process.

Indeed, the role of opinion leaders is central to the self-educating capacity of electorates. Within this process, however, education is not simply fact checking. In the words of Tocqueville (2000), a healthy democracy depends on the ability of individuals to act on the basis of their own self-interest, "rightly understood." Oftentimes this depends on the development of educated preferences – a crucial element of the social communication process.

At some point in time, the billionaire capitalist Warren Buffet developed a preference for the Democratic party and Democratic policy proposals. In some ways this may seem quite remarkable, but he is certainly not the first or the only person of great wealth to take public positions in support of liberal-leaning candidates and causes. In a similar yet converse way, working-class Tories have been a persistent phenomenon in British politics at least since Disraeli, and heterogeneous political preferences among the American working class have been a historically well documented phenomenon as well (Sombart 1976). Some might argue that these individuals are politically misguided, but we demur on this point. Who are we to argue that wealthy Democratic liberals or working-class Tories or Reagan Democrats are *necessarily* misguided?

Different people see the world differently, and self-defined interest is not necessarily a mechanical translation of objective circumstance into political preference. It is instead a subjective judgment that is idiosyncratic to individuals and the information and experience to which they are exposed. In this way, the process of political communication has more to do with the education of preferences than with the transmission of facts. All of this occurs in the context of noise and bias that are an inherent element in a complex process. While the process may appear hopelessly messy and radically decentralized, it is worth remembering that those who play central roles in the process tend to be those who spend the greatest amount of time and energy thinking and talking about politics.

Unlike the participants in our experiments, the preferences of citizens in the real world are *not* fixed. Indeed, much of the action in political communication relates to the negotiation of preferences, and these preferences are in play as an important target of persuasion. Hence, the goals and self-defined interests of citizens are best seen in this context. None of this discussion negates the very real potential for problems related to insufficient information and misinformation to arise, but it does call into question the explanations that point too quickly toward the failure of citizens to act on the basis of their own self-interests.

THE PROBLEM OF WRONG-HEADED EXPERTS

None of this suggests that experts are wise, insightful, or far-sighted. An example might clarify the issue. As this is being written, the Tea Party Movement occupies center stage in American politics. In many areas of the country, victory in a Republican Party primary is a virtual guarantee of a seat in the U.S. Congress. In many of these areas, Tea Party supporters occupy a position of great influence within the party. Tea Party support is crucial to victory in the Republican primary and hence to winning the congressional seat, and Tea Party opinion leaders play an important role in the process.

Indeed, Tea Party activists qualify as expert opinion leaders – both with respect to those who rise to elite status within the movement, as well as those who more modestly populate the corridors of everyday life. No one can deny that these grass-roots activists have been exceptionally successful, recruiting their friends and neighbors as new members within the movement. Our point is not that the Tea Party opinion leaders are necessarily wise or correct or far-sighted. Our only argument is that they have joined the ranks of the experts and activists who play a central role in democratic politics. These grass-roots participants are activists because they care about the outcome, are engaged by the process, and hence occupy positions of influence within countless processes of communication and influence. They are experts because they are able to articulate their own political positions in ways that are meaningful and persuasive to others.

Some readers might cringe either at the positions they take, or at an analysis that classifies them "expert." Our response is two-fold. First, even among the most elite and knowledgeable, experts make more than their fair share of judgmental errors (Tetlock 2005), and hence we are not arguing that experts necessarily get it right! Second, for students and supporters of democratic politics, the wrong-headed opinion leader comes with the terrain, both as a crucial actor within the political process and as an opinion leader who contributes to the shape and form of public opinion.

Sprague's (1980) insight is particularly important – democratic politics is best seen as a process that is perpetually at disequilibrium. Within this process, those in the corridors of power exercise and refine the fine arts of political manipulation (Riker 1986). And citizens, both individually and collectively, do their best to sort it out.

In short, the electorate *is* self-educating, but the education being provided is not aimed primarily at increasing comprehensive knowledge regarding policy problems or enhancing the civic quality of citizenship. To the contrary, opinion leadership is typically aimed at converting individuals to an opinion, movement, or cause. Hence, it looks much more like a political process and much less like a civic exercise.

None of this means that democratic politics is incapable of producing civic enlightenment, even though the process often appears dysfunctional and frequently misfires. In a democratic society, enlightenment is always a work in progress, with intermediate outcomes that are always less than perfect. Just as important, democratic politics tends to look particularly bad when it is compared to its utopian alternatives – alternatives that may be interesting to consider, but have thus far proven to be either impossible to realize or dangerous to embrace.

References

Abelson, Robert P. 1964. "Mathematical Models of the Distribution of Attributes Under Controversy." In Norman Fredriksen and Harold Gulliksen, eds. *Contributions to Mathematical Psychology*. New York: Holt, Rinehart, and Winston, 142–160.

1979. "Social Clusters and Opinion Clusters." In Paul W. Holland and Samuel Leinhardt, eds. *Perspectives on Social Network Research*. New York: Academic Press, 239–256

Achen, Christopher H. 1986. *The Statistical Analysis of Quasi-Experiments*. Berkeley: The University of California Press.

Achen, Christopher H. and W. Phillips Shively. 1995. *Cross Level Inference*. Chicago: University of Chicago Press.

Ahn, T. K., Robert Huckfeldt, and John B. Ryan. 2010. "Communication, Influence, and Informational Asymmetries among Voters." *Political Psychology* 31: 763–787.

Ahn, T. K., R. Huckfeldt, A. K. Mayer, and J. B. Ryan. 2010. "Politics, Expertise, and Interdependence within Electorates." In Jan E. Leighley, ed. *Oxford Handbook of American Elections and Political Behavior*. New York: Oxford University Press.

Ahn, T. K., R. Mark Isaac, and Timothy C. Salmon. 2009. "Coming and Going: Experiments on Endogenous Group Sizes for Excludable Public Goods." *Journal of Public Economics* 93: 336–351.

2011. "Rent-Seeking in Groups." *International Journal of Industrial Organization* 29(1): 116–125.

Ahn, T. K., R. Huckfeldt, A. K. Mayer, and J. B. Ryan. 2013. "Expertise and Bias in Political Communication Networks." *American Journal of Political Science* 57: 357–373.

Alford, John R., Carolyn L. Funk, and John R. Hibbing. 2005. "Are Political Orientations Genetically Transmitted?" *American Political Science Review* 99(2): 153–167.

Althaus, Scott L. 1998. "Information Effects in Collective Preferences." *American Political Science Review* 92: 545–558.

2004. *Collective Preferences in Democratic Politics: Opinion Surveys and the Will of the People*. New York: Cambridge University Press.

Alvarez, R. Michael and Garrett Glasgow. 2000. "Two-Stage Estimation of Non-Recursive Choice Models." *Political Analysis* 8: 147–165.

Amemiya, T. 1978. "The Estimation of a Simultaneous Equation Generalized Probit Model." *Econometrica* 46: 1193–1205.

Anderson, Christopher J. and Aida Paskeviciute. 2005. "Macro-Politics and Micro-Behavior: Mainstream Politics and the Frequency of Political Discussion in Contemporary Democracies." In Alan Zuckerman, ed. *The Social Logic of Politics*. Philadelphia: Temple University Press, 228–248.

2006. "How Linguistic and Ethnic Heterogeneity Influences the Prospects for Civil Society." *Journal of Politics* 68: 783–802.

Asch, Solomon E. 1955. "Opinions and Social Pressure." *Scientific American* 193: 31–35.

1963. "Effects of Group Pressure Upon the Modification and Distortion of Judgments." In Harold Guetzkow, ed. *Groups, Leadership and Men: Research in Human Relations*. New York: Russell and Russell, 177–190. Originally published by Carnegie Press, 1951.

Austen-Smith, David. 1990. "Information Transmission in Debate." *American Journal of Political Science* 34: 124–152.

Austen-Smith, David and Jeffrey Banks. 1996. "Information Aggregation, Rationality, and the Condorcet Jury Theorem." *American Political Science Review* 90(1): 34–45.

Austen-Smith, David and Timothy J Feddersen. 2009. "Information aggregation and communication in committees." Philosophical Transactions of the Royal Society of London – Series B: Biological Sciences 364 (1518): 763–769.

Axelrod, Robert. 1997a. "The Dissemination of Culture: A Model with Local Convergence and Global Polarization." *Journal of Conflict Resolution* 41: 203–26.

1997b. *The Complexity of Cooperation: Agent-Based Models of Competition and Collaboration*. Princeton, NJ: Princeton University Press.

Baker, Andy, Barry Ames, and Lucio Renno. 2006. "Social Context and Voter Volatility in New Democracies: Networks and Neighborhoods in Brazil's 2002 Elections." *American Journal of Political Science* 50: 382–399.

Baldassarri, Delia and Peter Bearman. 2007. "Dynamics of Political Polarization." *American Sociological Review* 72(5): 784–811.

Barabas, Jason. 2004. "How Deliberation Affects Policy Opinions." *American Political Science Review* 98(4): 687–701.

Barabasi, Albert-Laszlo. 2002. *Linked: The New Science of Networks*. Cambridge, MA: Perseus.

Barber, Benjamin. 1984. *Strong Democracy: Participatory Politics for a New Age*. Berkeley, CA: University of California Press.

Baron, David P. 1994. "Electoral Competition with Informed and Uninformed Voters." *American Political Science Review* 88(1): 33–47.

Bartels, Larry M. 1996. "Uninformed Votes: Information Effects in Presidential Elections." *American Journal of Political Science* 40: 194–230.

2002. "Beyond the Running Tally: Partisan Bias in Political Perceptions." *Political Behavior* 24: 117–150.

Bassili, John N. 1993. "Response Latency versus Certainty as Indices of the Strength of Voting Intentions in a CATI Survey." *Public Opinion Quarterly* 57: 54–61.

1996. "Meta-Judgmental versus Operative Indices of Psychological Properties: The Case of Measures of Attitude Strength." *Journal of Personality and Social Psychology* 71(4): 637–653.

Baybeck, Brady and Robert Huckfeldt. 2002. "Urban Contexts, Spatially Dispersed Networks, and the Diffusion of Political Information." *Political Geography* 21: 195–220.

Beck, Nathaniel and Jonathan N. Katz. 2001. "Throwing Out the Baby with the Bath Water: A Comment on Green, Kim, and Yoon." *International Organization* 55: 487–495.

Berelson, Bernard R., Paul F. Lazarsfeld, and William N. McPhee. 1954. *Voting: A Study of Opinion Formation in a Presidential Election*. Chicago: University of Chicago Press.

Berent, Matthew K. and Jon A. Krosnick. 1995. "The Relation between Political Attitude Importance and Knowledge Structure." In Milton Lodge and Kathleen M. McGraw, eds. *Political Judgment: Structure and Process*. Ann Arbor: University of Michigan Press, 91–110.

Bikhchandani, Sushil, David Hirshleifer, and Ivo Welch. 1992. "A Theory of Fads, Fashion, Custom, and Cultural Change as Informational Cascades." *Journal of Political Economy* 100(5): 992–1026.

Boudon, Raymond. 1986. *Social Theory and Social Change*. Berkeley: University of California Press.

Boudreau, Cheryl. 2009. "Closing the Gap: When Do Cues Eliminate Differences Between Sophisticated and Unsophisticated Citizens?" *Journal of Politics* 71(3): 1–13.

Boudreau, Cheryl, Seana Coulson, and Mathew McCubbins. 2008. "The Effect of Institutions on Behavior and Brain Activity: Insights from EEG and Timed-Response Experiments." Paper presented at the annual meeting of the Midwest Political Science Association, Chicago.

Boyd, Robert and Peter J. Richerson. 1985. *Culture and the Evolutionary Process*. Chicago: The University of Chicago Press.

Brady, Henry E. and Paul M. Sniderman. 1985. "Attitude Attribution: A Group Basis for Political Reasoning." *American Political Science Review* 79: 1061–1078.

Brown, Thad A. 1981. "On Contextual Change and Partisan Attributes." *British Journal of Political Science* 11: 427–447.

Budge, Ian. 1994. "A New Spatial Theory of Party Competition: Uncertainty, Ideology and Policy Equilibria Viewed Comparatively and Temporally." *British Journal of Political Science* 24(4): 443–467.

Bullock, John G. 2009. "Partisan Bias and the Bayesian Ideal in the Study of Public Opinion." *Journal of Politics* 71: 1109–1124

Burt, Ronald S. 1986. "A Note on Sociometric Order in the General Social Survey Network Data." *Social Networks* 8: 149–174.

    1992. *Structural Holes*. Cambridge, MA: Harvard Univ. Press.

Butler, David and Donald E. Stokes. 1969. *Political Change in Britain: Forces Shaping Electoral Choice*. London: Macmillan.

Buttice, Matthew, Robert Huckfeldt, and John Barry Ryan. 2008. "Political Polarization and Communication Networks in the 2006 Congressional Elections." In Jeffery J. Mondak and Donna-Gene Mitchell, eds. *Fault Lines: Why the Republicans Lost Congress*. New York: Routledge, 42–60.

Cai, Hongbin and Joseph Tao-Yi Wang. 2006. "Overcommunication in Strategic Information Transmission Games." *Games and Economic Behavior* 56(1): 7–36.

Calvert, Randall L. 1985a. "The Value of Biased Information: A Rational Choice Model of Political Advice." *Journal of Politics* 47: 530–555.

1985b. "Robustness of the Multidimensional Voting Model: Candidate Motivations, Uncertainty, and Convergence." *American Journal of Political Science* 29: 69–95.

Cameron, A. Colin and Pravin K. Trivedi. 2005. *Microeconometrics: Methods and Applications*. New York: Cambridge University Press.

Campbell, Angus, Philip E. Converse, Warren E. Miller, and Donald E. Stokes. 1960. *The American Voter*. Chicago: University of Chicago Press.

Carmines, Edward G. and James A. Stimson. (1989). *Issue Evolution: Race and the Transformation of American Politics*. Princeton, NJ: Princeton University Press.

Chaiken, Shelly and Yaacov Trope, eds. 1999. *Dual Process Theories in Social Psychology*. New York: Guilford Press.

Chambers, Simone. 2003. "Deliberative Democratic Theory." *Annual Review of Political Science* 6: 307–326.

Christakis, Nicholas A. and James H. Fowler. 2009. *Connected*. New York: Little, Brown and Company.

Coleman, James S. 1964. *An Introduction to Mathematical Sociology*. New York: Free Press

1988. "Social Capital in the Creation of Human Capital." *American Journal of Sociology* 94: S95–S120.

Condorcet, Marquis de. 1976. *Condorcet: Selected Writings*. Edited, translated and with an introduction by Keith Michael Baker. Indianapolis: Bobbs-Merrill.

Converse, Philip E. 1964. "The Nature of Belief Systems in Mass Publics." In D. E. Apter, ed. *Ideology and Discontent*. New York: Free Press, 206–261.

1969. "Of Time and Partisan Stability." *Comparative Political Studies* 2: 139–171.

Coughlan, Peter J. 2000. "In Defense of Unanimous Jury Verdicts: Mistrials, Communication and Strategic Voting." *American Political Science Review* 94(June): 375–393.

Crawford, Vincent P. 2003. "Lying for Strategic Advantage: Rational and Boundedly Rational Misrepresentation of Intentions." *American Economic Review* 93(1): 133–149.

1998. "A Survey of Experiments on Communication via Cheap Talk." *Journal of Economic Theory* 78: 286–298.

Crawford, Vincent and John Sobel. 1982. "Strategic Information Transmission." *Econometrica* 50(6): 1431–1451.

DeGroot, M. H. 1974. "Reaching a Consensus." *Journal of the American Statistical Association* 69: 118–121.

Delli Carpini, Michael X. and Scott Keeter. 1993. "Measuring Political Knowledge: Putting First Things First." *American Journal of Political Science* 37: 1179–1206.

1996. *What Americans Know about Politics and Why It Matters*. New Haven, Connecticut: Yale University Press.

Dogan, Mattei and Stein Rokkan, eds. 1974. *Social Ecology*. Cambridge, MA: M.I.T.

Downs, Anthony. 1957. *An Economic Theory of Democracy*. New York: Harper and Row.

Druckman, James N. and Kjersten R. Nelson. 2003. "Framing and Deliberation: How Citizens' Conversations Limit Elite Influence." *American Journal of Political Science* 47: 728–744.

Durkheim, Émile. 1984. On the Division of Labor in Society. Translated by W. D. Halls. New York: Free Press. Doctoral thesis, 1893.

1951. *Suicide*. Translated by John A. Spaulding and George Simpson. London: Routledge. Originally published 1897.

Erbring, Lutz, Goldenberg, Edie N., and Miller, Arthur H. 1980. "Front-page news and real-world cues: A New Look at Agenda-Setting by the Media." *American Journal of Political Science* 24(1), 16–49.

Erbring, Lutz and Alice A. Young. 1979. "Individuals and Social Structure: Contextual Effects as Endogenous Feedback." *Sociological Methods and Research* 7: 396–430.

Erikson, Robert S., Michael B. MacKuen, and James A. Stimson. 2002. *The Macro Polity.* New York: Cambridge University Press.

Estlund, David M. 1994. "Opinion Leaders, Independence, and Condoret's Jury Theorem." *Theory and Decision* 36: 131–162.

Eulau, Heinz. 1963. *The Behavioral Persuasion in Politics.* New York: Random House.

1986. *Politics, Self, and Society: A Theme and Variations.* Cambridge, MA: Harvard University Press.

1998. *Micro-Macro Dilemmas in Political Science.* Norman: University of Oklahoma Press.

Farrell, Joseph and Matthew Rabin. 1996. "Cheap Talk." *Journal of Economic Perspectives* 10: 103–118.

Fazio, Russell H. 1990. "A Practical Guide to the Use of Response Latency in Social Psychological Research." In Clyde Hendrick and Margaret S. Clark, eds. *Research Methods in Personality and Social Psychology.* Newbury Park, CA: Sage, 74–97.

1995. "Attitudes as object-evaluation associations: Determinants, consequences, and correlates of attitude accessibility." In R. E. Petty and J. A. Krosnick, eds. *Attitude Strength: Antecedents and Consequences.* Hillsdale, NJ: Erlbaum, 247–282.

Feddersen, Timothy and Wolfgang Pesendorfer. 1998. "Convicting the Innocent: The Inferiority of Unanimous Jury Verdicts under Strategic Voting." *American Political Science Review* 92(1): 23–35.

Fehr, Ernst and Simon Gächter. 2002. "Altruistic Punishment in Humans." *Nature* 415: 137–140.

Fehr, Ernst and Klaus M. Schmidt. 1999. "A Theory of Fairness, Competition, and Cooperation." *Quarterly Journal of Economics* 114(3): 817–868.

Festinger, Leon. 1957. *A Theory of Cognitive Dissonance.* Palo Alto, CA: Stanford University Press.

Finifter, Ada. 1974. "The Friendship Group as a Protective Environment for Political Deviants." *American Political Science Review* 68: 607–625.

Fiorina, Morris P. 1990. "Information and Rationality in Elections." In John A. Ferejohn and James H. Kuklinski, eds. *Information and Democratic Processes.* Urbana: University of Illinois Press, 329–342.

Fischbacher, Urs. (2007). "Z-Tree: Zurich Toolbox for Ready-made Economic Experiments." *Experimental Economics* 10: 171–178.

Fishkin, James S. 1991. *Democracy and Deliberation: New Directions for Democratic Reform.* New Haven: Yale University Press.

Fowler, James H. 2005. "Turnout in a Small World." In Alan Zuckerman, ed. *Social Logic of Politics.* New York: Temple University Press.

Fowler, James H. and Oleg Smirnov. 2005. "Dynamic Parties and Social Turnout: An Agent Based Model." *American Journal of Sociology* 110: 10710–1094.

Fowler, James H., Laura A. Baker, and Christopher T. Dawes. 2008. "Genetic Variation in Political Participation." *American Political Science Review* 102(2): 233–248.

Freeman, Linton C. 1979. "Centrality in Social Networks: Conceptual Clarification," *Social Networks* 1: 215–239.

Friedkin, N. E. and E. C. Johnsen. 1990. Social Influence and Opinions. *Journal of Mathematical Sociology* 15: 193–205.

Gamm, Gerald. 1999. *Urban Exodus: Why the Jews Left Boston and the Catholics Stayed.* Cambridge, MA: Harvard University Press.

Gerardi, Deeno and Leeat Yariv. 2008. "Information Acquisition in Committees." *Games and Economic Behavior* 62(2): 436–459.

Gerber, Alan and Donald Green. 1999. "Misperceptions About Perceptual Bias." *Annual Review of Political Science* 2: 189–210.

Gerling, Kerstin, Hans Peter Grüner, Alexandra Kiel, and Elisabeth Schulte. 2005. "Information acquisition and decision making in committees: A survey." *European Journal of Political Economy* 21(3): 563–597.

Gershkov, Alex and Balázs Szentes. 2009. "Optimal Voting Schemes with Costly Information Acquisition." *Journal of Economic Theory* 144(1): 36–68.

Gibson, James L. 1992. "The Political Consequences of Intolerance: Cultural Conformity and Political Freedom." *American Political Science Review* 86: 338–356.

2001. "Social Networks, Civil Society and the Prospects for Consolidating Russia's Democratic Transition." *American Journal of Political Science* 45: 51–69.

Gilens, Martin. 2001. "Political Ignorance and Collective Policy Preferences." *American Political Science Review* 95: 379–396.

Gimpel, James G., J. Celeste Lay, and Jason E. Schuknecht. 2003. Cultivating Democracy. Washington: Brookings Institution Press.

Gneezy, Uri. 2005. "Deception: The Role of Consequences." *American Economic Review* 95(1): 384–394.

Goodman, Leo. 1953. "Ecological Regressions and the Behavior of Individuals." *American Sociological Review* 18: 663–666.

1959. "Some Alternatives to Ecological Correlation." *American Journal of Sociology* 64: 610–624.

Granovetter, Mark. 1973. "The Strength of Weak Ties." *American Journal of Sociology*, 78: 1360–1380.

1978. "Threshold models of collective behavior." *American Journal of Sociology* 83(6): 1420–1443.

1985. "Economic Action and Social Structure: The Problem of Embeddedness." *American Journal of Sociology* 91(3): 481–510.

Green, Donald P. Soo Yeon Kim, and David H. Yoon. 2001. "Dirty Pool." *International Organization* 55 (Spring): 441–468.

Green, Donald, Bradley Palmquist and Eric Schickler. 2002. *Partisan Hearts and Minds: Political Parties and the Social Identities of Voters.* New Haven: Yale University Press.

Greer, Scott. 1961. "Catholic Voters and the Democratic Party." *The Public Opinion Quarterly* 25: 611–625.

Hafer, Catherine and Dimitri Landa. 2007. "Deliberation as Self-Discovery and Institutions for Political Speech." *Journal of Theoretical Politics* 19(3): 329–360.

Hauser, Robert M. 1974. "Contextual Analysis Revisited." *Sociological Methods and Research* 2: 365–375.

Heller, Joseph. 1961. *Catch-22.* New York: Simon and Schuster.

Huckfeldt, Robert. 1983a. "The Social Contexts of Political Change: Durability, Volatility, and Social Influence." *American Political Science Review* 77: 929–944.

1983b. "Social Contexts, Social Networks, and Urban Neighborhoods: Environmental Constraints on Friendship Choice." *The American Journal of Sociology,* 89: 651–669.

1990. "Structure, Indeterminacy, and Chaos: A Case for Sociological Law." *Journal of Theoretical Politics* 2: 413–433.

2001. "The Social Communication of Political Expertise." *American Journal of Political Science* 45: 425–438.

2007a. "Information, Persuasion, and Political Communication Networks." In Russell J. Dalton and Hans Dieter. Klingemann, eds. *Oxford Handbook of Political Behavior*. New York: Oxford University Press, 100–122.

2007b. "Unanimity, Discord, and the Communication of Public Opinion." *American Journal of Political Science* 51: 978–995.

2009a. "Citizenship in Democratic Politics: Density Dependence and the Micro-Macro Divide," in Mark Lichbach and Alan Zuckerman, eds. *Comparative Politics: Rationality, Culture, and Structure*. 2nd edition. New York: Cambridge University Press, 291–313.

2009b. "Interdependence, Density Dependence, and Networks in Politics," *American Politics Research* 37: 921–950.

(forthcoming). "Taking Interdependence Seriously: Platforms for Understanding Political Communication," in Kate Kenski and Kathleen Hall Jamieson, eds. *Oxford Handbook of Political Communication*. New York: Oxford University Press, PAGES.

Huckfeldt, Robert, Paul A. Beck, Russell J. Dalton, and Jeffrey Levine. 1995. "Political Environments, Cohesive Social Groups, and the Communication of Public Opinion." *American Journal of Political Science* 39: 1025–1054.

Huckfeldt, Robert, Paul A. Beck, Russell J. Dalton, Jeffrey Levine, and William Morgan. 1998. "Ambiguity, Distorted Messages, and Nested Environmental Effects on Political Communication." *Journal of Politics* 60: 996–1030.

Huckfeldt, Robert, Ken'ichi Ikeda, and Franz Urban Pappi. 2005. "Patterns of Disagreement in Democratic Politics: Comparing Germany, Japan, and the United States." *American Journal of Political Science* 49: 497–514.

Huckfeldt, Robert, Paul E. Johnson, and John Sprague. 2005. "Individuals, Dyads and Networks: Autoregressive Patterns of Political Influence." In Alan S. Zuckerman, ed. *The Social Logic of Politics: Personal Networks as Contexts for Political Behavior*. Philadelphia: Temple University Press, 21–48.

Huckfeldt, Robert, Paul E. Johnson, and John Sprague. 2004. *Political Disagreement: The Survival of Diverse Opinions within Communication Networks*. New York: Cambridge University Press.

Huckfeldt, Robert and Carol W. Kohfeld. 1989. *Race and the Decline of Class in American Politics*. Urbana: University of Illinois Press.

Huckfeldt, Robert, Carol W. Kohfeld, and Thomas W. Likens. 1982. *Dynamic Modeling*. Beverly Hills: Sage.

Huckfeldt, Robert, Jeffrey Levine, William Morgan, and John Sprague 1998. "Election Campaigns, Social Communication, and the Accessibility of Discussant Preference." *Political Behavior* 20: 263–294.

Huckfeldt, Robert, Jeffrey Levine, William Morgan, and John Sprague. 1999. "Accessibility and the Political Utility of Partisan and Ideological Orientations." *American Journal of Political Science* 43: 888–911.

Huckfeldt, Robert and Jeanette Morehouse Mendez. 2008. "Moths, Flames, and Political Engagement: Managing Disagreement within Communication Networks." *Journal of Politics* 70: 83–96.

Huckfeldt, Robert, Jeanette Mendez, and Tracy Osborn. 2004. "Disagreement, Ambivalence and Engagement: The Political Consequences of Heterogeneous Networks." *Political Psychology* 26: 65–96.

Huckfeldt, Robert, Matthew T. Pietryka, and Jack Reilly. 2014. "Noise, Bias, and Expertise in Political Communication Networks." *Social Networks* 36: 110–121.

Huckfeldt, Robert and John Sprague. 1987. "Networks in Context: The Social Flow of Political Information." *American Political Science Review* 81(4): 1197–1216.

1988. "Choice, Social Structure, and Political Information: The Informational Coercion of Minorities." *American Journal of Political Science* 32(2): 467–482

1993. "Citizens, Contexts, and Politics." In A. W. Finifter, ed. *Political Science: The State of the Discipline II.* Washington, D.C.: American Political Science Association, 281–303.

1995. *Citizens, Politics, and Social Communication: Information and Influence in an Election Campaign.* New York: Cambridge University Press.

Huckfeldt, Robert, John Sprague, and J. Levine. 2000. "The Dynamics of Collective Deliberation in the 1996 Election: Campaign Effects on Accessibility, Certainty, and Accuracy." *American Political Science Review* 94: 641–651.

Ikeda, Ken'ichi and Sean E. Richey. 2005. "Japanese Network Capital: The Impact of Social Networks on Japanese Political Participation." *Political Behavior* 27(3): 239–260.

Iyengar, Shanto. 1990. "Shortcuts to Political Knowledge: The Role of Selective Attention and Accessibility." In John A. Ferejohn and James H. Kuklinski, eds. *Information and Democratic Processes.* Urbana, IL: University of Illinois Press, 160–185.

Jackman, Simon and Paul M. Sniderman, (2006). "The Limits of Deliberative Discussion: A Model of Everyday Political Arguments." *The Journal of Politics* 68: 272–283.

Jackson, Matthew O. 2008. *Social and Economic Networks.* Princeton, NJ: Princeton University Press.

Jennings, M. Kent and Richard G. Niemi. 1974. *The Political Character of Adolescence.* Princeton, NJ: Princeton University Press.

Johnson, James. 1993. "Is Talk Really Cheap? Prompting Conversation Between Critical Theory and Rational Choice." *American Political Science Review* 87: 74–86.

Johnson, Paul E. (1996). "Unraveling in a Variety of Institutional Settings." *Journal of Theoretical Politics* 8: 299–331

Johnson, Paul and Robert Huckfeldt. 2005. "Agent-Based Explanations for the Survival of Disagreement in Social Networks." In Alan S. Zuckerman, ed. *The Social Logic of Politics: Personal Networks as Contexts for Political Behavior.* Philadelphia: Temple University Press, 251–268.

Kahneman, Daniel and Amos Tversky. 1973. "On the Psychology of Prediction." *Psychological Review* 80: 237–251.

Katz, Elihu. 1957. "The Two Step Flow of Communication: An Up-to-Date Report on an Hypothesis." *Public Opinion Quarterly* 21: 67–81.

Katz, Elihu and Paul F. Lazarsfeld. 1955. *Personal Influence: The Part Played by People in the Flow of Mass Communications.* New York: Free Press.

Kearns, Michael, Stephen Judd, Jinsong Tan, and Jennifer Wortman. 2009. "Behavioral Experiments on Biased Voting in Networks." *Proceedings of the National Academies of Sciences* 106: 1347–1352.

Kemeny, John G. and J. Laurie Snell. 1960. *Finite Markov Chains.* Princeton, NJ: Van Nostrand.

Kenny, Christopher. 1998. "The Behavioral Consequences of Political Discussion: Another Look at Discussant Effects on Vote Choice." *The Journal of Politics* 60(1): 231–244.

Kerr, Norbert L. and Cynthia M. Kaufman-Gilliland. 1994. "Communication, Commitment, and Cooperation in Social Dilemmas." *Journal of Personality and Social Psychology* 66: 513–529.

Key, V. O., Jr. 1949. *Southern Politics in State and Nation*. New York: Vintage Books. 1966. *The Responsible Electorate*. Cambridge, MA: Harvard University Press.

King, Gary. 2001. "Proper Nouns and Methodological Propriety: Pooling Dyads in International Relations Data." *International Organization* 55 (Spring): 497–507.

Klapper, Joseph T. 1960. *The Effects of Mass Communication*. New York: Free Press.

Klofstad, Casey A., Scott McClurg, and Meredith Rolfe. 2009. "Measurement of Political Discussion Networks: A Comparison of Two 'Name Generator' Procedures." *Public Opinion Quarterly* 73: 462–483.

Kotler-Berkowitz, Laurence. 2005. "Friends and Politics: Linking Diverse Friendship Networks to Political Participation." In Alan S. Zuckerman, ed. *The Social Logic of Politics*. Philadelphia: Temple University Press. 152–170

Krosnick, Jon A. and Petty, Richard E. (1995). "Attitude Strength: An Overview." In Richard E. Petty and John A. Krosnick, eds. *Attitude Strength: Antecedents and Consequences*. Hillsdale, NJ: Erlbaum, 1–24.

Kuklinski, James H. and Paul J. Quirk, "Reconsidering the Rational Public: Cognition, Heuristics, and Mass Opinion." In Arthur Lupia, Mathew McCubbins, and Samuel Popkin, eds. *Elements of Reason* (Cambridge University Press, 2000), 153–182.

Kuklinski, James H., Paul J. Quirk, Jennifer Jerit, David Schwieder, and Robert F. Rich. 2000. "Misinformation and the Currency of Democratic Citizenship." *The Journal of Politics* 62 (3): 790–816.

Kunda, Ziva 1990. "The Case for Motivated Reasoning." *Psychological Bulletin* 108(3): 480–498.
1999. *Social Cognition: Making Sense of People*. Cambridge, MA: MIT Press.

Lake, Ronald la Due and Robert Huckfeldt. 1998. "Social Capital Social Networks, and Political Participation." *Political Psychology* 19: 567–584.

Landa, Dimitri and Adam Meirowitz. 2009. "Game Theory, Information, and Deliberative Democracy." *American Journal of Political Science* 53(2): 427–444.

Langton, Kenneth P. and Ronald Rapoport. 1975. "Social Structure, Social Context, and Partisan Mobilization: Urban Workers in Chile." *Comparative Political Studies* 8: 318–344.

Lau, Richard R., David J. Andersen and David P. Redlawsk. 2008. "An Exploration of Correct Voting in Recent U.S. Presidential Elections." *American Journal of Political Science* 52(2): 395–411.

Lau, Richard R. and David P. Redlawsk. 1997. "Voting Correctly." *American Political Science Review* 91: 585–598.
2006. *How Voters Decide*. New York: Cambridge University Press.

Laumann, Edward O. 1973. *Bonds of Pluralism*. New York: Wiley

Lazarsfeld, Paul F., Bernard Berelson, and Hazel Gaudet. 1968. *The People's Choice: How a Voter Makes Up His Mind in a Presidential Campaign*. New York: Columbia University Press. First published in 1944.

Lazer, David, Brian Rubineau, Nancy Katz, Carol Chetkovich, and Michael Neblo. 2010. "The Coevolution of Networks and Political Attitudes." *Political Communication* 27: 248–274.

Levitan, Lindsey C. and Penny S. Visser. 2009. "Social Network Composition and Attitude Strength: Exploring the Dynamics within Newly Formed Social Networks." *Journal of Experimental Social Psychology* 45: 1057–1067.

Levine, Jeffrey. 2004. "Choosing Alone? The Social Network Basis of Modern Political Choice." In Alan S. Zuckerman, ed. *The Social Logic of Politics: Personal Networks as Contexts for Political Behavior.* Philadelphia: Temple University Press, 132–151.

Lewis, David K. 1969. *Convention: A Philosophical Study.* New York: Cambridge University.

Lodge, Milton, Kathleen M. McGraw, and Patrick Stroh. 1989. "An Impression-Driven Model of Candidate Evaluation." *American Political Science Review* 83: 399–420.

Lodge, Milton, Marco Steenbergen, and Shawn Brau. 1995. "The Responsive Voter: Campaign Information and the Dynamics of Candidate Evaluation." *American Political Science Review* 89: 309–326.

Lodge, Milton and Charles Taber. 2000. "Three Steps Toward a Theory of Motivated Political Reasoning." In Anthony Lupia, Mathew D. McCubbins, and Samuel L. Popkin, eds. *Elements of Reason: Cognition, Choice, and the Bounds of Rationality.* New York: Cambridge University Press, 183–213.

2013. *The Rationalizing Voter.* New York: Cambridge University Press.

Lord, Charles G., Lee Ross, and Mark R. Lepper. 1979. "Biased Assimilation and Attitude Polarization: The Effects of Prior Theories on Subsequently Considered Evidence." *Journal of Personality and Social Psychology* 37: 2098–2109.

Lupia, Arthur. 1992. "Busy Voters, Agenda Control, and the Power of Information." *American Political Science Review* 86: 390–403.

2005. "Deliberation, Elitism, and the Challenges Inherent in Assessing Civic Competence." Presented at the annual meeting of the International Society of Political Psychology, Toronto, July 2005.

Lupia, Arthur and Mathew D. McCubbins. 1998. *The Democratic Dilemma: Can Citizens Learn What They Need To Know?* New York: Cambridge University Press.

Luskin, Robert C. 1990. "Explaining Political Sophistication." *Political Behavior* 12(4): 331–361.

McClurg, Scott D. 2006. "The Electoral Relevance of Political Talk: Examining Disagreement and Expertise Effects in Social Networks on Political Participation." *American Journal of Political Science* 50(3): 737–754.

McKelvey, Richard and Peter Ordeshook. 1985a. "Elections with limited information: A fulfilled expectations model using contemporaneous poll and endorsement data as information sources." *Journal of Economic Theory* 36: 55–85.

1985b. "Sequential Elections with Limited Information." *American Journal of Political Science* 29: 480–512.

1986. Information, Electoral Equilibria, and the Democratic Ideal." *Journal of Politics* 48: 909–937.

1990. "Information and Elections: Retrospective Voting and Rational Expectations." In John Ferejohn and James Kuklinski, eds. *Information and Democratic Processes.* Urbana: University of Illinois Press, 281–312.

MacKuen, Michael B. 1990. "Speaking of Politics: Individual Conversational Choice, Public Opinion and the Prospects for Deliberative Democracy." In John A. Ferejohn and James H. Kuklinski, eds. *Information and Democratic Processes.* Urbana: University of Illinois Press, 59–99.

MacKuen, Michael B. and George E. Marcus. 2001. "Emotions and Politics: The Dynamic Functions of Emotionality." In James H. Kuklinski, ed. *Citizens and Politics: Perspectives from Political Psychology.* New York: Cambridge University Press.

McPhee, William N. 1963. *Formal Theories of Mass Behavior.* New York: Free Press.

McPherson, J. Miller and Lynn Smith-Lovin. 1987. "Homophily in Voluntary Organizations: Status Distance and the Composition of Face-to-Face Groups." *American Sociological Review* 52(3): 370–379.

McPherson, J. Miller, Lynn Smith-Lovin, and Matthew Brashears. 2006. "Social Isolation in America: Changes in Core Discussion Networks over Two Decades." *American Sociological Review* 71:3 (June, June, 2006): 353–375.

McPherson, J. Miller, Lynn Smith-Lovin, and James M. Cook. 2001. "Birds of a Feather: Homophily in Social Networks." *Annual Review of Sociology* 27: 415–444.

McPhee, William N. with Robert B. Smith and Jack Ferguson. 1963. "A Theory of Informal Social Influence." In William N. McPhee, *Formal Theories of Mass Behavior.* New York: Free Press, 74–103.

Madison, James. 1961. "Federalist #10." In Clinton Rossiter, ed. *The Federalist Papers.* New York: New American Library, 1961, 77–84. Originally published in 1787.

Maoz, Zeev. 2010. *Networks of Nations: The Evolution, Structure, and Impact of International Networks, 1816–2001.* New York: Cambridge University Press.

Marcus, George E., W. Russell Neuman, and Michael MacKuen. 2000. *Affective Intelligence and Political Judgment.* Chicago: University of Chicago Press.

Marsden, Peter V. 1987. "Core Discussion Networks of Americans." *American Sociological Review* 52: 122–31.

Marsden, Peter V. and Noah E. Friedkin. 1994. "Network Studies of Social Influence." In Stanley Wasserman and Joseph Galaskiewicz, eds. *Advances in Social Network Analysis.* Thousand Oaks, CA: Sage Publications, 3–25.

Matthews, Donald R. and James W. Prothro. 1966. *Negroes and New Southern Politics.* New York: Harcourt, Brace and World.

May, Robert M. 1973. *Stability and Complexity in Model Ecosystems.* Princeton, NJ: Princeton University Press.

    1974. "Biological Populations with Nonoverlapping Generations: Stable Points, Stable Cycles, and Chaos." *Science* 186: 645–647.

    1975. "Some Notes on Estimating the Competition Matrix". *Ecology,* 56(3): 737–741.

    1976. "Simple Mathematical Models with Very Complicated Dynamics." *Nature,* 261: 459–467.

May, Robert M. and Warren J. Leonard. 1975. "Nonlinear Aspects of Competition Between Three Species." *SIAM Journal of Applied Mathematics* 29(2): 243–253.

May, Robert M. and George F. Oster. 1976. "Bifurcations and Dynamic Complexity in Simple Ecological Models." *American Naturalist* 110(974): 573–599.

Maynard Smith, John. 1968. *Mathematical Ideas in Biology.* Cambridge, UK: Cambridge University Press.

    1974. *Models in Ecology.* Cambridge, UK: Cambridge University Press.

Mendez, Jeanette Morehouse and Tracy Osborn. 2010. "Gender and the Perception of Knowledge in Political Discussion." *Political Research Quarterly,* 63(2): 269–279.

Mendelberg, Tali. 2002. "The Deliberative Citizen: Theory and Evidence." In Michael Delli Carpini, Leonie Huddy, and Robert Y. Shapiro, eds. *Political Decision-Making, Deliberation and Participation: Research in Micropolitics* Vol. 6. Greenwich, CT: JAI Press, 151–193.

Mendez, Jeanette, and Tracy Osborn. 2010. "Gender and the Perception of Knowledge in Political Discussion." *Political Research Quarterly* 63(2): 269–79.

Michels, Robert. 1962. *Political Parties: A Sociological Study of the Oligarchical Tendencies of Modern Democracy.* Translated by Eden and Cedar Paul. New York: Free Press. First Published in 1911.

Middeldorp, Menno and Stephanie Rosenkranz. 2008. "Information Acquisition in an Experimental Asset Market." Tjalling C. Koopmans Research Institute Discussion Paper Series 8(25): 1–37.

Miller, Warren E. 1956. "One-Party Politics and the Voter Revisited." *American Political Science Review* 50: 707–725.

Miller, Warren E. and Donald E. Stokes. 1963. "Constituency Influence in Congress." *American Political Science Review* 57(1): 45–56.

Mondak, Jeffery J. 1995. "Media Exposure and Political Discussion in U.S. Elections." *The Journal of Politics* 57: 62–85.

Mondak, Jeffery J. 2010. *Personality and the Foundations of Political Behavior.* New York: Cambridge University Press.

Mondak, Jeffery J. and Adam F. Gearing. 1998. "Civic Engagement in a Post-Communist State." *Political Psychology* 19: 615–637.

Mondak, Jeffery J., Matthew V. Hibbing, Damarys Canache, Mitchell A. Seligson, and Mary R. Anderson. 2010. "Personality and Civic Engagement: An Integrative Framework for the Study of Trait Effects on Political Behavior." *American Political Science Review* 104(1): 85–110.

Mondak, Jeffery J. 1995. "Media Exposure and Political Discussion in U.S. Elections." *The Journal of Politics,* 57: 62–85.

Mondak, Jeffery J. and Adam F. Gearing. 1998. "Civic Engagement in a Post-Communist State." *Political Psychology,* 19: 615–637.

Mutz, Diana. 1998. *Impersonal Influence.* Cambridge University Press.

2002a. "The Consequences of Cross-Cutting Networks for Political Participation." *American Journal of Political Science* 46: 838–855.

2002b. "Cross-Cutting Social Networks: Testing Democratic Theory in Practice." *American Political Science Review* 96: 111–126.

2006. *Hearing the Other Side: Deliberative versus Participatory Democracy.* New York: Cambridge University Press.

Mutz, Diana C. and Paul S. Martin. 2001. "Facilitating Communication across Lines of Political Difference: The Role of Mass Media." *American Political Science Review* 95: 97–114.

Mutz, Diana C. and Jeffery J. Mondak. 2006. "The Workplace as a Context for Cross-Cutting Political Discourse." *Journal of Politics* 1: 140–155.

Nelson, F. D. and L. Olson. 1978. "Specification and Estimation of a Simultaneous Equations Model with Limited Dependent Variables." *International Economic Review* 19: 695–709.

Newey, W. K. 1987. "Efficient Estimation of Limited Dependent Variable Models with Endogenous Explanatory Variables." *Journal of Econometrics* 36: 231–250.

Nickerson, David. 2008. "Is Voting Contagious? Evidence from Two Field Experiments." *American Political Science Review* 102: 49–57.

Noelle-Neumann, Elisabeth. 1984. *The Spiral of Silence.* Chicago: University of Chicago Press.

Olson, Mancur. 1965. *The Logic of Collective Action: Public Goods and the Theory of Groups*. Cambridge, MA: Harvard University Press.

Ostrom, Elinor, James Walker, and Roy Gardner. 1992. "Covenants With and Without a Sword: Self-Governance is Possible." *American Political Science Review*, 86: 404–417.

Page, Benjamin I. and Robert Y. Shapiro. 1992. *The Rational Public: Fifty Years of Trends in Americans' Policy Preferences*. Chicago: University of Chicago Press.

Page, Scott E. 2007. *The Difference: How the Power of Diversity Creates Better Groups, Firms, Schools, and Societies*. Princeton, NJ: Princeton University Press.

Parker, Suzanne L., Glenn R. Parker, and James A. McCann. 2008. "Opinion Taking in Friendship Networks." *American Journal of Political Science* 52: 412–420.

Persico, Nicola. 2004. "Committee Design with Endogenous Information." *Review of Economic Studies* 71(1): 165–194.

Popkin, Samuel L. 1991. *The Reasoning Vote: Communication and Persuasion in Presidential Campaigns*. Chicago: The University of Chicago Press.

Price, Vincent and John Zaller. 1993. "Who Gets the News? Alternative Measures of News Reception and their Implications for Research." *The Public Opinion Quarterly* 57(2): 133–164.

Putnam, Robert D. 1966. "Political Attitudes and the Local Community." *The American Political Science Review* 60(3): 640–654.

Putnam, Robert D., Robert Lenardi, and Raffaella Y. Nanetti. 1993. *Making Democracy Work: Civic Traditions in Modern Italy*. Princeton, NJ: Princeton University Press.

Richey, Sean. 2008. "The Social Basis of Voting Correctly." *Political Communication* 25(4): 366–376.

Riker, William H. 1986. *The Art of Political Manipulation*. New Haven, CT: Yale University Press.

Rivers, D. and Q. H. Vuong. 1988. "Limited Information Estimators and Exogeneity Tests for Simultaneous Probit Models." *Journal of Econometrics* 39: 347–366.

Robinson, W. S. 1950. "Ecological Correlations and the Behaviour of Individuals." *American Sociological Review* 15: 351–357.

Rogers, William. 1993. "Regression Standard Errors in Clustered Samples." *Stata Technical Bulletin* 3 (13): 19–23.

Rolfe, Meredith. 2012. *Voter Turnout: A Social Theory of Political Participation*. New York: Cambridge University Press.

Rosenstone, Steven J. and John Mark Hansen. 1993. *Mobilization, Participation, and Democracy in America*. New York: Macmillan Publishing.

Ross, Lee, Gunter Bierbauer, and Susan Hoffman. 1976. "The Role of Attribution Processes in Conformity and Dissent." *American Psychologist* 31: 148–157.

Rousseau, Jean-Jacques. 1994. *The Social Contract or the Principles of Political Right*. New York: Oxford University Press. (Original work published 1762.)

Ryan, John Barry. 2010. "The Effects of Network Expertise and Biases on Vote Choice." *Political Communication* 27(1): 44–58.

2011a. "Accuracy and Bias in Perceptions of Political Knowledge." *Political Behavior* 33(2): 335–356.

2011b. "Social Networks as a Shortcut to Correct Voting." *American Journal of Political Science* 55: 753–766.

Sanders, Lynn M. 1997. "Against Deliberation." *Political Theory*, 25(3): 347–376.

Schattschneider, E. E. 1942. *The Semisovereign People. A Realist's View of Democracy in America*. New York: Holt, Rinehart and Winston.

1960. *The Semisovereign People. A Realist's View of Democracy in America.* New York: Holt, Rinehart and Winston.

Schelling, Thomas C. 1978. *Micromotives and Macrobehavior.* New York: Norton.

Schlag, Karl. 1999. "Which One Should I Imitate?" *Journal of Mathematical Economics* 31(4): 493–522.

Schneider, Mark, Paul Teske, and Melissa Marschall. 2002. *Choosing Schools: Consumer Choice and the Quality of American Schools.* Princeton, NJ: Princeton University Press.

Shepsle, Kenneth A. 1972. "The Strategy of Ambiguity: Uncertainty and Electoral Competition." *American Political Science Review* 66: 555–568.

Shively, W. Phillips. 1969. "'Ecological' Inference: The Use of Aggregate Data to Study Individuals." *American Political Science Review,* 63(4): 1183–1196.

Simon, Herbert A. 1957. *Administrative Behavior.* 2nd Edition. New York, NY: Macmillan.

1971. "Designing Organizations for an Information-Rich World." In Martin Greenberger, ed. *Computers, Communication and the Public Interest.* Baltimore, MD: The Johns Hopkins Press, 37–72.

1983. *Reason in Human Affairs.* Palo Alto, CA: Stanford University Press.

1985. "Human Nature in Politics: The Dialogue of Psychology with Political Science." *American Political Science Review* 79(2): 293–304.

Smith, Vernon L. 1982. "Microeconomic Systems as an Experimental Science." *The American Economic Review* 72 (5): 923–955.

Sniderman, Paul M. 1993. "The New Look in Public Opinion Research." In A. W. Finifter, ed. *Political Science: The State of the Discipline II.* Washington, D.C.: American Political Science Association, 281–303.

2000. "Taking Sides: A Fixed Choice Theory of Political Reasoning." In Anthony Lupia, Mathew D. McCubbins, and Samuel L. Popkin, eds. *Elements of Reason: Cognition, Choice, and the Bounds of Rationality.* New York: Cambridge University Press, 67–84.

Sniderman, Paul M., Richard A. Brody, and Philip E. Tetlock. 1991. *Reasoning and Choice: Explorations in Political Psychology.* New York: Cambridge University Press.

Sprague, John. 1980. "On Duverger's Sociological Law: The Connection between Electoral Laws and Party Systems." Prepared for delivery April 7–11, 1980, under the auspices of the Department of Political Science and the Shambaugh Fund of the University of Iowa, Iowa City, Iowa.

Sokhey, Anand Edward and Scott D. McClurg. 2012. "Social Networks and Correct Voting." *Journal of Politics* 74(3): 754–761.

Sombart, Werner. 1976. *Why Is there No Socialism in the United States?* Translated by Patricia M. Hocking and C. T. Husbands. White Plains, NY: International Arts and Sciences Press. Originally published in 1906.

Stimson, James A. 1999. *Public Opinion in America: Moods, Cycles, and Swings.* 2nd Edition. Boulder, CO: Westview Press

Stokes, Donald. 1963. "Spatial Models of Party Competition." *American Political Science Review* 57(2): 368–377.

Stone, Walter J. and Elizabeth Simas. 2010. "Candidate Valence and Ideological Positioning in House elections." *American Journal of Political Science* 54(2): 371–388.

Surowiecki, James. 2005. *The Wisdom of Crowds.* New York: Doubleday.

Taber, Charles and Milton Lodge. 2006. "Motivated Skepticism in the Evaluation of Political Beliefs." *American Journal of Political Science* 50: 755–769.

Tetlock, Philip E. 2005. *Expert Political Judgment: How Good Is It? How Can We Know?* Princeton, NJ: Princeton University Press.

Tingsten, Herbert. 1963. *Political Behavior: Studies in Election Statistics.* Translated by V. Hammarling. Totowa, NJ: Bedminster. Originally published in 1937.

Tocqueville, Alexis de. 2000. *Democracy in America.* Translated and edited by Harvey C. Mansfield and Delba Winthrop. University of Chicago Press. Originally published as two volumes in 1835 and 1840

Tversky, Amos and Daniel Kahneman. 1973. "Availability: A Heuristic for Judging Frequency and Probability." *Cognitive Psychology* 5: 207–232.

1974. "Judgment Under Uncertainty: Heuristics and Biases." *Science* 185(4157): 1124–1131.

1982. "Evidential Impact of Base Rates." In Daniel Kahneman, Paul Slovic, and Amos Tversky, eds. *Judgment under Uncertainty: Heuristics and Biases.* New York: Cambridge University Press, 153–160.

Verba, Sidney. 1961. *Small Groups and Political Behavior.* Princeton, NJ: Princeton University Press.

Verba, Sidney, Kay Lehman Schlozman, and Henry Brady. 1995. *Voice and Equality.* Cambridge, MA: Harvard University Press.

Visser, Penny S. and Robert R. Mirabile. 2004. "Attitudes in the Social Context: The Impact of Social Network Composition on Individual-Level Attitude Strength." *Journal of Personality and Social Psychology* 87(6): 779–795.

Walsh, Katherine Cramer. 2004. *Talking about Politics: Informal Groups and Social Identity in American Life.* Chicago: Univ. of Chicago Press.

Watts, Duncan J. 1999. "Networks, Dynamics and the Small World Phenomenon." *American Journal of Sociology* 105: 493–527.

2004. *Six Degrees: The Science of a Connected Age.* New York: Norton.

Weimann, Gabriel. 1982. "On the Importance of Marginality: One More Step into the TwoStep Flow of Communication." *American Sociological Review* 47 (6): 764–773.

1991. "The Influentials: Back to the Concept of Opinion Leaders?" *Public Opinion Quarterly* 55: 267–279.

Williams, Rick L. 2000. "A Note on Robust Variance Estimation for Cluster – Correlated Data." *Biometrics* 56(2): 645–646.

Wilson, James Q. 1973. *Political Organizations.* Princeton, NJ: Princeton University Press.

Wolfinger, Raymond E. and Stephen J. Rosenstone. 1980. *Who Votes?* New Haven: Yale University Press.

Young, H. P. 1988. "Condorcet's Theory of Voting." *American Political Science Review* 82(4): 1231–1244.

Zaller, John R. 1992. *The Nature and Origins of Mass Opinion.* New York: Cambridge University Press.

Zellner, Arnold and H. Theil. 1962. "Three-Stage Least Squares: Simultaneous Estimation of Simultaneous Equations." *Econometrica* 30: 54–78.

Index of key concepts and authors

Cambridge Studies in Public Opinion and Political Psychology

Karen Stenner, *The Authoritarian Dynamic*

Susan Welch, Timothy Bledsoe, Lee Sigelman, and Michael Combs, *Race and Place*

Cara J. Wong, *Boundaries of Obligation in American Politics: Geographic, National, and Racial Communities*

John Zaller, *The Nature and Origins of Mass Opinion*

Alan S. Zuckerman, Josip Dasovic, and Jennifer Fitzgerald, *Partisan Families: The Social Logic of Bounded Partisanship in Germany and Britain*